Supporting Multilingual Learners as They
Speak, **W**rite, **I**nteract, **R**ead, and **L**isten

The SWIRL Method

SUSAN B. KATZ

Foreword by Alma Flor Ada & F. Isabel Campoy

Solution Tree | Press

Copyright © 2025 by Solution Tree Press

Materials appearing here are copyrighted. With one exception, all rights are reserved. Readers may reproduce only those pages marked "Reproducible." Otherwise, no part of this book may be reproduced or transmitted in any form or by any means (electronic, photocopying, recording, or otherwise) without prior written permission of the publisher.

555 North Morton Street
Bloomington, IN 47404
800.733.6786 (toll free) / 812.336.7700
FAX: 812.336.7790

email: info@SolutionTree.com
SolutionTree.com

Visit **go.SolutionTree.com/EL** to download the free reproducibles in this book.

Printed in the United States of America

Library of Congress Cataloging-in-Publication Data

Names: Katz, Susan B., 1971- author.
Title: The SWIRL method : supporting multilingual learners as they speak,
  write, interact, read, and listen / Susan B. Katz.
Description: Bloomington, IN : Solution Tree Press, 2025. | Includes
  bibliographical references and index.
Identifiers: LCCN 2024041401 (print) | LCCN 2024041402 (ebook) | ISBN
  9781958590676 (paperback) | ISBN 9781958590683 (ebook)
Subjects: LCSH: English language--Study and teaching--Foreign speakers. |
  Multilingual persons--Education.
Classification: LCC PE1128.A2 K38 2025 (print) | LCC PE1128.A2 (ebook) |
  DDC 428.0071--dc23/eng/20241031
LC record available at https://lccn.loc.gov/2024041401
LC ebook record available at https://lccn.loc.gov/2024041402

Solution Tree
Jeffrey C. Jones, CEO
Edmund M. Ackerman, President

Solution Tree Press
President and Publisher: Douglas M. Rife
Associate Publishers: Todd Brakke and Kendra Slayton
Editorial Director: Laurel Hecker
Art Director: Rian Anderson
Copy Chief: Jessi Finn
Senior Production Editor: Tonya Maddox Cupp
Acquisitions Editors: Carol Collins and Hilary Goff
Content Development Specialist: Amy Rubenstein
Associate Editors: Sarah Ludwig and Elijah Oates
Editorial Assistant: Madison Chartier

For all my former multilingual students—
Donya, Devesh, Carlos, Sebastian, Daisy,
Jetzemany, Maria, and hundreds more—
and for the talented teachers who are and
will be serving multilingual learners
through the SWIRL method

ACKNOWLEDGMENTS

I am incredibly grateful to my outstanding editor, Tonya Maddox Cupp, whose patience, flexibility, and excellent editorial eye made *The SWIRL Method* possible. Thank you to Hilary Goff for acquiring this book. I also want to appreciate the entire Solution Tree team helping get *The SWIRL Method* into the hands of educators: Jamila Loving, Shavantay Minnis, Paige Spain, Danielle McDonald, Claudia Wheatley, Alissa Thompson, Riley Bogan, Kelsey Dallas, Reed Scott, Susan Rabel, Hector Barrera, Jamie Ferracioli, Darren Grissom, Jennifer Ivy, Todd Brakke, Mecco Mai, Leslie Richardson, Rowena Souder, and many more phenomenal people, all championing *The SWIRL Method*! I'm forever indebted to Alma Flor and Isabel for writing the foreword in support of this book. Thank you to Vanessa Flynn, Sharon Zinke, Allison Schweiger, WIDA, Jana Echevarría, Susanna Dutro, and many other experts whose stellar strategies are highlighted.

To my parents, Janice and Ray, my brother, Steve, and my sister-in-law, Jami: thank you for your encouragement. Thanks also go to Annie Boerm from whom I have learned so much about writing supports for ELs. Finally, to my friends and family who support me so wholeheartedly: Julia and Ira, Ann, Greg and Sofia, Lydia, Carla, Tanya, Laurie, Maureen, my nephews, Sam, Jacob, and David, Amparo, Michael, Michelle R., Michelle G., Esther, Ricardo, Alejandra, Deborah, Arden, Jen, Tami, Crystal, Bryan, Marji, Marcy and Pete, my Aunt Anita and my late Uncle Bob, Nena and Mel, Laura and Darren, Lara, Dr. Tracy Smith, Stacy, Pepe Gonzalez, and many more.

Solution Tree Press would like to thank the following reviewers:

Lauren Aragon
Instructional Specialist for
 Innovation & Development
Pasadena Independent School District
Houston, Texas

Becca Bouchard
Educator
Calgary, Alberta, Canada

Justin Fisk
Director of World Languages/ELL
Adlai E. Stevenson High School
 District 125
Lincolnshire, Illinois

Nathalie Fournier
French Immersion Teacher
Prairie South School Division
Moose Jaw, Saskatchewan, Canada

Kelly Hilliard
Math Teacher
McQueen High School
Reno, Nevada

Louis Lim
Principal
Bur Oak Secondary School
Markham, Ontario, Canada

Paula Mathews
STEM Instructional Coach
Dripping Springs ISD
Dripping Springs, Texas

Demetra Mylonas
Education Researcher
Calgary, Alberta, Canada

Melissa Saenz
Principal
Montwood Middle School
El Paso, Texas

Christie Shealy
Director of Testing and Accountability
Anderson School District One
Williamston, South Carolina

Lauren Smith
Assistant Director of Elementary
 Learning
Noblesville Schools
Noblesville, Indiana

Rachel Swearengin
Fifth-Grade Teacher
Manchester Park Elementary School
Olathe, Kansas

Visit **go.SolutionTree.com/EL** to download
the free reproducibles in this book.

TABLE OF CONTENTS

Reproducibles are in italics.

About the Author xi

Foreword xiii

Introduction 1
    Why This Book Is Crucial 2
    Why SWIRL Works for Multilingual/English Learners 5
    Who Multilingual/English Learners Are 7
    How to Use This Book 8

PART 1
The Elements of Learning a New Language 11

1 Setting Up the Classroom to SWIRL 13
    Culture and Language 14
    Culturally Responsive and Sustaining Teaching 18
    Strategies to Reinforce Culturally Responsive and Sustaining Teaching 25
    Conclusion 29

2 Understanding Language Acquisition and Proficiency Levels 31
    Language Theory in Brief 32
    The Five Hypotheses of Krashen's Theory of Second Language Acquisition ... 34
    Language Acquisition Proficiency Stages 37
    Assessments to Ascertain EL Level 39

The Comprehensible Input Debate 40
　　Motivation, Self-Esteem, and Anxiety 43
　　Instructional Approaches: Designated, Integrated, and Systematic ELD 44
　　Conclusion. 47

3 Planning Lessons 49
　　Turning Content Objectives Into Language Objectives 51
　　Writing Language Objectives 52
　　Conclusion. 75

PART 2
The SWIRL Elements 77

4 Speaking 79
　　The Research on Speaking 80
　　Activities and Strategies 83
　　Conclusion. 105
　　KWL Chart *106*
　　Cognitive Content Dictionary *107*
　　Octopi Have Tentacles *108*
　　Four Layers of the Rain Forest *109*
　　Sweet Harriet *110*
　　Process Grid *111*

5 Writing 113
　　The Research on Writing 115
　　Activities and Strategies 116
　　Conclusion. 138
　　Writers' Workshop Conference Tool *139*
　　Note-Taking Place Mat *140*
　　Writing a Biography *141*

6 Interacting 143
　　The Research on Interacting. 144
　　Activities and Strategies 146
　　Conclusion. 160

7 Reading 161
   The Research on Reading 163
   Activities and Strategies 167
   Conclusion 184

8 Listening 187
   The Research on Listening 189
   Activities and Strategies 190
   Conclusion 201
   Clock Partners *202*

Epilogue 203

References and Resources 207

Index 233

ABOUT THE AUTHOR

Susan B. Katz is a National Board Certified Teacher and an award-winning, best-selling, Spanish-bilingual children's book author with Scholastic, Penguin Random House, Simon & Schuster, Callisto, Capstone, Heinemann, Lerner (*Sesame Street*), Little Bee Books, and NorthSouth Books. She served as a Spanish-bilingual teacher and literacy coach for over thirty years. Her book *The Story of Ruth Bader Ginsburg* hit number eighteen on Amazon's overall book bestseller list and number nine among all kids' books. Susan has written over eighty published books, including *Share Your Love*, which is a National Parenting Product Award winner, and *Gaudí: Architect of Imagination*, which earned a starred review from *School Library Journal*.

Susan writes and translates curriculum with a focus on access and equity for English learners. She is an internationally renowned keynote speaker, professional development facilitator, and literacy coach.

To learn more about Susan's work, visit her website (www.susankatzbooks.com).

To book Susan B. Katz for professional development, contact pd@SolutionTree.com.

FOREWORD

By Alma Flor Ada and F. Isabel Campoy

Our words are intended to echo Susan's SWIRL method—a seminal work that advances a field to which we have dedicated decades training teachers, creating quality bilingual literature, and researching transformational education. *The SWIRL Method* will undoubtedly become a universal, groundbreaking, go-to professional development guidebook on how to best serve multilingual learners in classrooms, teachers' colleges, and homes. This innovative framework does the following.

- Ensures that students' diverse backgrounds, home languages, and heritage cultures are valued in an asset-based, culturally sustaining classroom
- Provides English learners with frequent, formative opportunities to speak, write, interact, read, and listen
- Differentiates instruction while gradually releasing responsibility
- Creates a stellar pedagogical resource to use for professional development, professional learning communities, classroom implementation, and observations

We have had the pleasure of knowing and working with Susan for more than twenty-five years. She is a pioneering expert in effectively teaching multilingual learners. Through SWIRL, Susan does teachers, administrators, English learner and multilingual learner coordinators, migrant educators, literacy coaches, and instructional leaders the favor of gathering and presenting dozens of best practices in one user-friendly, research-based manual.

Bilingualism and multilingualism are powerful assets. Being bilingual and biliterate significantly expands a child's communication skills. In a multicultural society, learning a new language is a complex issue, as students each enter school with different degrees of bilingualism and English language proficiency.

In *The SWIRL Method*, Susan offers clear, well-researched strategies and structures that give teachers and staff an actionable, efficient methodology and lessons to support multilingual learners. SWIRL readers will also come away with a full understanding of the joys and challenges involved in the privilege of becoming bilingual.

We believe that this book will become a must-have classroom curriculum and training resource because of its attention to the following.

- **Transferability of skills:** All languages, despite having different phonemes, syntax, and semantics, enable us to express knowledge, connect ideas, and communicate emotions.
- **Memory:** Because memory is crucial to language acquisition, the author provides activities for students to develop memory via visual, auditory, and articulatory methods.
- **Academic vocabulary development:** An ample, active vocabulary bridges the gap and leads to effective communication and improved equity.
- **Critical thinking:** From mathematical concepts to Socratic seminars, SWIRL is a springboard to analyze problems, hypotheses, and literature using critical thinking skills collaboratively and individually.
- **Student voice and choice:** Whether students are acquiring receptive language through listening and reading or productive language when speaking, writing, and interacting, this book infuses student agency into all aspects of language development.

The SWIRL Method details clear, effective strategies and scaffolds that orient educators as to how to fully tap into multilingual learners' potential. Students in a SWIRL classroom will gain the superpower of bilingualism that liberates them to become leaders, clear communicators, and cooperative, compassionate citizens.

Susan's book is a transformative educational resource that will contribute to achieving a just society—the essential basis for a universal, lasting, peaceful coexistence on earth. As professors, authors, and multilingual learners ourselves, we give our highest recommendation, praise, and full support of Susan B. Katz's *The SWIRL Method: Supporting Multicultural Learners as They Speak, Write, Interact, Read, and Listen.*

INTRODUCTION

To have another language is to possess a second soul.
—Charlemagne

If you're a K–12 classroom teacher instructing students whose home language is something other than English, *The SWIRL Method* is for you. Inside this book is a toolbox of strategies that support English learners' speaking, writing, interacting, reading, and listening skills so these students become confident, competent, and fluent in English. This book helps English language development (ELD; formerly referred to as *English as a second language*) and content-area teachers, multigrade, multisubject teachers, and single-subject teachers scaffold for English learners (ELs). This book's SWIRL method is geared toward general education teachers, instructional coaches, ELD pull-out and push-in teachers, administrators with small or large EL student populations, bilingual or dual language teachers, and resource specialists. You might have one or two English learners, multilingual learners might be the majority of your class, or you might have an entire roster of EL students.

Speaking, writing, interacting, reading, and listening (SWIRL) are the skills multilingual learners need in order to learn the English language. *The SWIRL Method* offers research-based, time-tested best practices for teachers who educate English learners, from newcomers to long-term English learners (those who have received instruction in English for years but have not yet tested as English proficient).

I come to this conversation as a seasoned, Spanish-bilingual educator and literacy coach. Since 1990, I've taught thousands of English learners, from prekindergartners to high school seniors, from newcomers to long-term EL students. My students have spoken Spanish, Portuguese, Farsi, Arabic, Vietnamese, Chinese, Mien, Russian, Mam (a Guatemalan language that is only spoken, not written), Bulgarian, and myriad other languages at home. My work morphed into coaching teachers and delivering professional development on best practices for teaching English learners, both nationally and internationally.

Often, when I meet with teachers, they say, "My students are not advancing; they are not exiting out of being classified as English learners. I don't understand why." The answer is simple: if we want students to speak, write, and read English fluently, we need to give them ample opportunities to do so with fidelity and accountability. This book's strategies help you create, structure, and monitor those opportunities.

But first, let me explain why this book's topic is important.

Why This Book Is Crucial

Three issues make this book's strategies crucial for educators: (1) the prominence of ELs in primarily English-speaking countries, (2) the limited preparation many teachers report having for teaching ELs, and (3) ELs' specific academic challenges and current overall achievement data.

The United States and other primarily English-speaking countries, such as Canada, Australia, and England, have an increasing number of students whose first language is something other than English. The following statistics highlight why all these countries' educators must know how to teach students who are English learners, also referred to as *multilingual learners* (MLs; formerly MLLs).

- Approximately 25 percent of all students in the United States—or roughly 12.5 million students—are ELs (National Education Association, 2020).

- The majority of EL students in the United States—77 percent—speak Spanish (Bialik, Scheller, & Walker, 2018); however, there are also high concentrations of students who speak Mandarin, Portuguese, Farsi, Vietnamese, Arabic, Haitian Creole, and other languages.

- Populations in the United States are trending such that "by 2050, one in three people in the U.S. will speak Spanish" (Thompson, 2021).

- One in eight Canadians predominantly speak a language other than English or French at home (Statistics Canada, 2022).

- Canadian populations speaking a South Asian language at home—Gujarati, Punjabi, Hindi, or Malayalam, for instance—grew markedly from 2016 to 2021 (Statistics Canada, 2022).

- Most international business is conducted in English, regardless of what continent you are on (Gajjar, 2023).

Since the vast majority of ELs in the United States are Spanish speakers—over 70 percent—this book addresses how to leverage Spanish more than other languages. I recognize and respect that languages such as Chinese, Vietnamese, French, Haitian Creole, Portuguese, Arabic, Punjabi, and Farsi are also very prevalent in the United States and Canada (National Center for Education Statistics, 2024).

Most academic instruction in schools across the United States, Canada, England, and Australia is delivered in English (Relocate Magazine, 2022). Yet the vast majority of educators are not required to complete professional development focused on teaching English learners; most report feeling unprepared to teach ELs (Grant, Yoo, Fetman, & Garza, 2021; Najarro, 2023). Regarding professional development, in short, "preparation of teachers who can successfully instruct English learners has not kept pace with the number of ELs in classrooms" (Grant et al., 2021, p. 62).

Also, educators must watch out for mistaken underrepresentation or overidentification of EL students in special education. Harvard University scholars note:

> Students who are learning English at school tend to be diagnosed with learning disabilities two to three years later than their native English-speaking peers, and they're underrepresented in special education before the third grade—likely because their teachers assume their reading challenges are rooted in developing language rather than readiness to read. (Tatter, 2018)

This underrepresentation or overidentification can lead to academic issues (American University School of Education, 2020). While we don't want to give ELs watered-down text or assume they have dyslexia or other reading challenges, we also don't want their true reading challenges or other disabilities to go ignored. For example, I taught a first-grade student named Sebastian. He was a Spanish speaker whose family was from Mexico. Sebas, as his friends and family called him, was enthusiastic, exuberant, and social, and he struggled in reading. One day, I noticed that he squinted at the board quite a bit. I asked his mom when he'd last had his eyes checked. Not only was Sebas learning to read in two languages, but a doctor later diagnosed him as nearsighted. This completely changed his academic trajectory. I'm pleased to say that when I last saw him, Sebas was on his way to an outstanding university, where he was going to study to become a pharmacist. His LinkedIn profile says that his areas of research include organic chemistry, toxicology, and antibody discovery.

That's an encouraging anecdote, but let's examine how multilingual students are doing academically in general. Long-term assessment data paint a dire picture, since

National Assessment of Educational Progress (n.d.) reports 5 percent of EL students as proficient or above in reading and mathematics in 2022, whereas 33 percent of non-EL students were at that same proficiency level. When we examine graduation rates, it is important to note that having a high school diploma increases one's employment opportunities and earnings: "In 2015–16, 84 percent of students nationwide graduated from high school on time. . . . For ELs the rate was 67 percent" (U.S. Department of Education, 2019).

There are many causes of this inequity, and a school must consider many essential questions when planning how best to serve its multilingual learners.

- Will English language development be designated to a separate lesson that has language in the foreground and content in the back, or will it be integrated into content areas throughout the day?
- If EL students need thirty minutes or more of designated ELD at their level per day, and not just integrated ELD, who will deliver that instruction?
- Will the students be pulled out, or will a teacher push in?
- Will the classroom teacher deliver ELD lessons? If so, what will other students be doing at those times?
- Do teachers want to mix students between classrooms to create homogeneous groups by language proficiency?
- What materials and resources will the teacher use?
- Is there a plan to make EL student groups flexible and fluid?
- Will the teacher speak the ELs' home language to support them with cognates and processing?
- What languages will the teacher speak to their students during ELD? Will any home languages be allowed or encouraged?

Many teachers feel unprepared, under-resourced, or understaffed to meet English learners' needs. They have students in a range of proficiency levels in a single class, and they don't have enough time, resources, or training to adequately address those varying needs. This is where the SWIRL method comes in: speaking, writing, interacting, reading, and listening in English throughout the day with accountability and scaffolding to support ELs.

Why SWIRL Works for Multilingual/English Learners

The SWIRL method centers on the following five actions, each of which is connected to activities and strategies in its respective chapter.

1. **Speaking:** Oral production of words, phrases, sentences, and ideas
2. **Writing:** On-paper or electronic expression of words, phrases, sentences, and ideas
3. **Interacting:** Collaboration and cooperation with others to produce language
4. **Reading:** Decoding and comprehension of complex texts in a variety of genres
5. **Listening:** Auditory processing of words, phrases, sentences, and ideas

Each of these forms of communication is critical to learning English, which is a very complex language. In fact, English is so complex that "when researchers look at language complexity, they remove English because it is off the charts confusing" (Silverzweig, 2020)! Most, if not all, of its rules have exceptions. Many English words are not spelled phonetically, so it is hard to sound them out. Meanwhile, written words in Spanish and other Latin-based languages clearly correlate with the spoken sounds (for example, *mesa*, which is Spanish for "table," sounds just as it's spelled, whereas *table* has a silent *e*). Spanish is a transparent language, as it contains fewer than fifty letters and letter combinations that produce its sounds. English is an opaque language with 219 sounds for the consonant combinations and an additional 342 sounds for the vowels.

Ideally, you can incorporate several SWIRL elements into every lesson and use all five SWIRL elements throughout a school day (or at least each week). Students already engage in many of the elements during the course of a day; however, consciously encouraging students to speak to each other, write down their thoughts, interact in varying configurations, read different texts, and listen each day takes intention, planning, consistency, flexibility, and a willingness to gradually release the responsibility of learning to students. With the ubiquity of technology, many teachers rely on computer programs for reading assessments and activities. While students may look engaged in these lessons—and might be into them—they are not speaking or interacting during these activities. They are passively listening and reading. Reflect on whether you are prompting students to listen and read much more often than they speak, interact, and write. Be aware that many multilingual students may present as orally fluent; however, their writing and reading comprehension fall short in terms of rigorous academic vocabulary, grammar, and expression.

Balancing the elements of SWIRL is a delicate dance. Your SWIRL practice may be incremental, but it will impact students' language acquisition over time. Combining the five interconnected elements, shown in figure I.1, in instruction each day ensures that students have sufficient opportunities to practice, apply, and be assessed in English. Ultimately, our goal is for students to become fluent speakers, writers, and readers of English—to be able to communicate and think critically in two or more languages. This is additive bilingualism, not subtractive. We want them to gain English as a language while maintaining their home language.

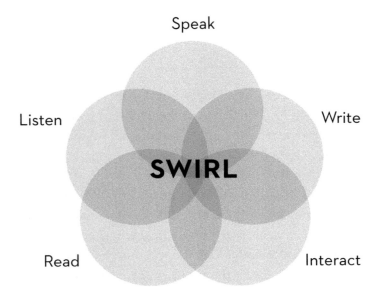

Figure I.1: The interconnected elements of SWIRL.

Ideally, you will evenly integrate these elements into your instruction—20 percent of your instructional time dedicated to each component of SWIRL. You have roughly 360 minutes per day, so that is about seventy minutes per SWIRL element for elementary schoolers (taking noninstructional time into account). If you teach a single subject at a middle or high school for seventy-five minutes, dedicate about fifteen minutes each to speaking, writing, interacting, reading, and listening every period. The great news is that there is so much overlap. Many lessons will combine elements of SWIRL—writing with reading, listening with speaking, and so on. Each lesson should include one form of comprehensible input (listening, reading) and one form of output (speaking, writing). The bridge (defined in chapter 1, page 13) is where interacting comes into play.

Who Multilingual/English Learners Are

Throughout this book, I interchangeably refer to students as *English learners* (*ELs*), *emergent multilingual students* (*EMSs*), and *multilingual learners* (*MLs*). *Multilingual learner* is the most up-to-date term at the time of publication. Still, many schools refer to such students as *English learners*.

Regardless of the term we use as teachers, we do not perceive or label multilingual students as if they have a deficit. Rather, being multilingual is an asset. Also, our objective is to *add* a language, not to subtract one. Consider the assets that bilingual and multilingual students bring to the classroom. For example, Spanish speakers may know the word *historia*, which helps them know the words *history*, *historical*, and *historian*. This is just one aspect of an approach to bilingual education known as *translanguaging*.

Translanguaging is a "different view of bilingualism and multilingualism" (Vogel & García, 2017, p. 1). It considers learning a new language to be a dynamic, social process—not a linear, individual one. In this framework, students' home language is seen as an asset, not a deficit. Sara Vogel and Ofelia García (2017) of CUNY Graduate Center write:

> The theory posits that rather than possessing two or more autonomous language systems, as has been traditionally thought, bilinguals, multilinguals, and indeed, all users of language, select and deploy particular features from a unitary linguistic repertoire to make meaning and to negotiate particular communicative contexts. Translanguaging also represents an approach to language pedagogy that affirms and leverages students' diverse and dynamic language practices in teaching and learning. (p. 1)

It is worthwhile to note that "most Spanish speaking, EL students are U.S. citizens" (Sanchez, 2017). The majority of the students I have taught were born in the United States. Their parents may have been born in Mexico, Central America, or South America, but most of my students have been U.S. citizens. When EL students enter kindergarten, they may have spoken only Spanish (or another first language) at home. In addition, there is a common perception that the parents of such students don't have a formal education and didn't graduate from high school or college. While that may sometimes be true, this is a generalization. Parents of EL students have been nurses, doctors, lawyers, and teachers in their home countries. Some have taken on manual labor (cleaning houses, doing construction, and nannying, for example) in their new country of residence simply because their degrees did not transfer. Whatever their education or profession, parents overwhelmingly want a solid education for their children. They count on educators to teach their children the skills needed to succeed.

To be clear, this book advocates for the inclusion of multiple languages and cultures in the classroom. I was, after all, a dual immersion teacher for my entire teaching career. That being said, encouraging students to learn English—*in addition to*, not *instead of*, their home language—is not a xenophobic nor an ethnocentric goal. English is the most spoken language in the world (International Center for Language Studies, 2024) and, therefore, a key to college and career readiness.

We want to continue to urge students to maintain their first language at home, in their community, with family members, and with any peers and educators at school who may share that cultural linguistic connection.

How to Use This Book

This book is divided into two parts.

Part 1 contains chapters 1–3. These beginning chapters take a deep dive into how to create language objectives and what the theory of language acquisition is. Chapter 1 sets up your work with English learners by providing culturally responsive and sustaining teaching strategies to employ in your classroom. Chapter 2 offers very brief overviews of various language acquisition theories, focusing on linguist Stephen D. Krashen's (1982) five hypotheses about second language acquisition. You also get a synopsis of the six stages of language acquisition, as well as a look at proficiency stages and assessments. Chapter 3 helps you turn content objectives from state or provincial standards into language objectives and create a lesson plan with approaches, strategies, and activities specifically geared toward multilingual learners. If you feel like you got a solid foundation of these chapters' components in your credentialing program, or through professional development, please feel free to skim or skip the chapters. You can also come back to them should you have questions along the way or need a refresher on language acquisition theory or proficiency levels.

In part 2, chapters 4–8 are about, respectively, speaking, writing, interacting, reading, and listening (also known as SWIRL or SWIRLing). I've implemented and coached others to utilize many of the SWIRL strategies and activities presented in these chapters. Accompanying each strategy, you'll see a SWIRL icon that capitalizes the predominant facets the strategy incorporates. For example, the paint chip vocabulary strips strategy says *SWIrl* because, although students are reading and listening, the primary cognitive and language demands involved are speaking, writing, and interacting as students brainstorm synonyms with their group to expand their academic vocabulary. You are free to skip around the chapters, and the strategies they include, but I encourage you to peruse all five SWIRL chapters at some point. Otherwise, you might just be SRLing (for example) and not giving students enough opportunities to write and interact.

Although each chapter examines a specific aspect of language acquisition, these aspects all tie together and complement each other. Speaking and listening are the crux of interacting. After students read a text, writing and speaking naturally flow, and vice versa. The SWIRL elements are all interlaced. Give students adequate opportunities to practice each of these skills every day. Obviously, some days or lessons weigh one area more heavily than another, but keeping these five SWIRL components in mind when designing lessons is ideal. Table I.1 lists each activity for each element in SWIRL. Keep in mind that nearly all activities involve more than one element.

A school where I provided professional development and coaching for ELD teachers needed help enacting SWIRL. Initially, every class I walked into had students reading on laptops or writing independently. The environment was quiet, which teachers often feel is more controlled (and more desirable). But students weren't talking. They weren't interacting. Their teachers weren't requiring them to use their English in a way that they could get feedback and be held accountable. Within a week of receiving training to implement SWIRL, the teachers were having the students do jigsaws, give presentations, and engage in debates and discussions. The teachers and students felt a palpable increase in the amount of airtime being dedicated to students' use of their English language skills.

This school has students in grades 6–8, a quarter of whom are identified as English learners. In 2020, seven of the school's students were reclassified as English language proficient (formerly known as fluent English proficient) when they passed their English proficiency test. Only seven out of over 250! The year prior, two students were reclassified. Clearly, there is more work to be done. We can't expect students' English to improve if they are (literally and figuratively) on mute.

If your students use SWIRL elements daily, their confidence and competence in speaking, writing, interacting, reading, and listening in English will soar. Let's start to SWIRL!

Table 1.1: Activity by Element

Speaking	
Purposeful Partnerships (page 84)	Paint Chip Vocabulary Strips (page 97)
Hand Up, Stand Up (page 86)	Songs (page 100)
Jigsaw (page 87)	Trivia (page 101)
Sentence Frames, Starters, and Stems (page 88)	Along the Lines (page 102)
KWL T-Chart (page 92)	Hot Seat (page 103)
Cognitive Content Dictionary (page 95)	Process Grids (page 104)

Writing	
Word Families (page 118)	Poetry (page 130)
Interactive Journaling (page 120)	Biographies (page 132)
Writers' Workshop (page 122)	Cooperative Strip Paragraphs (page 133)
Peer Editing (page 128)	Persuasive Essay Writing (page 137)
Place Mat Note Taking (page 129)	Informational or Expository Writing (page 137)

Interacting	
Think-Pair-Share (page 148)	Four Corners (page 156)
Classroom Feud (page 150)	Snowball (page 157)
Dice Discussions (page 151)	Memory (page 158)
Socratic Seminar (page 151)	Salute (page 159)
Swimming the Spectrum (page 154)	Who Am I? (page 159)

Reading	
Academic Vocabulary (page 167)	Including Informational, Nonfiction, and Complex Texts (page 175)
Anchor Charts (page 168)	Compound, Root, and Base Words (page 177)
Mirrors, Windows, and Sliding Glass Doors (page 169)	Pronunciation, Accuracy, and Fluency (page 178)
Making Connections (page 171)	Checking Comprehension (page 180)
Roles for Books Clubs (page 172)	Idioms (page 182)
Rime Magic (page 173)	Homonyms and Homophones (page 183)

Listening	
Active Listening and Body Language (page 191)	Partner and Group Conversations (page 197)
Story as Input (page 194)	Narrative Input (page 199)
Chunked Audio and Video for Processing (page 197)	Total Physical Response (page 200)

PART 1
The Elements of Learning a New Language

Have you ever tried to learn another language, or traveled to a country where you did not speak the language? It can be exciting, intimidating, gratifying, and overwhelming—sometimes all in one day! For this reason, educators must take many considerations into account when planning and delivering instruction for multilingual learners. The SWIRL method empowers these students to speak, write, interact, read, and listen throughout the day. Balancing the five SWIRL elements ensures that students can communicate effectively and access content equitably.

Before we dive into SWIRL activities and strategies, let's first explore how to set up a culturally responsive and sustaining classroom. Next, we'll delve into language acquisition theory as well as various English proficiency levels. Then, we'll learn how to deliver comprehensible input. Also, it is essential to identify whether your classroom will offer designated, systematic, or integrated ELD lessons, or a combination of these delivery methods. Using your district standards, you will learn how to convert content objectives into student-friendly language objectives.

If you already have a solid hold on language acquisition theory, culturally sustaining teaching, and the creation of language objectives, please feel free to consult part 2's chapters for specific strategies on each SWIRL element. All of this is in service of your English learners, and it is well worth your while because you will see them blossom when you provide rich, frequent, meaningful, and purposeful opportunities to SWIRL.

CHAPTER 1

Setting Up the Classroom to SWIRL

*Meeting the needs of all students starts with
knowing who your students are.*
—Elena Aguilar

A core proposition to which National Board Certified Teachers adhere is knowledge of students (National Board for Professional Teaching Standards, n.d.). As educators, it is incumbent on us to get to know students' abilities; likes and dislikes; interests; home languages; English language levels (entering, emerging, developing, expanding, bridging, or reaching); and primary, secondary, and tertiary learning preferences (such as auditory, musical, kinesthetic, visual, and linguistic) so we can incorporate these as we plan instruction. We want students to feel comfortable in class so they take risks, both academically and socially. Millions of students are counting on us to give them agency and incorporate their home languages, cultures, and customs into our classrooms. Failure to do so may limit their academic and social success (Gay, 2015; Minocha, 2024).

This differentiation for multilingual learners takes a variety of forms, depending on whether yours is an elementary or secondary classroom. Furthermore, you may have a student who is verbally fluent, but whose reading or writing is still well below grade level. You may be serving newcomers or long-term English learners in middle or high school classes. How can you make the content accessible? If the majority of your students are fluent in English, how can you teach them while also adequately supporting multilingual learners by meeting them where they are? In short, SWIRL strategies in this book vary depending on students' English language levels, ages, and grade levels. You know your students best, so choose which strategies will address their specific needs.

Ideally, you are cognizant of EL students and plan instruction that incorporates elements such as language objectives, independent think time, purposeful partnering of students during think-pair-share, team tasks, diverse books, and connections to cognates. It all starts, however, with setting a classroom tone in which all learners' home cultures and languages are valued.

Culture and Language

As teachers, we value language because it is a key component of any culture. It is the way students communicate with their parents, siblings, cousins, grandparents, aunts and uncles, and community members. They think in their home language, dream in it, and, in my experience, prefer to express emotions in it. Nursery rhymes, pop songs, and traditional music in home languages build core memories that stimulate brain development and instill a sense of pride. Home cultures also include foods, celebrations, customs, crafts, and myriad other components.

When a multilingual learner steps into the classroom, they bring with them a treasure trove of home language and cultural components. Our job is to embrace these cultural and linguistic assets and fold them into discussions, literature, projects, and presentations.

We want to encourage students to maintain their home language outside of class with family and friends and in class, even if it is not a dual immersion program. Not every state, province, county, or school offers classroom instruction in additional languages, like Spanish, French, and Chinese, but we want students to continue to speak, read, and write in their home language. Whether MLs are in a one- or two-way dual language immersion program, or in a transitional early- or late-exit program, the goal is for students to become bilingual and biliterate, meet or exceed grade-level expectations, and develop cross-cultural competence (Center for Applied Linguistics, 2016). This work with their home language helps keep students connected to their family as well as to their family's homeland and makes them more qualified for college and career opportunities.

Three Levels of Culture

To understand the breadth of what multicultural education really means, examine founding theorist's Nitza M. Hidalgo's (1993) three levels of culture.

1. **The concrete:** This is the most visible and tangible level of culture and includes the most surface-level dimensions such as traditional clothes, music, food, and games. These aspects of culture often provide the focus for multicultural festivals or celebrations.

2. **The behavioral:** This level of culture clarifies how we define our social roles, the language we speak, and our approaches to nonverbal communication. The behavioral level includes gender roles, family structures, political affiliations, and other items that position us organizationally in society.

3. **The symbolic:** This level of culture holds our values and beliefs. It can be abstract, but it most often is the key to how individuals define themselves. It includes value systems, customs, spirituality, religion, worldviews, beliefs, and more.

Culture involves many components beyond language, such as literature, landmarks, art, dance, friendships, milestones, rituals, diet, forms of kindness, and surname origins (González, 1974; Intercultural Development Research Association, n.d.).

Speaking of dance, an example of asset-based cultural integration that involved dance came early in my career. I am a dancer (salsa, samba, merengue), but I was unfamiliar with the traditional Mexican dances that originated where many of my students and their families were from. The particular region, Jalisco, has a specific step known as the *zapateado* and a quintessential white dress that girls there often wear. I invited some of my students and their mothers to teach our whole class the dance, and we performed it for the school's international festival. The families took much pride in sharing this cultural tradition through the music, the movement, and even the making of traditional costumes; it increased parental involvement. And I saw students shining with pride as they danced in the costumes. Teaching other students traditional dance steps from Jalisco made them feel like they had an asset to offer to their peers.

Not everyone is a dancer, but you can ask your students to explore the three levels of their cultural identity in an art, text, music, or multimedia project. Hidalgo (1993) asserts:

> Your most important multicultural education resources are the students in your classes and, instead of trying to define what is culturally important to them through special celebrations or additive techniques, it is our responsibility to draw them into the conversation, allow them to define themselves, and start there in the development of multicultural education.

You can be a culturally responsive and sustaining teacher by asking your students to engage in this way, which enhances the sense of belonging for students who are often underrepresented.

Benefits of Maintaining Home Language

I spent my entire teaching career serving as a Spanish immersion teacher, so I am a firm proponent of students' becoming bilingual and biliterate. Establishing a classroom where home language, culture, and customs are invited and included enables more risk taking and develops a sense of belonging (Colorín Colorado, 2023). You can offer the following additional facts to any peers who might be tempted to exclude diverse languages and cultures in their classrooms:

> **Second language development:** A strong foundation in the home language facilitates the learning of a second language.
>
> **Social-emotional development:** Children who see that their home language is valued build a positive and healthy self-identity and stronger sense of pride in their cultural and linguistic heritage.
>
> **Cognition:** Bilingual students are generally flexible thinkers and problem solvers and have an easier time understanding math concepts and solving word problems [once they are truly fluent in both languages].
>
> **Future employability:** There is a growing need for individuals who are proficient in two or more languages in today's world economy and socio-political climate. (IRIS Center, 2015)

At schools in predominantly English-speaking countries, English is often seen as the *language of power*. It is the primary method of communication on the playground, in the cafeteria, and for most academic instruction. To help a student maintain skills in their heritage language, invite the student to use their first language as a springboard for processing their thoughts orally and in writing. Since the majority of teachers who serve ELs deliver instruction in English, it is also important that those educators keep a cognate list of Latin-based words and their similar-sounding or similarly spelled counterparts (such as *history/historia*, *valid/válido*, and *animal/animal*). Another strategy is to invite students to read resources in their first language to gather background information on a topic.

In a dual immersion program, using cognates to compare the two languages' phonology (sound system), morphology (word formation), syntax, grammar, and pragmatics (language use) is known as *bridging*:

> The bridge occurs once students have learned new concepts in one language.... [You] undertake contrastive analysis and transfer what they have learned from one language to the other. The bridge is also the instructional moment when teachers help students connect the content area knowledge and skills they have learned in one language to the other language. (Beeman & Urow, 2012, p. 1)

We want students to learn English, but our goal is not for them to lose their first language, a phenomenon referred to as *subtractive bilingualism*, in the process (Lambert, 1974). As dual language instruction pioneer Rosa Molina says, "No child has to lose a language to learn a language" (as cited in *The Madera Tribune*, n.d.). Research shows multiple reasons why it is essential that students maintain their multilingual skills.

- English learners who continue developing their home language achieve more academically in the long run than students who lose their language of origin when learning English (National Clearinghouse for Bilingual Education, 2000).

- Losing a home language harms a student's relationships with family members. Ensuring a student is well-versed in their home language "allows for more meaningful communication that can facilitate respect for these relationships" (Triebold, 2020).

I have seen many students over my career answer their parents or grandparents in English even though they completely understand them in their home language. This may communicate to their elders that English is more important and lead to some distancing between family members.

Knowing another language is an asset. The concept of *asset-based education* involves honoring and incorporating all the cultures represented in your classroom, at your school, and in your community as well as those that may not be represented. In chapter 7 (page 161), for example, we talk about books as mirrors, windows, and sliding glass doors to diverse cultures.

Experiences While Learning a New Language

Newcomers go through several emotional stages when learning a new language, just as they go through cognitive and linguistic phases (Althen, 2003). Being aware of these four stages may help educators help these students.

1. **Euphoria:** There is excitement about their new surroundings.

2. **Culture shock:** There may be overwhelm, frustration, anger, or resentment toward the new culture.

3. **Acceptance:** Gradual acceptance of this experience and place is occurring.

4. **Assimilation or adaptation:** They embrace and adapt to their surroundings and the new culture and language.

Please note many, but not all, newcomers may be facing trauma from experiences at international borders as refugees and other sources of trauma. One resource for trauma-informed education is Debbie Zacarian, Lourdes Alvarez-Ortiz, and Judie Haynes's (2017) *Teaching to Strengths: Supporting Students Living With Trauma, Violence, and Chronic Stress.*

Culturally Responsive and Sustaining Teaching

Culturally responsive and sustaining teaching is another way to help build positive relationships with your EL (and other) students since "understanding the cultural beliefs, values, and attitudes of culturally and linguistically diverse children is an important first step in developing a warm and caring relationship with the child and family" (López & Páez, 2021, p. 17). Being an asset-based educator means that you take the time to get to know your students' customs and cultures—and view them as assets.

Post some basic words in your EL students' home language. Invite the students and their families to share various aspects of their home language and culture so they feel welcome and respected and other students learn about diverse cultures. Sharing this cultural information cultivates respect and helps the classroom better represent the diverse society in which we live. The ultimate goal is to create a classroom of students who love learning, who are held to high expectations at which they excel, and who feel seen and know their needs are being met. This is the essence of culturally responsive teaching, which is a way of instructing "that uses students' customs, characteristics, experiences, and perspectives as tools for better classroom instruction. Students of color see themselves and their communities as belonging in academic spaces" (Will & Najarro, 2022). Classroom teacher and educational consultant Nikki Williams Rucker (2019) explains that cultural responsiveness "encourages students to feel a sense of belonging and helps create a space where they feel safe, respected, heard, and challenged."

The need for cultural relevance applies not only to students whose first language is something other than English but also to other historically marginalized student groups (such as Black, Muslim, Jewish, disabled, and deaf students; Ladson-Billings, 1995). Culturally responsive instruction calls for students to develop critical perspectives that challenge societal inequalities. Author and prominent pedagogical theorist Gloria Ladson-Billings (1995) proposes that classrooms employ three main components, distilled in the following list, to attain and maintain cultural responsiveness.

1. **Student learning:** This includes intellectual growth, moral development, problem solving, and reasoning. In elementary classrooms, this may include conflict resolution, class meetings, and collaborative conversations. In middle and high school classrooms, it can include student-led Socratic seminars (see page 151), team projects, and debates.

2. **Cultural competence:** This includes skills that affirm and appreciate students' culture of origin while simultaneously supporting the development of fluency in at least one other culture. This might require stocking the classroom library with diverse books at the elementary school level and promoting foreign language learning at the middle and high school levels.

3. **Critical consciousness:** This includes identifying, analyzing, and solving real-world problems, specifically those that lead to societal inequalities. The older the students, the more imperative it is that they understand and solve social and political issues pertaining to other countries and cultures.

These components need not appear in every lesson, but they should be central to a teacher's overarching approach and pedagogy. Culturally sustaining classrooms "perpetuate and foster—to sustain—linguistic, literate, and cultural pluralism as part of the democratic project of schooling" and include materials and practices that incorporate the products and traits listed in table 1.1 (page 20).

Culturally sustaining teaching closes the teacher-student gap as the teacher learns about the cultural nuances that may impact trusting relationships and potentially impede student achievement. An example of a cultural nuance is how your students' parents originally learned how to do division, multiplication, and the like. These are taught differently in various countries (and their teaching has changed over time in the United States). Knowing the methodologies used helps you aid parents in supporting students at home and dispel any confusion that families may have about homework assignments.

In her book *Culturally Responsive Teaching and the Brain: Promoting Authentic Engagement and Rigor Among Culturally and Linguistically Diverse Students*, Zaretta Hammond (2015) asserts, "By third grade, many culturally and linguistically diverse

Table 1.1: Products and Traits of Culturally Responsive and Sustaining Asset-Based Classrooms

What Culturally Sustaining Classrooms Do	How to Accomplish or Incorporate the Culturally Sustaining Classroom Trait
They connect to students' background knowledge and experiences.	Country reports; cooking events; in-depth research into other cultures; texts and diverse books in the classroom library used for read-alouds and book clubs; anchor charts labeled with home language words; family and student interest forms and home language surveys collected at the start of the year or during conferences
They build on students' home languages through the use of cognates, crosslinguistic connections, and invitations for students to share ideas in their home language and bring literature from another language into the research process.	Cocreated cognate chart (page 26); think-pair-share in the home language; student groupings by home language; diverse books in the classroom library; translated home communications
They get to know students' linguistic repertoires (for example, the languages they speak and their literacy levels in those languages) and academic profiles.	Students' data-based English language levels, as well as information on the degree to which students speak, read, or write in their home language; academic profile information; parents' skill levels in their home language and in English (which help with ascertaining the level of support students have at home)
They recognize variations of English and require a range of academic and social registers.	*Academic registers* ("school speak" and vocabulary used in textbooks, articles, assignments, assessments, and presentations) and *social registers* (casual language students use with peers at lunch, on the playground, and between classes)—for example, "We did it!" (social register) versus "Our hypothesis proved accurate based on the data from our experiment" (academic register)
They offer consistent and integrated content and language support.	Complimentary language objectives connected to content objectives (standards) specific to the words, phrases, or tenses students are expected to use in order to demonstrate comprehension and their ability to manipulate language; support with sentence frames, word banks, adequate independent think time, or turn-and-talk opportunities
They invite students to develop oral language by discussing a variety of topics.	Partner, group, or whole-class discussion; oral language reports; hot-seat games; research projects
They respect and integrate home languages and cultural customs.	Properly pronouncing students' names; learning about cultural customs such as Día de los Muertos (Day of the Dead), Chinese and Vietnamese New Year, Ramadan, and Rosh Hashanah; inviting students to share their cultural customs; labeling the room in various languages; displaying a map that shows where students' families or ancestors are from; sharing songs, books, poems, and recipes in students' primary languages; highlighting cognates for Latin-based languages

students are one or more years behind in reading. . . . Culturally responsive teaching is one of our most powerful tools for helping students find their way out of the [achievement] gap" (p. 14).

Culturally responsive and sustaining teaching asks that educators comprehend and dig into implicit bias, pedagogical and instructional practices, and cultural connections.

Implicit Bias

Creating a truly culturally responsive and sustaining, asset-based classroom means taking a hard look at one's own implicit biases. Implicit biases may, for example, include presuming a student doesn't read or write in English simply because they speak with an accent, or presuming a parent isn't well educated because they are currently doing manual labor. As I mentioned, many of my students' parents achieved advanced degrees in their countries of origin but had not yet earned their degrees in the United States.

Award-winning social psychologist Anthony Greenwald, who does research in the field of cognition, explains that implicit bias "shapes conscious thought, which in turn guides judgments and decisions" (Mason, 2020). If you want to examine your own implicit biases by taking a survey, visit https://implicit.harvard.edu/implicit/takeatest.html to try Harvard University's Implicit Association Tests. These tests give you an honest, objective look at what implicit biases you might hold.

You may also want to ask yourself some questions based on guidance from Rucker (2019), who specializes in diversity, equity, inclusion, and belonging:

> Are you operating from a place of critical care within your classroom—a place that marries high expectations with empathy and compassion? Are your students, regardless of socioeconomic status or background, being held to high standards? Has your past interaction with a particular race of people impacted your ability to communicate with parents?

Greenwald also explains that making decisions objectively, instead of subjectively, is a step toward reducing implicit bias:

> Once you know what's happening, the next step is what I call discretion elimination. . . . When [subjective] decisions are made with discretion, they are likely to result in unintended disparities. But when those decisions are made based on predetermined, objective criteria that are rigorously applied, they are much less likely to produce disparities. (Mason, 2020)

Increasing student choice and voice is a way to ensure that your own biases around, say, what books to read aloud do not impact students' learning or sense of belonging. Also, to ensure objectivity, middle and high school teachers can employ anonymous grading where students use a number or code instead of their name on any assessments. Drawing sticks with students' names on them, for example, can help ensure equal participation, which is another way to reduce implicit bias. Once you start examining where your implicit biases lie, you can adjust your practices to ensure that no student is being underestimated or pigeonholed into a certain group, level, or set of expectations.

Pedagogical and Instructional Practices

After acknowledging your implicit biases and adjusting your approach, you must take a look at your pedagogical and instructional practices as well. Here are some questions to ask yourself about your curriculum and instruction.

- Do you use a variety of books that reflect the students in your classroom and diverse cultures around the globe (with these books acting as mirrors, windows, and sliding glass doors; see chapter 7, page 161)?
- Do you give students the chance to choose what they read?
- Are science, social studies, and other topics presented from several points of view and driven by students' interests?
- Do students have voice and choice in where they sit and who they are partnered with? For example, can they partner up with students who speak the same home language to process a passage before they respond in writing?
- Are students required to participate in holiday activities (for December holidays, Halloween, Thanksgiving, Valentine's Day, and so on)? Are they able to share the holidays they celebrate at home, such as Día de los Muertos, Lunar New Year, Rosh Hashanah, or Ramadan?
- Do students get a chance to share about their families' cultures and customs? Are there presentations and projects, such as country reports and international cooking days, that allow students to elaborate on their cultural customs and help their peers learn about other cultures and places?
- Are families welcomed in to explain about their traditions, clothing, food, and celebrations alongside their children?

- Do you communicate with students and their families in multiple languages—through the use of a translator or an online translation tool—since keeping all families informed is crucial to helping parents and caregivers support students at home?
- Do you encourage students to share words or phrases from their home languages to propel understanding of English and also to share the richness of their multilingualism?

As a literacy coach, I taught several students in my ELD groups who were from Iran and Yemen. A few of the girls wore hijabs; one of the girls wore a hijab when she was in her home country but didn't in the United States. One day, I drove two sisters home because they had stayed after school to make up a test. At their house, I didn't get out of the car, but I waved to their mother, who stood at the front door. The next day, I asked the girls why their mom did not have a hijab on, as I'd never seen her without one before. I commented on how beautiful her long hair was.

"Ms. Katz," they giggled, "we don't wear our hijabs at home with our father and brother—only when we are out of the house, like at school." I didn't know that, and my interest in learning more about their customs and culture connected us in a new way. They felt like experts in an area where I had little to no experience. When I acknowledged how I'd learned something from them, the girls felt seen and respected.

Cultural Connections

When you are considering embracing different cultures in your classroom, know that it is important to "incorporate cultural studies into our curriculum . . . to cultivate in our students a sense of awareness, empathy, and respect" (McGraw Hill, 2017).

For example, as a bilingual educator, I worked among many immersion teachers who all wanted to honor and include students' cultures. Early in my career, I saw that some of my students' families celebrated Thanksgiving, but not all of them had the traditional turkey, stuffing, and mashed potatoes meal. I decided to have a multicultural cooking day in my first-grade classroom during Thanksgiving week. It consisted of setting up centers at which various parents taught students how to make recipes from their cultural cuisines. Parents taught my students how to make sushi, enchiladas, and a variety of other recipes. Families got to participate, sharing part of their culture, and students got to cook dishes that represented the families' traditional food.

Similarly, my colleagues who taught fourth and fifth grade had their classes do country reports. Students would pair up—one or both of them being from the country they were researching—and create a trifold poster with information and artifacts about the country. As a culminating event, the teachers invited the students' families to presentations in the evening. The student pairs featured the sports, famous people, languages, populations, and major exports of their countries, from Panama to Portugal. This also served to enlighten students about the various cultures represented in the class. Some schools and classrooms create a map that shows where their students' families or ancestors are from. Students each place a flag (or flags) on the map and use string to connect the flags to the city the school is in, demonstrating how we are all interconnected.

The following list includes other dynamic, engaging ways to include culturally relevant topics in your class (McGraw Hill, 2017).

- **Literature:** Ensure that students have access to a wide array of diverse books in which they can see themselves, their peers, and other cultures represented. I firmly believe that students need to see themselves in the books they read to feel valued and seen. In choosing texts, be mindful of school, community, or state or provincial guidelines that influence (and sometimes inhibit) text choice. Even if you find your options limited in this way, don't shy away from being creative within those guidelines. I had a high school English teacher who put up a sign that read *Editorial* when he was presenting something the district didn't approve and photocopied books about topics such as nuclear disarmament if he wasn't permitted to purchase them. Please know I am acutely aware of the book banning taking place in many states and countries; however, censorship should not negatively impact students' right to read.

- **News:** At the middle and high school levels, allow students to share current events and engage in healthy debates about political and social issues.

- **Pop culture:** Encourage students to incorporate the music they listen to, the fashion they wear, and their extracurricular activities into presentations. For example, students can use spoken word to incorporate rhythm into their literacy skills.

The better you know your students (and speak with them about how their cultures are unique), the easier it is to include such practices.

Strategies to Reinforce Culturally Responsive and Sustaining Teaching

Culturally responsive and sustaining teaching encompasses several specific strategies—cognates, tiered vocabulary, concepts of print, and language structure transfers—that acknowledge and incorporate students' home languages, cultures, and customs. The following sections discuss each of these, but (big picture) note that while you can (and should!) take steps like making sure the names in mathematical word problems are ethnically diverse and representative of students' cultures, culturally sustaining teaching goes far beyond integrating diverse names, posting flags, and briefly mentioning holidays. It means creating an environment in which students feel welcomed, valued, and accepted for who they (and their families) are. Consider asking bicultural students how they view themselves. For example, one year, I had a student who was Black and Latinx and another who was Vietnamese and Black. We discussed how they believed others saw them versus how they self-identified. Do this not to put students on the spot but, rather, to listen to their experiences at school, and in society, in an effort to understand them better.

Now, let's look at some strategies.

Cognates

If there is one essential strategy for ELs, especially Spanish, French, Portuguese, and Haitian Creole speakers, it is the use of cognates. *Cognates* are words that sound similar and are spelled similarly in two languages. Latin-based languages like Spanish, French, Italian, and Portuguese have lots of words that resemble words in English, where the root, or base, word might be similar (for example, *demonstration/demostración*, *solar system/sistema solar*, and *bicycle/bicicleta*). There are over twenty thousand cognates between Spanish and English (Montelongo, Hernández, & Herter, 2016), so having a routine set up to identify, record, and reflect on cognates is essential. Many cognates are considered tier three vocabulary (subject-specific words that are not often used; you can read more about tiered vocabulary on page 27). Beyond literature, cognates with Latin roots are particularly important for extracting meaning from academic vocabulary in science, social studies, and mathematics. (Cognates do not work to compare English to Arabic, Vietnamese, or Chinese, among other languages.)

Teaching cognates explicitly signals to EL students, "You've come in with a knowledge base that puts you at an advantage, not a disadvantage. Your home language is the perfect springboard to learning English."

In this book, we focus on Spanish-to-English cognates, since over 75 percent of the English learners in the United States are Spanish speakers; however, you will encounter much more diversity in your students. For example, in 2023, the National Center for Education Statistics noted an increase in Portuguese and Haitian Creole speakers who immigrated to the United States. Cognates sometimes—not always, but often—apply across Latin-based languages. Consider *opinion*, for example, which is *opinión* in Spanish, *opinião* in Portuguese, and *opinyon* in Haitian Creole. Cognates are a strategy for success. Out of fourteen award-winning picture books, researchers pulled at least four cognates from each (Calderón et al., 2003).

The following are some different types of cognates.

- **Perfect cognates:** These words are spelled exactly the same, but their pronunciations are slightly different. *Chocolate/chocolate* is an example. In English, you say *chalk-a-lit*, while in Spanish, the same word is pronounced *cho-ko-la-tay*. Other examples are *jaguar/jaguar* (pronounced *jag-gwar* in English and *ha-guar* in Spanish) and *animal/animal* (emphasizing the first syllable in English and the last syllable in Spanish).

- **True cognates:** These words look very similar but are pronounced differently. These are so close that any reader can discern the similarity. Examples include *history/historia*, *opinion/opinión*, and *salt/sal*.

- **False cognates:** These words look like they are cognates, but they are not. For example, students often assume that the Spanish word *embarasada* means "embarrassed" in English. Alas, it means "pregnant," the confusion about which can be quite embarrassing! In English, you might eat a pie, but in Spanish, you would not want to eat a *pie*, which means "foot." My own brother once called me from Mexico, desperately seeking soap at the corner store. He was asking for *sopa*, which in Spanish means "soup." *Soap* in Spanish is *jabón*.

Building a growing cognate list is helpful, as words will come up organically through reading. See table 1.2 for an example.

Visit the Colorín Colorado website (https://tinyurl.com/55c757pj) to see a more complete list of cognates. You might want to keep a T-chart of cognates and encourage students to keep adding to it as an anchor chart. Offer a signal (such as linking both thumbs and pointer fingers in a chain) that students can silently show to indicate they have identified a cognate when reading aloud or tackling new academic vocabulary. To add the cognate to the T-chart, you can either use sticky notes or

Table 1.2: Cognates List

English	Spanish
accident	accidente
accompany (to)	acompañar
activities	actividades
adventure	aventura
atmosphere	atmósfera
biography	biografía
camouflage	camuflaje
catastrophe	catastrophe
distance	distancia
extraordinary	extraordinario(a)
ferocious	feroz
importance	importancia

write directly on the anchor chart. For grades 3–12 students, note that prefixes are also similar enough to help extract meaning (for example, *disappear/desaparecer*).

Tiered Vocabulary

You likely are already familiar with the concept of tiered vocabulary words, which fall under culturally sustaining teaching. The following well-established three-tiered system helps teachers choose vocabulary words from read-aloud books (Beck, McKeown, & Kucan, 2002).

- **Tier one:** These are high-frequency words such as *book*, *red*, and *apple*. No direct classroom instruction is needed in order to ascertain their meaning, as most ELs acquire these words outside of school.

- **Tier two:** Vocabulary words that fall into this category are heard or used often; are used across several content areas; are important for meaning making; or connect to other words (Kucan, 2012). Examples include *incredible*, *satisfy*, and *tolerate*.

- **Tier three:** These are subject-specific words that are more sparsely utilized, like *aphid*, *antenna*, and *pollen*. Teachers need to explicitly cover the meanings of tier three words, also known as *academic vocabulary*. You can read more about academic vocabulary in chapter 7 (page 161).

Because it is important to set the bar high and expect *all* students to use academic vocabulary, never water down content or vocabulary for English learners. Scaffolding while holding high expectations is the key to gaining proficiency.

Concepts of Print and Language Structure Transfers

Recognizing linguistic differences helps you understand potential areas of confusion. For example, students with Farsi, Arabic, or Hebrew as their home language read from right to left, not from left to right. Their books open from what English speakers consider the back as well, so differences like these need to be explicitly taught to students who learned to read in Arabic, Hebrew, Farsi, and similar languages.

The following list provides some common examples of differences that you will encounter. Knowing these can help you anticipate stumbling blocks.

- **It:** In many Asian languages, such as Chinese, Hmong, Korean, and Vietnamese, people do not use the pronoun *it* as a subject. So, for example, students may ask, "What time?" instead of "What time is it?" In some languages, like Haitian Creole, Vietnamese, and Chinese, possessive pronouns are omitted or placed after the noun—for example, "This car is of him" (instead of "This is his car") or "He raised hand" (instead of "He raised his hand").

- **Have:** Another example is the use of the verb *have* in Spanish. You may hear students say, "She has seven years" (*Tiene siete años*) instead of "She is seven years old." Or a student might say, "I have hunger" (*Tengo hambre*) as opposed to "I am hungry." The Spanish verb *tener* (meaning "to have") expresses a temporary status. Teach these verb usages in English.

- **Adverbs:** In some languages, such as Hmong, adverbs are used twice to say something is happening a lot, such as "I run fast fast." Fluent English speakers would say, "I run really fast."

- **Double negatives:** English avoids double negatives, but in Spanish and Haitian Creole, it is acceptable to say, "They don't like nothing." In English, one would say, "They don't like anything."

- **Word order:** English typically puts the adjective (descriptor) before the noun. In many other languages, the adjective goes after the noun. For example, *red car* would be *carro rojo* in Spanish.

Other structures such as articles, pronouns, and commands are outlined in Hampton-Brown's (2000) *Language Transfer Issues: For English Learners*.

Clearly, few teachers will speak all the languages represented in their classrooms. Lean on the students and families to provide home-language words that you can add to anchor charts, classroom labels, homework directions, and so on. Big buddies—like kindergartners matched with fifth graders or a senior English-proficient student mentoring a newcomer ninth grader—can also help with transcribing stories, reading texts in students' home language, and explaining academic vocabulary. This is a place where generative artificial intelligence (AI) can help, if peers are unavailable.

Conclusion

Our world is a beautiful, diverse, fascinating mix of cultures, languages, customs, and communities. The classroom is a microcosm of society at large. Our students' academic and social success depends on creating a culturally responsive and sustaining learning environment in which all students' cultures, languages, and experiences are included, valued, and respected.

From literally reading books and words on the walls that are in their home language to seeing people and places that represent themselves in books and other media, students will take bigger risks and participate more if they feel seen, heard, and represented. Also, it is incumbent on us as educators to examine, acknowledge, and keep in check our implicit biases. While there are entire books on culturally responsive, culturally sustaining pedagogy and instruction, I wanted to discuss it here before we dive into SWIRL strategies. We can't expect students to speak, write, interact, read, and listen unless they feel like their languages, cultures, and lived experiences are reflected, recognized, and valued.

CHAPTER 2

Understanding Language Acquisition and Proficiency Levels

Language and culture are the frameworks through which humans experience, communicate, and understand reality.
—Lev Vygotsky

Whether you've learned a second language yourself or you teach English learners, you know that there are many nuances to acquiring a second language. It is essential for teachers of multilingual learners to know how best to deliver instruction so that students can learn key academic vocabulary, grammatical structures, and strategies like using context clues, identifying root words, and springboarding off rhyming families or cognates when spelling and reading.

Researchers compare learning a language to learning how to tie shoelaces or count in that it requires much repetition and reinforcement (Ghazi-Saidi & Ansaldo, 2017). Language learners also benefit from receiving verbal and nonverbal praise from adults as they acquire words, phrases, and sentences.

This chapter provides an overview of essential language theories; language acquisition proficiency stages and assessments; comprehensible input; the role of motivation, self-esteem, anxiety, and affective filter in language acquisition; and ELD instruction (including designated, integrated, and systematic ELD). The goal is to give you the lay of the land in terms of how people best acquire a second language and how to assess students' language proficiency.

Language Theory in Brief

Knowing the basics of major language theories is crucial because it gives us, as educators, insight as to how and when students learn language. In researching *first* language acquisition, behaviorist B. F. Skinner (1953, 1957) claimed that children imitate their parents', teachers', or caregivers' language. Rewards are given for successfully spoken words and phrases. Unsuccessful utterances, sounds, or nonsensical words are not rewarded and, Skinner (1953, 1957) asserted, are therefore forgotten.

Professor of linguistics Noam Chomsky (1965) theorized language acquisition is innate, claiming that people's brains are wired to acquire language from birth. If this theory is true, then it benefits both students and teachers in that children are essentially language sponges. It is natural for them to learn language, as evidenced by immersion programs in which students can emerge bilingual and biliterate after six years of instruction (California Department of Education, 2024).

Child development psychologist Jean Piaget (1936) theorized that language happens as a child develops, and that a child must understand a concept prior to acquiring the specific language forms and functions to express that concept. This means that the language to process mathematical and scientific concepts, as well as transference of literacy skills, happens naturally after a student understands the concepts in their home language.

Finally, psychologist Jerome S. Bruner (1967), known for his work on human cognition, emphasized the importance of interactions between children and their parents, teachers, and caregivers in the development of language. In his study on developmental psychology and how children learn, Bruner (1967) uses the term *scaffolding* to describe a series of instructional practices in which the teacher gives guidance and, over time, reduces the level of assistance they offer. Many sentence frames, team tasks, word banks, and other strategies for multilingual learners in the SWIRL method fall under this initial scaffolding pedagogy.

These major language development theories are summarized in table 2.1. As a classroom teacher, harness the important impact that modeling of language has on students. It is an essential skill for survival.

Those theories all apply to, say, a baby learning its primary language. This book focuses more on an elementary or secondary student learning a new language, often English in the United States, Australia, England, or Canada, in addition to already knowing their home languages.

Table 2.1: Theories of Language Acquisition

Theory and Creator	Central Idea
Behaviorist (Skinner, 1953)	Children mimic adults. Correct words, phrases, and language are reinforced when children get the object they ask for, are given rewards, or receive praise.
Innateness (Chomsky, 1968)	All children are born with innate language-learning capabilities.
Cognitive (Piaget, 2001)	Language is merely one component of a child's overarching intellectual development.
Interaction (Bruner, 1975)	Interaction between caregivers and children is the most important aspect of language development.

As mentioned earlier, translanguaging—while a subtly different pedagogy and philosophy from valuing a student's home language as an asset—is transformative:

> Research has indicated that translanguaging has been directly connected to positive identity formation, lesson completion, increased participation, expanded vocabulary, and learning gains in math and reading (Breton-Guillen, 2020; Canagarajah, 2011; Creese & Blackledge, 2010; Gort & Sembiante, 2015; Makalela, 2015; Musanti & Rodríguez, 2017). Ultimately, translanguaging not only contributes to increased academic success, but to the social-emotional wellbeing of the emergent bilingual [student] as they journey through their scholastic careers. (Dougherty, 2021, p. 21)

For second language acquisition, three main theories branch off the pioneering psychologists' theories listed in table 2.1.

1. **Nativist:** At birth, children already have an innate ability to learn language, process the rules, and expand their vocabulary (Chomsky, 1965).

2. **Environmentalist:** A child's upbringing and experience, or their nurture, prove more important in language development than their natural abilities. Environmentalists do not completely reject innate factors (Skinner, 1957).

3. **Functionalist:** The focus is on how language enables people to meet their needs, explore ideas, question, argue, express themselves, be entertained, and figure out the world around them (Prutting & Kirchner, 1987).

Linguist and educational researcher Stephen D. Krashen (1982) extrapolated ideas from these basic theories of language acquisition and applied them to second language acquisition. Ask any immersion or English language development teacher, and they will likely have heard of Stephen Krashen.

The Five Hypotheses of Krashen's Theory of Second Language Acquisition

Krashen's *input hypothesis* asserts that language input must be delivered at the student's level, and just a bit beyond it, so as to be both understandable and challenging. Many call this space of instruction the *zone of proximal development* (Vygotsky, 1978), in which a student is challenged but can comprehend and process enough to be successful. This space also is sometimes referred to as *productive struggle* or *desirable difficulty*. Here, a student is approximating answers and can make meaning by asking clarifying questions, leveraging their vocabulary and resources, or partnering with a peer or group for support.

This is why it is important for students to spend most of their reading time on books that are "just right"—those they can accurately read and comprehend 95 to 98 percent of the time (Betts, 1946). That being said, teacher and author Donalyn Miller (2017) points out:

> Reading level measurements apply to the texts children read, not the children themselves.... Requiring students to read books "at their level" at all times limits children's reading choices and derails intrinsic motivation to read, which is driven by interest, choice, and reader's purpose—not reading level. While we don't want students laboring to read text that is too difficult for them to comprehend, or burn through books that provide little intellectual challenge, we must be mindful of how reading level systems affect how children see reading and themselves as readers. Reading levels are meant to guide, not limit or define children's reading choices.

Back to Stephen Krashen, who is widely thought of as the patriarchal theorist of second language acquisition. Krashen's (1989) five central hypotheses, listed here, are worth spending some time on because they impact instructional strategies such as giving wait time, allowing students to partner up before they share with the whole group, and ensuring that inputs (vocabulary, texts, and videos) are comprehensible.

1. **Acquisition-learning hypothesis:** *Acquired* language and *learned* language are different production and performance systems. In the acquired system, a person gains a second language in a similar way to how they learned their first language. In class and elsewhere, interactions in the target language enable students to communicate in a meaningful way. On the contrary, the learned system entails formally learning through instruction, grammar rules, and tests. Krashen further distinguishes these two approaches by saying that a "deductive approach in a teacher-centered setting produces 'learning,' while an inductive approach in a student-centered setting leads to 'acquisition'" (Schütz, 2019). In short, Krashen believes that acquisition is more important than learning.

2. **Monitor hypothesis:** Monitoring happens when the following occur.
    - The learner has enough time to course-correct.
    - The learner focuses on form or thinks about accuracy.
    - The learner knows the rule.

    A student with low self-esteem may over-monitor their English language production. Krashen (1989) argues that monitoring should be limited to correcting errors that allow students to sound more polished. Recall how you felt when a teacher marked your paper with what looked like fireworks of failure. When I conference with EL students during writers' workshop (see page 122), I pick the most salient errors that I want them to correct. I don't fix every error—and really, prompt a student to self-correct with my guidance—when I know they are publishing that piece. *They* hold the pen or pencil.

    A nonexample follows.

    > *Student: I eat muffin breakfast.*
    >
    > *Teacher: Was the muffin that you ate for breakfast good?*

    An example follows.

    > *Student: I go school on car.*
    >
    > *Teacher* (not correcting "go to"): *You go by car?*

3. **Input hypothesis:** The input hypothesis focuses on acquisition, not learning, as Krashen (1989) claims that students progress through

a natural order of language acquisition when receiving input (speaking, reading, or listening) one level beyond their current level of comprehension. So, listening to an audio story or reading a text slightly more advanced than their current level of production expands their vocabulary and comprehension. Students will have productive struggle in this sweet spot and grow academically as a result (Vygotsky, 1978).

4. **Affective filter hypothesis:** This hypothesis claims that variables including a student's motivation, anxiety, and self-confidence impact second language acquisition. I can attest to the importance of lowering students' affective filter, as this makes them much more willing to take risks both academically and socially. This plays out in the classroom as lowering students' anxiety and increasing their willingness to take risks by giving them sufficient opportunities to process information before they are put on the spot. Having independent think time, turning and talking, writing before speaking, and processing in their home language are examples of how to lower students' affective filter.

   Krashen (1989) also claims that the more motivated the learner, and the lower their anxiety, the better set up for success they are in terms of second language acquisition. A student who lacks motivation, has low self-esteem, or has high anxiety will struggle because the affective filter is high. A high affective filter impedes language acquisition. A low affective filter is necessary, but not enough on its own, to ensure language acquisition.

5. **Natural order hypothesis:** This says everyone learns language in the same way, and language has a natural progression—preproduction, early production, speech emergence, intermediate fluency, and advanced fluency. The hypothesis indicates fewer stages than those given in the next section, but the basic progression is similar. Krashen (1989, 2019) does not favor posting or teaching grammar rules and vocabulary lists or giving spelling tests, listen-and-repeat drills, or overcorrections in classrooms. He does support continuous exposure to meaningful, memorable language (via comprehensible input) to allow speech to emerge spontaneously. He highlights, for example, the silent or sponge phase in which a child may not produce language but is soaking it up, which aligns with the natural order theory. Another key concept is acknowledging that multilingual learners may first speak in words or phrases, not complete sentences, like how they first produce words in their home language during development as a toddler.

Keep these hypotheses in mind while you read about the stages through which someone progresses as they acquire a second language.

Language Acquisition Proficiency Stages

Language acquisition has certain proficiency stages (which most people go through as they acquire a new language). From being silent as they soak up everything to beginning to produce language and, finally, to becoming English language proficient, remember: This is a marathon, not a sprint! In my experience, many students first develop their listening and reading (more passive) skills and later master their speaking and writing (more active) skills. There are always outliers. For example, I'm a stronger speaker than reader in my second and third languages (Spanish and Italian), but that is not typical.

Table 2.2 (page 38) describes the WIDA (2020) acquisition stages. These are the most common descriptions for the levels of language acquisition (what used to be labeled *levels 1, 2, 3, 4, 5,* and *6*). The stages correlate with Krashen's (1989) descriptors: (1) silent or receptive, (2) early production, (3) speech emergence, (4) intermediate fluency, and (5) continued fluency, respectively.

The areas where I saw emergent multilingual students struggle the most—far and away—were writing and reading comprehension. Objective research bears this out as well (Cho, Kim, & Jeong, 2019).

Please note that students might perform at varying levels, depending on the SWIRL skill demanded of them. For example, a student may be emerging in speaking but developing in reading.

Much can be said about the progression of these stages, and for that, I refer you to the following resources, which are widely considered best practice as of this writing.

- ***WIDA English Language Development Standards Framework, 2020 Edition: Kindergarten–Grade 12* (WIDA, 2020):** The majority of U.S. states assess multilingual learners based on WIDA standards.

- ***California English Language Development Standards: Kindergarten Through Grade 12* (California Department of Education, 2014):** This source distills acquisition into three stages of language acquisition.

- ***Province of British Columbia: English Language Learning (ELL) Standards* (British Columbia Ministry of Education, 2017):** This source includes similar stages.

- ***English as an Additional Language or Dialect Teacher Resource* (Australian Curriculum, Assessment and Reporting Authority, 2015):** This source suggests four stages.

Table 2.2: WIDA Proficiency-Level Descriptors

Proficiency-Level Descriptor	Student Ability to Identify Point of View in a Narrative Text
Entering	Identify language that indicates narrative points of view (for example, "I" versus "he," "she," or "they") from illustrated texts using word or phrase banks with a partner. In the beginning of the second language acquisition process, students learn vocabulary and terms that allow them to communicate basic needs for social and academic tasks. This silent, or sponge, phase can last anywhere between six weeks and six months.
Emerging	Identify language that indicates narrative points of view (for example, "he felt scared") from illustrated texts using word or phrase banks with a partner. In this second stage, learners collect new words, begin to say some of these words, and may even begin speaking in short phrases by combining words. This phase usually lasts several months to a year.
Developing	Categorize passages based on narrative points of view from illustrated texts using word or phrase banks with a partner. By this third stage, second language learners have several thousand words at their disposal. Learners communicate in short phrases and sentences as their second language begins to click for them. This phase can last several months to years.
Expanding	Compare narrative points of view in extended texts using graphic organizers with a partner. Now, learners communicate in complex sentences using conjunctions to connect related clauses. Students connect language, ideas, concepts, and thoughts. Complex conversations begin and students may start thinking in their second language. This phase may last several years.
Bridging	Compare and contrast narrative points of view in extended texts. This long-lasting stage is one in which learners acquire accuracy with complex academic and social language. This phase may last several years.
Reaching	This is the ultimate goal—English language proficiency—and usually takes between five and seven years to attain according to many second language acquisition experts (Cummins, 1984; Filmore, 1989; Krashen, 1989; Snow & Hoefnagel-Höhle, 1978).

Source: © 2020 by WIDA. Adapted with permission.

Some tools and structures for assessing EL skills and describing their proficiency levels exist. Even if your state or province, district, or school does not use standards such as those given in table 2.2, or the listed publications, you can focus on WIDA's key language uses (*narrate*, *inform*, *explain*, and *argue*) and assess how well students speak, write, interact, read, and listen in those four areas. As students move through the stages of language acquisition, continue leveraging their home languages and cultures as you celebrate their advances in English. A combination of observing language and monitoring progress—informally and formally assessing students—best informs your instruction so you can target the specific language forms, functions, and skills students need to focus on improving.

Assessments to Ascertain EL Level

Student assessments inform instruction, ensure accurate placement of students in designated ELD groups, monitor progress, and eventually serve a key role in exiting students from formal ELD instruction. Your school, district, or state or province may use a specific assessment to ascertain students' English language levels. For example, if you teach in Texas, you might use the Texas English Language Proficiency Assessment System (www.texasassessment.gov/telpas.html) to assess your English learners' proficiency. Typically, your EL coordinator, literacy coach, or principal will make sure you have access to the assessment that your district or school uses. That said, throughout the year, formative assessments should allow you to create and reform fluid groups and serve students at their particular English level.

No matter what the assessment, it is important to note that oral language is weighted more heavily in kindergarten than, say, fourth grade. That is because kindergartners have much more practice with their oral skills than their reading comprehension or writing. As students progress through the grade levels, the expectation is that their reading and writing skills expand. Therefore, areas like reading comprehension and writing are weighted more heavily in the upper grades on English proficiency exams. The exception to this is that newcomers' skills will likely all be at the entering or emerging level, independent of what grade they are in.

WIDA's language targets may be helpful even if you don't use WIDA standards for formal assessment because their specific key language uses—narrating, arguing, informing, and explaining—incorporate specific applications for science, social studies, and mathematics.

For assessing reading specifically, literacy researcher Marie Clay's (2000) running record system helps teachers analyze when students do the following as they read a given passage: make an error, self-correct, use phonics to decode, use morphemes (the smallest units of words, such as root words), and substitute or omit a word. Running records allow you to learn how fluent students are and, specifically, what impediments students have in accurately decoding words or comprehending a text.

I want to emphasize the importance of ongoing formative assessments in addition to the formal, mandated state or provincial tests. Higher-stakes initial or annual assessments inform groupings and instruction, while ongoing formative assessments may help you plan day-to-day lessons, regroup students, or scaffold. Listen-fors and look-fors, such as the following, are equally important as you work with English learners on a daily basis.

- Is the student using correct grammar?
- Is the student pronouncing words accurately?
- Can the student readily access academic vocabulary and integrate it when communicating?
- Does the student use correct sentence structure and spelling when writing?
- Is the student showing signs of being ready to work at a more advanced level?

Keep notes on every student, either in a binder or on an app like PowerSchool, Schoology, Google Classroom, or even Kahoot! I liked having a binder with pages for each student, and some teachers use sticky notes, which they add to the pages.

The Comprehensible Input Debate

In his seminal research, Krashen (1985) says that second language acquisition requires that learners receive and understand comprehensible language input. *Comprehensible input* is language that learners understand even though they might not yet grasp all the vocabulary, grammar, or structures in it—growth mindset!

The comprehensible input theory became widely accepted as the foundation of second language learning around 2019 (Lewis, 2020). It says that when a teacher, parent, or peer models speaking or writing in language that a student can understand, but the student is a bit challenged by the language, that leads to linguistic improvement. This theory aligns with Vygotsky's (1978) zone of proximal development, applying it specifically to second language acquisition.

In class, introduce new concepts using grammar or vocabulary with which the acquirers of a second language are already familiar. For example, you might read a passage or show a video about shopping at a store to introduce unfamiliar clothing items or a new tense, with the bulk of the vocabulary and grammar already being in students' repertoires. You must know the proficiency levels of the students in your classroom in order to tailor comprehensible input strategies for them. Newcomers will need more visuals and repetition than, say, long-term English learners. You can ascertain students' levels through formal (summative) and informal (formative) assessments.

Teachers need a toolbox of comprehensible input strategies to differentiate for varying English language levels. Using, for example, only short reading passages with comprehension questions will not allow you to fully utilize students' English abilities. Students might get frustrated or confused if new information is not presented in a way that they can comprehend. Consider the following example strategies in addition to cognate information (page 25).

- Strategically form groups according to instructional purpose and language demands.
- Choose mostly tier two words, and some tier three words (page 27).
- Use sentence frames to scaffold the structure and grammar, enabling students to produce a complete sentence as a response.
- Amplify meaning by paraphrasing, naming synonyms, listing examples, using gestures, sharing pictures, or presenting realia.
- Provide or cocreate anchor charts, graphic organizers, or other visuals.
- Build background knowledge with videos and demonstrations.
- Discuss target vocabulary (taught words) and teach language for explaining, asking questions, agreeing or disagreeing, and justifying ideas.
- Include oral presentations, academic writing, and discourse, and adapt them to the situation or audience.
- Provide opportunities for students to discuss ideas before writing.
- Have students summarize information they've heard in peer-to-peer conversations.

As teachers present comprehensible input, such as the verbal input of *teacher talk*, students need time to process and respond, be that verbally, in writing, or in the form of total physical response. For example, if you say to a group of students, "Hold up your blue book," while modeling that act, students will then show you that they understand by lifting up their blue books. The debate lies in how teachers may balance the amount of teacher talk time with student processing and response time. Consider the following.

- The brain needs time to chunk information and make sense of it (Bor, 2022). For example, if you play a thirty-minute audio story without pausing to discuss what students understand, you are overloading them.
- Educators need to check for understanding. That could mean listening to students speak in pairs or circulating throughout the room to look at their writing.
- Educators need students to hear themselves speaking often in order for them to recognize when language sounds accurate or "off." Krashen's (1982) take on this is the following:

  > We are generally not consciously aware of the rules of the languages we have acquired. Instead, we have a "feel" for correctness. Grammatical sentences "sound" right, or "feel" right, and errors feel wrong, even if we do not consciously know what rule was violated. (p. 10)

Consider this example from when I observed several world language classes at the high school level. In one classroom, I noticed the teacher was speaking 75 percent of the time. Students were occasionally asked to turn and talk, or write, in response to the teacher's questions. A few times, they were prompted to respond orally to the whole class. I also observed several students who seemed confused and unable to respond to the questions. This was a high-level French class. In a different class at that same school, students were asked to speak from the moment their lesson began. The teacher started out with a check-in, then eased her way into showing a video and having students respond to the video content, first in writing and then verbally to the whole class. This Spanish 3 class felt more inviting and engaging than the French class in which the teacher was doing most of the talking. Students had more opportunities to practice the language, and far fewer chances to tune out and get off task.

Let's also consider linguist Merrill Swain's (1995, 2000, 2005) *comprehensible output* theory. It states that students need scaffolding (for example, the aforementioned sentence frames, anchor charts, and think-pair-share) in order for input (texts they read, information you say, and videos they watch) to be comprehensible. Swain (1995, 2000, 2005) *also* argues that recognizing a gap in one's own knowledge of the target language allows for real learning. Multilingual learners require equal opportunities to speak, write, interact, respond, and listen in their target language for authentic, accurate, and meaningful communication to happen.

Motivation, Self-Esteem, and Anxiety

To learn a new language, students need to feel motivated, confident in their abilities, and safe. When a student feels pressured—or like classmates are ridiculing their mistakes or the teacher is overcorrecting them—they will inevitably shut down. Teachers should aim for students' affective filter to be as low as possible (Oteir & Al-Otaibi, 2019) because when *negative affect* (the experience of emotions such as fear, shame, or frustration) gets too high, the students may be unable to learn. Researchers who ascribe to the affective filter theory explain that a "language teacher can minimize the students' anxiety by following certain strategies such as focusing on the message, neglecting the form, and not insisting on early production unless the teacher feels that the students are ready" (Oteir & Al-Otaibi, 2019, p. 312).

Keeping students' affective filter low is a nuanced pedagogical practice. In addition to the many scaffolds and strategies presented in part 2 (page 77), here are some strategies I've found helpful.

- **Value students' assets** by springboarding off their home languages (for example, by using cognates), their cultures, their experiences, and their identities. This is a WIDA recommendation and a best practice in a culturally responsive and sustaining classroom.

- **Give students voice and choice** whenever and however you can. Allow students to choose what they read and write about, who they partner with (about half the time), and how they demonstrate what they learned (such as via oral presentation, written essay or reflection, or presentation slide deck).

- **Develop vocabulary** by using the Frayer model (figure 2.1, page 44), discussing shades of meaning through activities like paint chip vocabulary strips (page 97), and previewing new vocabulary prior to reading. Focus on tier two words, which are less frequently used academic vocabulary, and integrate some more complex tier three words. Spend less time on tier one words unless working with newcomers. Incorporate polysemous (multiple meaning) words such as *palm* (a tree, part of your hand).

- **Extend language** by providing sentence frames, starters, or stems as scaffolds. Teach students to use the "Yes, and" strategy, which shows them how to build on each other's ideas.
- **Provide a print-rich environment** with word banks, co-constructed anchor charts, cognate lists, chants, labeled visuals, and graphic organizers on display around the room for reference.
- **Give positive and actionable feedback** during student turn-and-talks, one-on-one conferences, and small-group instruction. Consistently acknowledge both effort and accuracy. Also, choose your battles in terms of correcting one or two words and not every single word a student says or writes.

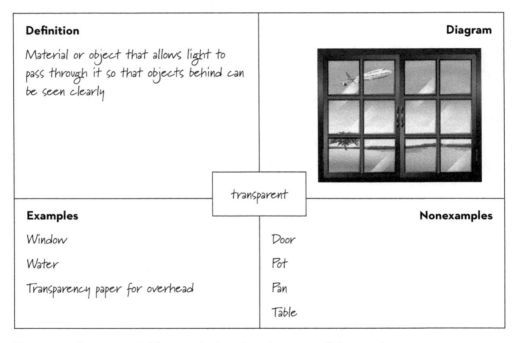

Figure 2.1: Frayer model for vocabulary development of the word *transparent*.

Visit **go.SolutionTree.com/EL** *for a free reproducible version of this figure.*

Instructional Approaches: Designated, Integrated, and Systematic ELD

There are myriad methods through which educators can deliver English language development. During designated or integrated approaches, systematic ELD may be implemented.

Your school, district, or state or province may mandate thirty minutes of *designated ELD* instruction to target students' particular English proficiency level. This is protected time "during the regular school day when teachers provide lessons for English learners to develop English language proficiency" (Ybarra & Hollingsworth, n.d.).

Or, you may be in a district that encourages a more *integrated ELD* model:

> In the integrated ELD model, educators teach language and content simultaneously by designing lessons focused on content standards with scaffolding that supports emergent multilingual students at their respective language proficiency levels. With integrated ELD, students experience explicit language development opportunities throughout the school day—not just [during ELD lessons]. (Scardina & Johnson, 2024)

Programs such as Guided Language Acquisition Design® (GLAD; https://ntcprojectglad.com or https://begladtraining.com) offer thematic integration of language, which makes for a print-rich environment where academic vocabulary is integrated across content areas.

Susana Dutro and Michelle Thelander's E.L. Achieve (www.elachieve.org) offers a strategic program, called Systematic ELD, that progresses through developmental units designed to grow ELs' proficiency. They also offer what they call Constructing Meaning resources for teaching the language needed to comprehend and demonstrate understanding of grade-level work (integrated ELD). Dutro's solo and collaborative work provides a sequence of vocabulary, grammatical structure, and syntax lessons that progress over time (Dutro, 2016; Dutro & Kinsella, 2010; Dutro & Moran, 2003; Dutro, Núñez, & Helman, 2016).

Designated Versus Integrated ELD

Designated and integrated ELD are not mutually exclusive as approaches. You can combine, alternate, or switch strategies. Many districts require that teachers spend a certain amount of time (typically thirty minutes per day) delivering direct ELD instruction at the learner's level (Calderón, Slavin, & Sánchez, 2011). Some schools group students according to EL level and share or mix groups of students between classes to address their specific language needs. Others rely on the teacher to group multiple EL levels together during ELD lessons. Some research shows increased oral proficiency in students who receive designated ELD and, on that note, a significant positive impact of designated ELD compared to integrated ELD alone (Edelman et al., 2022).

Whatever the format or structure, designated ELD instruction differs from regular content lessons in that it is language objective forward, with content in the background. For example, if you're doing a lesson on the plant life cycle, the plant phases are part of your science lesson for all students. During the ELD lesson, you may label a graph with the vocabulary, have students turn and talk to restate the cycle phases to their partner, or ask students to draw and label their own graph. The emphasis is on *input* (what the students are listening to you say or what they read) and *output* (what they are saying or writing), modeling, and overall English language production. This is a sacred space and time for you to work exclusively with your EL students. It is usually conducted in a small group of four to six students.

Some teachers take more of an integrative approach. This requires them to weave ELD strategies into lessons that they are delivering to the whole class or to a small mixed group of students at varying English language proficiency levels. The theory is that all students can benefit from the strategies you employ for ELs, such as visual anchors and an emphasis on academic vocabulary. Integrated ELD also addresses a logistic concern, in that some teachers may not have the time or resources to meet separately with ELs at each proficiency level.

Systematic ELD

Systematic ELD's ultimate goal is to shift the ratio of teacher talk to student talk from 85 percent teacher and 15 percent student to the opposite—15 percent teacher talk and 85 percent student talk—and shift English learner participation from 2 percent to 85 percent (Kostadinovska-Stojchevska & Popovikj, 2019). That aligns with education academic John Hattie's (2015) discovery that teacher talk should be minimal, and that careful consideration needs to be paid to what students are saying and the kinds of questions they ask.

Simply shifting the ratio of teacher talk to student talk isn't enough (Hattie, 2015). We need to find ways to spark productive classroom discussions. Systematic ELD is thematic (featuring words and activities about community helpers, fruits and vegetables, or animals, for example) and focused on real-life, applicable themes. Often, teachers receive an EL group or are assigned students, but they have no concrete resources for teaching ELD lessons. You can follow the lessons, deliver them by sequential steps, and see real progress among your ELs.

I used systematic ELD as a literacy coach and found it to be a valuable resource. The instruction concentrates on how English works. It is student centered and follows a language scope and sequence, focusing on tier one, tier two, and tier three vocabulary, and utilizing sentence structures at, or slightly beyond, the learner's level.

It draws on the rhythm and cadence of English, idioms, grammatical structures, formal and informal registers, and rules of discourse (E.L. Achieve, n.d.). Systematic ELD covers the forms of English (grammar) and functions (purpose); the forms of vocabulary, syntax, and grammar all influence how well a function performs. Systematic ELD monitors and limits teacher explanation in service of making sure students have adequate time to produce language in English.

Conclusion

The theories surrounding how students learn English are an important base that we need to understand to best serve multilingual learners. Knowing students' English language level (entering, emerging, developing, expanding, bridging, or reaching) helps us scaffold and support students with specific ELD lessons and opportunities to process language through differentiated instructional methods. Ongoing formative assessments help keep students' English language level groupings and instruction fluid to meet their needs.

Krashen's (1982, 2017, 2018, 2019) theory of second language acquisition informs us that comprehensible input is important to students' success in acquiring English (or another foreign language). Supporting your students via the mandatory designated ELD time, or integrated ELD lessons and strategies, so that they do not remain long-term ELs, is incumbent on us.

We want students to be fluent, graduate from high school, attend and graduate from college, and have successful careers. To reach this North Star, it is essential to keep students' affective filters as low as possible, and their confidence as high as possible, so they take risks both socially and academically. Allowing students to, for example, think or write about a story, then speak to a partner, and then share out with the whole group—as opposed to calling on raised hands immediately after posing a question for reflection—builds up their confidence and encourages ELs to take risks.

CHAPTER 3

Planning Lessons

A well-developed lesson plan is a road map of a wise educator. An educator's expertise is reflected in [their] lesson plan. It is the architecture of a teacher's expertise.

—Rajeev Ranjan

Planning lessons, like learning another language, takes time to master. When planning a lesson for English learners, you must turn content objectives (What are you teaching? That is, what standards are you required to teach about content areas?) into language objectives (How will students use language to meet those requirements with academic language skills? For instance, will they speak to a partner? Write a paragraph? Read a book and then compare two characters in a Venn diagram?). From there, you build a classroom lesson. This chapter helps you design lessons with clear content and language objectives in mind to meet the needs of your multilingual learners.

Let's begin with some self-reflection so you can gauge where you are with your EL lessons. Here are some questions to consider.

- Are you providing visible sentence stems or frames?

- Do you know which phase of language acquisition (EL level) each student is currently at? Many states use WIDA standards (2020; see chapter 2, page 31) but, whatever the assessment, teachers should know each student's English language proficiency level so they can properly group their students, choose appropriate texts, provide scaffolds, and differentiate instruction.

- For Spanish speakers, are you leveraging cognates (such as *car/carro* and *imagine/imaginar*)? There are over twenty thousand cognates between Spanish and English.

49

- Do students have tasks that require them to SWIRL: speak, write, interact with others, read content, and listen attentively?
- Are you providing differentiated scaffolds throughout the day that call on students to use academic vocabulary and accountable talk?
- Do you identify and display both the lesson objective (the *what*, or content standard) and the language objective (the *how*, or a specific method through which students will use their English language skills to demonstrate that they understand the content)?

If this feels overwhelming, there's good news: many language skills are acquired over time. So, if you are working, for example, on having students correctly use verbs and verb conjugations, that language objective may be displayed for days or weeks. While you might have several language objectives up at the same time, some will be long-term goals. The other encouraging element is that, often, students will be speaking about, interacting through, and listening to what they are reading or writing. It all ties together.

When you design your lessons with SWIRL elements in mind, you should integrate and balance all these cognitive demands in your students' day. Of course, this looks different depending on where students are on their proficiency journey. And it takes practice to keep all five SWIRL elements in mind as you create language objectives from content objectives.

Before the rest of the book dives into classroom activities, this chapter explains how to plan a lesson or unit for an EL student, which generally breaks down into the following steps.

1. Know your content objectives.
2. Turn each content objective into a language objective.
3. Write each language objective in student-friendly language as an *I can* statement.
4. Incorporate scaffolds (such as gradual release of responsibility, cognate connections, student partners for think-pair-share, and sentence frames) with certain activities. Ensure a mixture of speaking, writing, interacting, reading, and listening opportunities every single day, if not every lesson.

This chapter will prepare you to plan where best to integrate the different scaffolds and strategies described in subsequent chapters.

Turning Content Objectives Into Language Objectives

Why is it important for ELs to have clear content objectives *and* language objectives? No matter what state, province, territory, or country you teach in, there are a set of standards that comprise *what* you will teach. Those are your *content objectives* and are, in general, non-negotiable. For English learners (and, one might argue, for all students), it is imperative to also articulate *how* they will learn and demonstrate knowledge of those content objectives. What specific academic language, grammar, or spelling conventions do they need to be able to say, read, or write in order to demonstrate that they understand and can respond in English? The answer determines your *language objectives*.

Language objectives address the following questions: What language will students use to communicate and express their comprehension? How will they express their knowledge—by speaking, writing, interacting, reading, listening, or a combination thereof?

Like content objectives, language objectives need to be written in student-friendly language that makes them readily accessible. To get where they need to go, students need to be able to clearly see and say where they are going. Integrating language objectives with content objectives grants students access to the content. For example, a content objective might be, "Retell the events of a story in order." The language objective might state, "Use the terms *in the beginning, in the middle,* and *at the end* when retelling the events of the story in order orally to a partner." Understanding the what (content objective) and the how (language objective) increases engagement, output, and overall achievement. It also allows you to assess students more effectively.

Students need teachers to articulate explicit objectives and to say how they will demonstrate that they have achieved these goals. Research shows that visible objectives help students focus their attention on what they need to learn (Duchastel, 1979; Marzano, Pickering, & Pollock, 2001; Orr, Csikari, Freeman, & Rodriguez, 2022). Specific objectives given prior to a lesson give students clear direction and a target to work toward. English learners, especially, stay more focused on their instructional path when they know their purpose.

Figure 3.1 (page 52) shows examples of content objectives aligned to language objectives (also sometimes referred to as *language targets*).

Content Objective	Language Objective
Compare and contrast two texts.	Discuss the similarities and differences between the two books with your partner, and write three sentences using descriptive adjectives and comparison words (such as *similar, different,* and *same*).
Describe the life cycle of a frog.	Use basic adjectives to describe frogs (*green, venomous, fast, jumpy, bright*). Examples follow. • The frog is green. His feet are sticky. • A green frog has sticky feet. • The tiny, green frog has powerful legs.
Learn the causes of the American Revolution.	Be able to orally explain the connection between the French and Indian War and the American Revolution.

Source for standard: California Department of Education, n.d.a, n.d.c.

Figure 3.1: Content objectives converted into language objectives.

While it might seem cumbersome and daunting to write a language objective for every lesson, I assure you that it will be well worth your while. Once you've established language objectives that accompany content standards, you will reuse them in the future. Springboard off your state or provincial ELD standards, WIDA standards, or both. Collaborate with other teachers at your grade level (on site or in the district) to write language objectives; then collaborate across grade levels to align the preceding and following years' objectives with those at your grade level. Professional collaboration improves the effectiveness of implementing language objectives (Orr et al., 2022).

The Sheltered Instruction Observation Protocol (SIOP®), in which many teachers of multilingual learners are trained, calls on teachers to post language objectives, making them observable and measurable (Echevarria, Vogt, & Short, 2017). *Measurable* falls under the SMART goals protocol, which defines goals that are *specific, measurable, attainable, results oriented,* and *time bound* (Conzemius & O'Neill, 2014; Doran, 1981).

The following sections help you write language objectives and then recraft them in student-friendly language.

Writing Language Objectives

Follow these steps to turn a content objective into a language objective (Morgan, n.d.).

1. Look at your content standards, one by one, and pinpoint each desired outcome. For example, imagine that the content standard

is to summarize an informational text about chameleons. You are expecting a five-paragraph essay from students, with topic sentences and supporting details.

2. Identify the language skills required. For example, students need to use correct grammar and tense when summarizing and include scientific terms such as *camouflage*, *scales*, *habitat*, and *species*. This is the language objective, or language target.

3. Figure out the specific language (words, tenses, or terms) students need to demonstrate their understanding of the concept, text, or task, and decide how students will demonstrate their knowledge. Will they speak to a partner, share with the whole class, or do a written reflection? Will they read a text and respond by making a slide deck or presentation?

4. Consider your specific students' English language proficiency levels (table 2.2, page 38) and include scaffolding or modifications where appropriate. Perhaps you want students to include the countries in which chameleons can be found. A language objective for newcomers may read, "Identify proper nouns by underlining them." A more advanced multilingual learner's objective may read, "Identify and name all proper nouns orally and in writing."

While the language objective remains almost the same, independent of the individual student's language proficiency level, you can differentiate the level of support through scaffolds. An example might be varying the number and difficulty of sentence frames depending on whether the student needs substantial, moderate, or light support. Ideally, students state out loud or silently read the content and language objectives before launching into a lesson. There are two scaffold tiers—(1) the action requested of the student and (2) the proficiency level. For example, you might ask a student to describe, compare, explain, discuss, or summarize. For each of those requests, you target the frame toward the student's English language abilities (entering or emerging, developing, or expanding). Consider the following examples (Colorín Colorado, n.d.a).

Describe a plant cell.

- **Entering or emerging:** The plant cell has _____.
- **Developing:** The cell has _____, which helps it _____.
- **Expanding:** I can infer that the cell is _____, since it has _____.

Compare plant and animal cells.

- **Entering or emerging:** Plant and animal cells both have _____.
- **Developing:** Like the plant cell, the animal cell also contains _____.
- **Expanding:** Some similarities between the plant and animal cell include _____.

As you work on language objectives, keep in mind how long the project, lesson, or task will take. Table 3.1 covers other considerations.

Table 3.1: Considerations When Writing Language Objectives

What to Ask	How to Integrate Into the Lesson
Consideration	
What students should know and be able to do with their newly learned language (otherwise known as *function* [*purpose*], *form* [*structure*], and *fluency*)	
What vocabulary, forms, and functions will students need for the task at hand?	For vocabulary (subject-specific words, adjectives, nouns, proper nouns), consider cocreating a word bank or anchor chart to which students can refer.
Do they need to know a certain tense (present, past, or future)?	
Does anyone need a grammar or vocabulary minilesson?	For event sequencing, clearly model how you use specific vocabulary and language patterns by writing in front of the class and by doing think-alouds (Dutro & Moran, 2003; Miles & Bailey-McKenna, 2016).
If foundational skills (phonics, grammar, decoding, and fluency) are the focus, how can you also encourage meaning making (comprehension) and a love of learning?	
Are they required to write or say events in order for sequencing?	For decoding skills, compare sounds or symbols from home language alphabets or characters to those in English.
What specific vocabulary will you listen for or look for?	
How will they show you that they understand? (Giving students a choice or combining product types is best practice so they show what they know via their primary learning modality.)	
Consideration	
The student's English proficiency level (which is important because scaffolds will differ based on that proficiency) and which scaffolds will support students as they use the language needed to perform the language function	

What is each student's zone of proximal development? Will they be able to achieve this goal with substantial, moderate, or light support?	While you want multilingual learners to meet grade-level content objectives, a student with emerging English skills in, say, fourth grade may need to focus on identifying nouns before identifying proper nouns.
Consideration	
What prior knowledge students have or do not have (since prior knowledge helps students contextualize and comprehend new ideas)	
What background knowledge do students need to access this information? How can you springboard off students' current knowledge of the topic to introduce the current unit? If they have little or no background knowledge on the topic, how will you front-load some information and vocabulary prior to launching the unit?	"Plan short prompts or questions to *activate prior knowledge* about the text's concepts, themes, historical background, vocabulary, connections, and experiences, allowing students to realize they know something about the upcoming topic" (Nickelsen & Dickson, 2022, p. 59). Build background knowledge and simultaneously value students' linguistic assets by leveraging cognates. Also known as *building schemata*, building background knowledge includes narrative input charts, cognitive content dictionaries, and labeling and drawing charts. Singing and chanting help ELs retain information and engage. Making content visual with anchor charts, color coding, or underlining helps build schemata too. *Dictation*, which falls under foundational skills and also mimics the Spanish *dictado*, is when a teacher reads a word, phrase, or sentence aloud as students write it down. Teachers then either write the correct spelling and punctuation on the board (and students self-correct) or check students' papers as an assessment tool.
Consideration	
Cultural relevance and whether the content is relatable and meaningful for students (whether it represents and reflects your class makeup)	
How can you invite students to share their culture and language as a springboard to learning?	Leveraging Spanish, French, and Haitian Creole cognates—for example, in Spanish, *history/historia*, *editor/editora*, and *animal/animal*—encourages students to view and use their home language vocabulary as an asset. Making other crosslinguistic connections, such as with prefixes (*sub-*, *in-*, *dis-*, *des-*) and punctuation (upside-down question marks in Spanish), helps ELs apply knowledge they already have in their home language to English.

CONTINUED →

What to Ask	How to Integrate Into the Lesson
Consideration	
Which strategies to use (including but not limited to scaffolding, interventions, adaptations, gradual release of responsibility, think time, and brain breaks)	
What strategies make the language accessible? How will you keep students engaged, accountable, and in their zone of proximal development?	Put students in pairs, triads, or small groups to practice using academic language—key vocabulary, grammar, or phrases needed to understand and respond to texts, academic discourse, and formal writing assignments (Dutro & Moran, 2003; Miles & Bailey-McKenna, 2016). Students should practice different ways to become more flexible—accessing prior knowledge, using anchor charts such as word banks and diagrams, or turning and talking before writing or speaking. Having multiple means of processing input ensures students are less likely to have cognitive overload, feel frustrated, or give up (Dutro & Moran, 2003; Miles & Bailey-McKenna, 2016). Scaffold responses by allowing students to turn and talk before you ask anyone to share with the whole class. Knowing your students' English proficiency levels helps you plan an objective and a lesson that let them have productive struggle. Partnering newcomers with more English-proficient students increases the likelihood that they will take risks and view peers as resources in addition to the teacher. In mathematics, for example, a student's zone of proximal development may be different than it is in English language arts (because they may be familiar with and able to do numerical calculations when the task is not entirely based on new vocabulary). A list of tried-and-true classroom strategies that you're almost certainly using for all the students in your classroom follows this table (page 58) so you can see how they work with EL students.

Consideration
When and how to use technology to differentiate for varying learning modalities (visual, kinesthetic, auditory, and tactile)

What technology might you use to support instruction in all SWIRL elements?	There are pros and cons to using technology with ELs. On the pro side, programs like Curriculum Associates' i-Ready allow for differentiated reading lessons and progress monitoring. It may also create low-pressure situations and have engaging visuals and music, in addition to encouraging rewards as students progress through various levels and tasks.
	On the con side, often technology means students are listening and reading more and speaking, interacting, and writing less. There also is general concern about how technology impacts students' attention spans (one study found that since 2000, the average attention span has decreased from twelve seconds to eight seconds; McSpadden, 2015).
	Consider scaffolds during technology use as well, such as displaying closed captions on a video or chunking content by pausing the video or audio to give students time to discuss, process, and ask questions.

Consideration
How to assess language objective mastery

How will you assess that students read or heard the content and can respond verbally or in writing? (The same language objective is usually at play; however, you may give more support to newcomers than to long-term ELs, for example, though every student still gets assessed.)	Assessment *as* learning involves strategies such as self- and peer assessment, student choice in research subjects, and identification and selection of the way students communicate (orally or in writing, for instance) to process information and convey what they are learning (Gottlieb, 2016).
	Assessment *for* learning may include student-generated rubrics and real-time feedback to students (Gottlieb, 2016).
	Assessment *of* learning consists of looking at evidence of learning and matching it to standards to see if they were met; teachers also evaluate products, performances, projects, and presentations (Gottlieb, 2016).

As mentioned in the table, the following list includes strategies you're likely familiar with that have a meaningful impact on EL students. The parenthetical SWIRL capitalizations indicate which language competencies students use during each.

- **Anchor charts (SWIRL):** Display vocabulary charts, Venn diagrams, T-charts, and so on. Refer back to them in support of student output. For example, a chart might list nouns and adjectives in English and all the languages your EL students use at home.

- **Collaborative conversations (SwIrL):** Give students prompts and then invite them to move around the room and talk in pairs or groups about their answers. For example, you might have students discuss what evidence they found in a text, how they drew a conclusion, or how their idea and their partner's idea match (or don't). Specific activities for collaborative conversations might also include four corners (page 156) and along the lines (page 102), both of which have participants speak, interact, and listen (and potentially write and read, such as on charts during four corners).

- **Turn-and-talk (SwIrL):** Talking to a peer, as opposed to having to raise their hand and speak in front of the whole class, is a much less risky proposition for those who are still tentative about their language skills. Maintaining a low affective filter is an important ingredient of turn-and-talks, as are sentence frames, questions, and turn-taking protocols (Riches, 2021). Also known as *think-pair-share* and *10/2* (after the teacher speaks for ten minutes, they give students two minutes to process the input by talking to someone), this purposeful partnering should happen throughout the day. Some teachers assign partners, and others allow students to choose. The majority of teachers do a combination of these. The following partnering points are important as well.
    - Often, the students in a pair or partner grouping should have different English language proficiencies so they can support each other and have English language models besides the teacher.
    - Consider partnering students of similar English language levels if the task is differentiated based on proficiency.
    - Also partner students who speak the same home language so they can first process content in their home language before being prompted to speak in English.

- **Sentence frames and stems (SWIRL):** A sentence frame basically is a sentence that contains empty spaces to which students add words. An example is, "One character in the story who acted brave was _____ because _____." This activity helps scaffold students' production of complete sentences with key vocabulary. A sentence stem or starter is the beginning of a sentence that students finish, such as, "The main idea of this text was _____." Stems are open-ended and help students launch their writing or speaking so the language demands do not seem overwhelming.

- **Student menu (SWIrL):** This gives students choice in how they show you what they've learned. For example, a menu might give students options to talk to a partner, meet with their table group, or think quietly. Other choices can include to write a response, raise their hand, check a resource, or request help from a peer (some teachers call this "phone a friend"). You may not give students choice in every task, but knowing that they can ask for help from a peer if they are called on and feel stuck gives them a way to navigate anxiety. Being able to lean on peers, interact, and choose the way that they demonstrate their learning lowers their affective filter.

- **Writing before responding (SWIRl):** Getting to write about a prompt or question before sharing their response with a partner, a group, or the whole class helps many students process information, gather their thoughts, and lower their affective filter. For example, you can ask students to jot down unfamiliar words, character traits, or predictions they have about what will happen next in the text.

The following student-friendly content objectives apply to a third-grade lesson.

- Students will research the solar system using multiple digital and print resources.
- Students will use scientific terms such as *asteroid*, *comet*, and *galaxy* to describe the solar system.
- Students will be able to ask and answer questions about the text, orally and in writing, using complete sentences.

The student-friendly language objective would be this: "I can use scientific terms such as *orbit*, *asteroid*, *planet*, *comet*, and *galaxy* to describe the solar system orally and in writing."

The teacher would follow this procedure.

1. Identify different features of the solar system, like the sun, the moon, the planets, comets, and asteroids.
2. Ask each student to choose one solar system feature to research. Work with students as they choose their topics to be sure that each feature, including each planet, is chosen.
3. Talk about where students might find information on their topics (books, online articles, magazines, and newspapers).
4. Review these steps to doing research: question, search, analyze, compose, and share (reflected in the following steps).
5. Have students determine what they would like to know about their solar system topic. Help them create specific questions that articulate what they want to find out.
6. Tell students they should use both online and traditional sources for their research. Encourage them to check as many sources as time allows.
7. Limit students' online research to websites that have been vetted for safe use.
8. Ask students to organize their information and make a poster, drawing, diorama, mural, or papier-mâché planet to show what they learned about their topic. One group I taught decided to do a newscast about their solar system topic.
9. Tell students that, when they do research, they need to make a list of the resources they used, called a *bibliography*.
10. Have students set up and share their finished work in a classroom galaxy, present to other students, or share with families.

Now comes the assessment. You could use the rubric in figure 3.2 to evaluate student work.

This is just one example to give you a sense of how to plan, execute, and assess a lesson with multilingual learners in mind. The following sections further examine the considerations listed in table 3.1 (page 54): function and form, rigor, student-friendly wording, and strategies for multilingual learners.

4 Exemplary Understanding	3 Competent Understanding	2 Developing Understanding	1 Emerging Understanding
Uses unique, well-vetted research sources Shows extended thinking in addition to information synthesis Creates a product that is thorough, neat, and creative	Uses well-vetted research sources Shows basic application and information synthesis Creates a product that is thorough and neat	Uses unreliable or insufficient research sources Shows how and why, but little or no information synthesis Creates a product that is incomplete or difficult to read	Uses unreliable research sources or relies on self Shows no information synthesis Creates a product that is incomplete and difficult to read

Figure 3.2: Example rubric to assess student work in the solar system unit.

Function and Form

In crafting your language objectives, it is imperative to keep the forms and functions of the English language in mind. *Language function* is the purpose (why the student is using the language—to what end). Do they need to do the following?

- Express wants and needs
- Sequence events
- Give their opinion
- Inform others about a topic
- Analyze literature
- Summarize stories or others' arguments

Language forms refer to the structures of language (vocabulary, syntax, and grammar).

You may want to consider the following foci and terms when writing language objectives (Dutro & Moran, 2003). If you teach ELD lessons (either designated or integrated), be sure to have the functions and forms articulated in the language objectives.

Functions	Forms	Fluency
Tasks: What are the communicative purposes English learners must be able to navigate?	**Tools:** What are the discourse and grammatical tools needed to communicate for different purposes?	**Trying it out:** What do English learners need in order to develop accurate and fluent language?

Functions
- Express social courtesies
- Participate in discussions
- Give and follow directions
- Express needs, likes, and feelings
- Ask and answer questions
- Describe people and things
- Describe places and locations
- Relate observable events
- Express time and duration
- Classify and compare
- Express cause and effect
- Predict
- Summarize
- Draw conclusions
- Make generalizations

Forms
- Syntax—word order
- Subject-verb agreement
- Conventions for formal and informal use
- General and specific nouns
- Verb tenses
- Auxiliary verbs
- Conjunctions
- Pronouns and articles
- Adjectives
- Adverbial phrases
- Prepositional phrases
- Sentence variation and complexity

Fluency
- Clear modeling of how to purposefully use a range of vocabulary and language patterns
- Structured peer practice using taught language
- Practice using learned language in various ways to develop flexibility
- Frequent and varied opportunities to communicate ideas orally
- Frequent and varied opportunities to apply learned language in different ways, both orally and in writing

As noted, you will keep in mind the forms and functions of the English language.

- **Common forms:** These are the structures of language needed for a particular function. Examples include vocabulary, sentence structure (subject + verb + object), nouns (such as plural nouns, possessive nouns, and proper nouns), pronouns, verbs, verb tenses, modals (*can, could, should,* and so on), adjectives (such as comparative and superlative adjectives), adverbs, prepositional phrases, and conjunctions.

- **Common functions:** These are the purposes for which someone is using language. Examples include retelling, describing, summarizing, identifying cause and effect, comparing and contrasting, analyzing, sequencing, expressing wants and needs, arguing an opinion, persuading, classifying, drawing conclusions, and informing.

You might include some of the following key words and phrases in your language objectives for a smattering of language functions.

- **Compare and contrast:** *Same, alike, similar, both, different, difference, unlike*
- **Persuade:** *One reason that, should, should not, for example*
- **Sequence:** *In the beginning, in the middle, at the end, first, next, then, finally, in conclusion*
- **Analyze:** *More, less, as evidenced in, the data show, least, greatest*
- **Clarify:** *Why, how, I wonder, what if*
- **Draw a conclusion:** *In summary, I noticed, I identified, I surmised, my takeaways were*

Rigor

Educational psychologist Benjamin Bloom's (1956) revised taxonomy (Anderson & Krathwohl, 2001) underscores the demands placed on students and aligns those with specific verbs that give the gist of the tasks at hand. In the following list, the least rigorous task appears first, with *create* as the most rigorous task.

- **Remember:** Recall or restate a fact, summary, or story element after hearing or reading it.
- **Understand:** Comprehend concepts and explain them to others.
- **Apply:** Manipulate information or use it to build on and further your knowledge base.
- **Analyze:** Delve into comparing, contrasting, drawing conclusions, or making hypotheses about a theory or text.
- **Evaluate:** Discern and make decisions about an article or text, given concrete information or opinions. Form an opinion of your own.
- **Create:** Make, design, or ideate a project, presentation, or slide deck.

Starting a language objective with a concrete verb tells students specifically what they will be doing. Examples include "*Identify* the main characters," "*Compare* and *contrast* two books," and "*Support* your opinion using facts from the text" (Anderson & Krathwohl, 2001). The following lists provide verbs you can use when writing content and language objectives (Echevarria, Vogt, & Short, 2017).

Verbs for Content Objectives	**Verbs for Language Objectives**
Knowledge: List, identify, locate, memorize, review, label, describe, define, name, match	**Listening:** Tell, role-play, identify, listen, recognize, point, show, follow directions
Comprehension: Recall, reproduce, summarize, explain, demonstrate, translate, rephrase	**Speaking:** Name, discuss, rephrase, ask, answer, predict, say steps in a process, pronounce, repeat, respond, state, summarize, retell, explain, tell, use
Application: Predict, compare, contrast, solve, classify, categorize, show, apply, make, build a replica	**Reading:** Preview, read aloud, find specific information, find the main idea, identify, skim, explore
Synthesis: Build a model, combine, compile, compose, construct, create, design, elaborate, test, infer, predict, hypothesize, invent, design	**Writing:** List, summarize, ask and answer questions, create sentences, state and justify opinions, write, contrast, classify, record
Evaluation: Choose, decide, recommend, select, justify, defend, support	**Developing vocabulary:** Define isolated words, define words in context, find words and construct meaning

Figure 3.3 underlines the verbs in the language objectives.

<u>Discuss</u> the similarities and differences between the two books with your partner, and <u>write</u> three sentences using descriptive adjectives and comparison words (such as *similar*, *different*, and *same*).

Use adjectives to <u>describe</u> frogs (*green*, *slimy*, *fast*, *smooth*) to a partner (or in a paragraph).

Be able to orally <u>explain</u> the connection between the First and Second World Wars.

Figure 3.3: Underlined verbs in example language objectives.

As you craft the language objectives, keep newcomers, long-term ELs, and students with disabilities in mind, in addition to the bulk of your ELs, who may be emerging, developing, expanding, or bridging.

Newcomers

When a student first comes to an English-speaking country and starts school, whether that is in kindergarten, fifth grade, or tenth grade, they are considered a newcomer. Newcomers need specific and, often, substantially more intense and frequent support. At this initial stage, students require extra scaffolding, and may even need to be partnered with a student or staff member who can help translate for them.

Among newcomers, there are two main types.

1. **Students with interrupted formal education (SIFE), who often recently immigrated to the country and did not receive a grade-level-equivalent education in their home country:** Literacy in their home language, academic vocabulary, and independent study skills may be lacking.

2. **Students who arrive at or near grade level with developmentally appropriate skills in their home language and present school transcripts:** These newcomers are likely to progress quicker than SIFE because they have foundational skills on which to build (like how to read, write, speak, and so on).

It is worthwhile to take some time to consider the unique challenges that newcomers face. Whether you have a kindergartner who has only been spoken to in Haitian Creole at home, or a seventh grader whose family recently emigrated from Guatemala, teaching newcomers is arguably one of the hardest, yet most rewarding, parts of being an educator.

You may need to use some of the following strategies to help onboard newcomers, both SIFE and non-SIFE. The Scaffolds, Interventions, and Adaptations section in this chapter (page 71) has more ideas.

- Assign a buddy who speaks the student's home language. The buddy can translate directions, explain assignments, and help the newcomer navigate a world that is incomprehensible to them.

- Partner the student with a fluent English speaker who can help during turn-and-talks, group tasks, and so on.

- Determine if someone at the district, or in your building, can assess the student's literacy abilities in their home language. Find out whether the student knows the alphabet in their home language and can read and write in that home language.

- Provide visual cue cards for actions like going to the bathroom, drinking water, needing a break, being hungry, and feeling sick so that the newcomer can point to a visual in order to communicate an immediate need. Laminate the cards and put them on a ring-binder clip so the student can flip to the one they need to communicate.

- Learn some basic words and phrases in the student's home language (*hello, thank you, you're welcome, good job,* and *yes* or *no*). You may want to do this for all multilingual students, but it is especially crucial to help newcomers feel welcome, know that their language is valued, and keep their affective filter lower (Krashen, 1989).

- Talk to the student's parents or guardians to see if they speak any English and can provide support at home, or if you are the sole source of English language input. If the parents don't speak English and you don't speak their language, see if another staff member or district personnel can help you translate parent letters, homework directions, and so on. If all else fails, translator apps can be helpful.

- Meet one-on-one with the student—ideally daily—or if your school delegates this responsibility to another teacher, have a dedicated EL teacher or aide work with the student one-on-one or in a small group to build their vocabulary and expose them to spoken and written English. Designated ELD requirements for students vary region to region, but many EL students are required to receive designated ELD for thirty minutes daily.

- Use rhymes, songs, chants, and videos to engage and encourage newcomers through music and oral language. (I highly encourage this.)

My personal experience includes mainly Spanish speakers; however, I did teach English language development to several groups of newcomers over my career. One group included a girl from Iran and two sisters from Yemen. The Iranian girl knew very basic words when she arrived in fifth grade—*hello*, *thank you*, *please*. I taught her English. By the time she entered middle school, she was fluent in English, and by the end of middle school, you could no longer tell that English was not her first language. She went on to thrive and, as of the publication of this book, just graduated from a major California university, is teaching fourth grade, and is starting a simultaneous master's program in the fall.

It's also important to note that this student and her mother fled their home country because her father was abusive. So, being able to trust teachers—and adults in general—came slowly for her (and her mother). Eventually, I earned their trust and assisted in writing the letter that helped the student's mother get political asylum in the United States. Many students will arrive to school with traumatic experiences from their home countries (and en route). Be gentle. Have patience. Show them respect. Use realia, visuals, and total physical response (such as, "Bring me your book" and "Take out your pencil"). Display and provide books with characters who look like and speak the same languages as your students. Listen and learn. Smile a lot and look into their eyes. They want to learn, be part of the class discussion, and read aloud. It may just take some time, so be kind and compassionate.

Long-Term ELs

Long-term English learners also have particular needs to address. These are students who have been in school for six or more years and are still not English language proficient. Why is this such a prevalent phenomenon? I would argue that not enough time has been dedicated to demanding that they SWIRL. All too often, middle school and high school students are silently responding to reading comprehension questions on computers. Perhaps they are not required to use enough academic vocabulary, to respond to texts in writing, or to give oral presentations.

Long-term English learners might present as fluent in social conversations, but literacy tasks and rigorous coursework may prove challenging for them. Aside from a few grammar or word choice mistakes, they can sound fluent. But they are not yet passing the writing and reading sections of the state or provincial English language test. As the quantity and complexity of texts increase, long-term ELs are expected to meet the same academic standards as their English-fluent peers. The problem is that they continue to be labeled as *EL* and put in lower-level secondary classes, where they fall more and more behind.

According to the Migration Policy Institute, "29 percent of the foreign-born population (ages 25 and older) has *less* than a high school diploma, compared to 9 percent of U.S.-born adults" (Sugarman, 2019, p. 4). The National Center for Education Statistics (2019) found that students still designated as ELs have the second-to-lowest graduation rate, at just over 69 percent; the U.S. average is 85.8 percent.

Long-term ELs, who often face extenuating circumstances such as poverty, transiency (their parents are migrant farmworkers, for example), or a lack of support in school or at home, are more likely to be identified as requiring special education and more often enrolled in remedial classes. So when working with EL students who truly have a learning disability, teachers must distinguish between their challenges rooted in the disability (dyslexia, auditory processing disorder, or dysgraphia) and those challenges that are part of the language acquisition process.

Student-Friendly Wording

The Common Core State Standards, WIDA standards, and individual state and provincial standards (such as California's ELD standards, which many educators consider cutting edge) are written in edujargon that most students, regardless of what their primary language is, cannot understand. Once you write your language objectives, the next step is to rewrite them in student-friendly language (often using *I can* statements).

It may seem tedious, but writing objectives in student-friendly terms helps students understand, internalize, and articulate what they are learning. *I can* statements get to the gist of the objectives. Visit www.youtube.com/watch?v=Tr3uqF7YObo to watch a video explaining why *I can* statements are so important and how to create them (Willmar Public Schools, 2013). In the video, the teacher explains that students cannot be expected to reach a goal they do not understand. Often, standards are written in complex and lengthy language that isn't comprehensible at their age or, in the case of English learners, at their proficiency level. Here are a few example objectives.

- I can compare and contrast two stories.
- I can use context clues to help me understand the text.
- I can write a paragraph summarizing five facts from a nonfiction text.

Many teachers post the objective somewhere in the classroom or project it on their SMART Board. Some even have the students say the content and language objectives out loud. It can be as simple as the following exchange (which you can have the class read in unison or have one student read aloud).

> *Teacher: What are we going to learn today?*
>
> *Students (as they read the content objective): I can compare and contrast two books.*
>
> *Teacher: How will we show that we can do that?*
>
> *Students (as they read the language objective): I can use language like* the same, different, alike, *and* both *to compare when writing and presenting a Venn diagram.*

Have students read and reread the objective by either having them read it chorally or asking a volunteer. Let them marinate in it for a bit. Give them a few minutes to react to the *I can* statement and, perhaps, give a thumbs-up when they believe that they understand the objective.

Many studies between 1995 and 2011 revealed that explicitly naming the learning targets for students positively impacts learning at various grade levels and in different subject areas (Andrade, Du, & Mycek, 2010; Black, Harrison, Lee, Marshall, & Wiliam, 2004; Higgins, Harris, & Kuehn, 1994; Moss, Brookhart, & Long, 2011; Orr et al., 2022; Ross, Hogaboam-Gray, & Rolheiser, 2002; Ross & Starling, 2008; Seidel, Rimmele, & Prenzel, 2005). One analysis explains it this way:

When students understand exactly what they're supposed to learn and what their work will look like when they learn it, they're better able to monitor and adjust their work, select effective strategies, and connect current work to prior learning (Black et al., 2004; Moss et al., 2011). (Brookhart & Moss, 2014, p. 28)

Figure 3.4 features an example sixth-grade reading standard. Notice how the example flows from the content standard to the language objective to student-friendly language.

Content standard: "Compare and contrast texts in different forms or genres (e.g., stories and poems; historical novels and fantasy stories) in terms of their approaches to similar themes and topics" (RL.6.9).

Language objective: Create a Venn diagram, with a partner, using academic vocabulary from the two texts to say what is the same, what is different, and what features both contain.

I can **statements:**

- I can <u>compare</u> two texts. (Reading)
- I can <u>draw and label</u> a Venn diagram with specific features that are the same, different, and shared. (Writing)
- I can <u>discuss</u>, with my partner, how the two texts are different and alike. (Interacting/speaking/listening)

Source for standard: National Governors Association Center for Best Practices [NGA] & Council of Chief State School Officers [CCSSO], 2010.

Figure 3.4: Example *I can* statements.

Display the language objective on the board or in a presentation. Highlight key vocabulary, underline verbs, circle new words—mark up the statements to make them user friendly. Figure 3.5 (page 70) includes an example.

At the end of the lesson, have students self-assess if they met the objective. For example, prompt partners to meet with another pair to share their Venn diagrams and then self-assess whether they feel like they included all the relevant differences and similarities. Fist to five is a way for them to show how they feel like they have done on a scale of 0 to 5 (with a fist, or zero fingers up, meaning, "I do not understand this well," and five fingers up meaning, "I understand this perfectly").

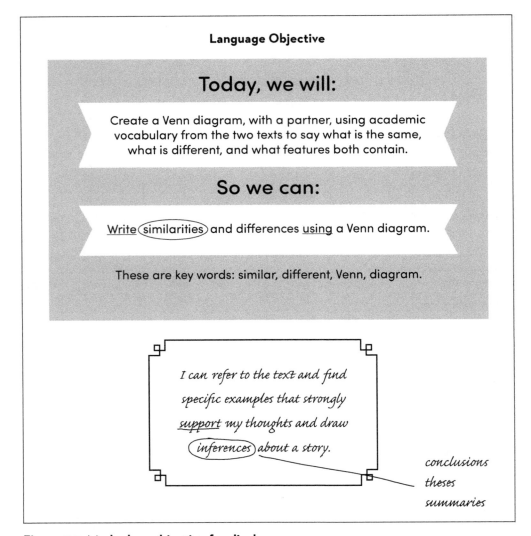

Figure 3.5: Marked-up objective for display.

Strategies for Multilingual Learners

While many of the strategies described in this section (such as displaying anchor charts with academic vocabulary) may benefit non-ELs, these resources are essential for English learners to acquire language skills. A classroom lesson may involve the following research-based EL strategies, which are discussed here: scaffolds, interventions, and adaptations; gradual release of responsibility; think time; brain breaks; and technology.

Scaffolds, Interventions, and Adaptations

Scaffolds are supports that you provide to help a student navigate a task. They can be especially valuable tools for EL students as interventions, adaptations, and differentiation. Sentence stems and anchor charts are two examples of resources that ease language demands by making some vocabulary and structures more readily available. *Interventions* target a specific skill with which a student needs extra practice (such as using Rime Magic for middle-sound chunks and fluency, page 173). *Adaptations* alter the task in some way so that a student can achieve success. For example, a five-paragraph essay for a newcomer might become *one* paragraph and be dictated to and scribed by a fluent student.

As you get to know your students' language abilities, you become more agile in providing or directing them to the right supports at any given time. Multitiered system of supports (MTSS), or response to intervention (RTI), has tiered instruction that your EL students may need. To outline those tiers succinctly, Tier 1 is whole-class instruction. Tier 2 is interventions for students who need help becoming proficient in grade-level standards, and Tier 3 is intensive student support (Mattos et al., 2025). More specifically, Tier 1 instruction is delivered to the whole class, regardless of home language or English language level. Tier 2 supplements this and may be done in a small group, one-on-one, or in partners. Tier 3 instruction refers to intervention strategies that happen based on specific needs—English language level, giftedness, and need for remediation, for instance.

Tiers 2 and 3 may include some or all of the following strategies, but in the case of Tier 1 core instruction, these pieces are pivotal.

- **Slowing down:** As a teacher, your own pace and clarity of speech matter so much, since "students who are at the beginning levels of language proficiency benefit from teachers who slow down their rate of speech, use pauses, and enunciate clearly while speaking" (Echevarría, Vogt, & Short, 2017, p. 97). (I know I have been guilty of speaking too fast and had to consciously slow down, pause to check for understanding, and allow for processing. That shift led me to provide my students with more comprehensible input.)

- **Visuals and gestures:** Whenever possible, use visuals (images or realia) for vocabulary or gestures to describe words. Ask students to repeat those movements so the meanings get imprinted in their muscle memory; for example, they might use their fingers to show the letter C when they make a connection to a text.

- **Flexibly grouped students:** Consider the instructional purpose and language demands. Then, either purposefully partner students of varying English language levels, group them by home or heritage language, or let them choose who they feel most comfortable with their as language partner. Allowing grouping changes is essential, so students don't get pigeonholed, too dependent on a partner, or stuck at a certain level.

- **Strategically grouped students:** Whether you homogeneously or heterogeneously group students by their EL level, be purposeful in your partnerships. It is helpful for a newcomer to have a partner who is more fluent in English so they can make sense of the lesson. At times, though, you want to let students with the same home language turn and talk so they can process content in their first language. Other times, placing students at the same proficiency level together benefits their learning.

- **Language awareness:** This includes understanding how language works—everything from directionality (reading left to right in English, which is the opposite of languages like Arabic, Farsi, and Hebrew) to sentence structure (adjective before noun in English versus noun before adjective in Spanish) and subject-verb agreement (many Asian languages do not conjugate verbs based on singular or plural).

- **Gradual release of responsibility:** Typically, this approach follows an instructional framework of *I do* (teacher modeling), *we do* (whole-class creation), *two do* (partner or group practice), and *you do* (independent work; Fisher & Frey, 2021). You might be tempted to hold English learners' hands to the point where you (or another student) become a crutch. Gradual release allows students to have agency, interact with peers, and actively participate in the process of learning English. The gradual release phases also allow you, as the facilitator, to circulate, listen in, and do some formative assessment.

- **Think time:** Calling on students raises their affective filter (contributing to anxiety), which lowers their willingness to take risks academically and socially. Before you call on students, have them turn and talk or engage in prewriting, or after you call on them to answer a question, count silently to fifteen. Stopping to let students process gives their brains time to formulate a thought and the accompanying language to respond. It allows their synapses to connect concepts and recall background knowledge or vocabulary (Rowe, 1972; Stahl, 1994). Increasing the wait time between posing a question and calling on students from even one to five seconds significantly increases participation, and also has the following academic and behavioral benefits:

- Increases in the length of student responses
- Increases in the number of unsolicited appropriate responses
- Increases in responses from students categorized as low-performing
- Increases in student-to-student interactions
- More thoughtful and contemplative answers, including speculation and alternative answers
- Decreases in students not responding or saying "I don't know"
- Decreases in discipline problems
- Increases in student achievement (IRIS Center, 2018, p. 1)

- **Brain breaks:** If you're struggling to manage your class, or to engage a lot of your students, try offering them a brain break that lasts somewhere between three and five minutes (Willis, 2016). When you pause your direct instruction and give students a brain break, their neurons can catch up with all the new knowledge they are acquiring (Buch, Claudino, Quentin, Bönstrup, & Cohen, 2023). This also has the perk of benefiting any neurodivergent students you might have in your classroom (Bateman, 2018). Brain breaks that achieve these outcomes can include the following, and these are just for starters: stretching, taking deep breaths, listening to a calm song, doing a free write or read, or watching a relaxing video. Some brain breaks can include learning, such as watching word chant videos. A brain break is commonly misconstrued as a break, or pause, in the learning process. But it is actually "the period when our brains compress and consolidate memories of what we just practiced" (National Institutes of Health, 2021).

Technology

Using technology to support independent reading, spelling, and writing practice can benefit ELs if it is done in moderation, monitored by teachers, and is of high interest. Programs like i-Ready, Popplet, Quizlet, and others can allow you to assess students' progress and individualize instruction. I have seen many students enjoy and experience success on i-Ready.

That being said, teachers (and students) must not become too dependent on technology. Nothing replaces speaking, writing, interacting, reading, and listening to others, and doing these things with real books. Letting these students work online might be easier, especially if you're overwhelmed by the gamut of EL levels in your class, but that doesn't help multilingual learners in the way interaction does, nor can you assess their oral proficiency if you don't talk with them or listen to them talk to other students. If you use technology, remember that "it is important to give [students] frequent and varied opportunities to interact with English-speaking peers " (Altavilla, 2020).

The following and other online programs have adaptations and scaffolds for English learners.

- Khan Academy (www.khanacademy.org) translates its curriculum into many languages.
- Newsela (https://newsela.com) provides articles at different Lexile levels, many in both English and Spanish.
- ThinkCERCA (www.thinkcerca.com) offers leveled texts and an audio option.

Of course, generative AI has entered the chat. Its introduction provides unique opportunities for meeting English learners' needs. Teachers might consider using it to tailor lessons to students' needs by analyzing their strengths and struggles, and to assess students' skills and correct writing assignments for grammar, sentence structure, and vocabulary (while making sure to provide students with oral feedback). They might also use AI to translate texts into home languages, and let students use chatbots as interactive conversation partners in a pinch.

Before your school or district invests in a technology, vet the program and make sure it meets your students' needs. For example, not all technologies accurately register the pronunciation of multilingual learners (Ashwell & Elam, 2017; Coniam, 1999; Derwing, Munro, & Carbonaro, 2000). School and district leaders are responsible for deciding "what linguistic group it treats as 'standard'" and considering "whether [the technology's] design is appropriate for use with the given students and at the intended grade level" (Altavilla, 2020). Recommendations will vary based on grade level, English proficiency, and possibly even home languages that the technology can accommodate.

Again, everything in moderation—especially when replacing human feedback and interaction with technology. Rarely do programs and apps require students to speak, interact, or write as much as they require them to read and listen.

Conclusion

Lesson planning includes identifying content and language objectives (with the language forms and functions integrated) and rewriting those in student-friendly language. It also covers considering the various scaffolds students might need in order to experience success. Anchor charts, sentence frames, turn-and-talks, think time, and opportunities to process information all help students access academic vocabulary and process input. Your lesson plan is like a map to a destination. Being transparent with your students by sharing the language objective lets them know where they are going and how you will help them get there.

PART 2
The SWIRL Elements

During my thirty-year career in education, I was a Spanish immersion teacher for preK–5 students and a literacy coach for grades K–12. Throughout that time, I taught students whose home languages were Spanish, Arabic, Farsi, Mam, Laotian, Bulgarian, Portuguese, Vietnamese, and several others. As a consultant, I coach teachers in classrooms where the vast majority of students are multilingual learners. What I have learned through hundreds of observations and lessons—and what the prominent researchers concur with—is that multilingual learners need to be speaking, writing, interacting, reading, and listening every single day.

There is overlap among these SWIRL facets, of course. Students may read two texts (reading), talk to a partner (speaking, interacting, listening), and then fill out a graphic organizer comparing the texts (writing). In that instance, they are doing all five SWIRL elements. The chapters in part 2 share strategies and scaffolds to prop up ELs when they *speak*, hold them accountable when they *listen* and *read*, and have them *write* poetry, argumentative essays, and research reports. You will find many activities aimed at getting MLs to *interact* with one another, one-on-one or in small groups, because their affective filter is lower than when responding in front of the whole class. Decreasing whole-class call-and-response increases their social and academic risk-taking, so more learning can occur. Providing diverse books, as well as shoring up skills to tackle complex texts, is the focus of the reading chapter. Finally, you'll read about activities and strategies that encourage active listening as students *interact* and speak.

As such, each strategy in these chapters has the SWIRL acronym next to it to indicate which SWIRL elements are involved. The SWIRL elements that are mainly required for the activity appear in uppercase letters. For example, it might say *SwIrL* next to an activity, meaning that the activity does not require much writing or reading; the language demands are mainly in the realms of speaking, interacting, and listening.

The SWIRL method described in this book is not an exhaustive list of strategies. It is a framework by which you can expand your instructional repertoire and measure if you are leaning too heavily on one or two of the elements and excluding certain forms of communication to the detriment of your students. Balance is key in the SWIRL method!

CHAPTER 4

Speaking

The person doing the speaking is doing the learning.
—Jennifer York-Barr

Often, speaking is the first piece of the puzzle that clicks into place, or starts to be a proficient skill, for MLs. Basic interpersonal communication skills (BICS), or playground English, are the elements of socialization students develop in order to play with their peers ("Throw me the ball") and meet their basic needs ("I am hungry"). That social language "is meaningful, cognitively undemanding, and non-specialized. It takes the learner from six months to two years" to acquire (Colorín Colorado, n.d.b). This social language is learned first because students need it for their social and physical survival. But there are levels of discourse.

Remember that we acquire a second language in stages. Newcomers or entering ELs may point to or hold up an object before they are ready to speak. Single words or phrases might be the way they communicate until full sentences flow. As emergent multilingual learners advance through the stages of language acquisition, we expect them to integrate more academic vocabulary, use correct grammar, and communicate in complete sentences.

It is a well-known, natural part of language acquisition to *sponge*, or be in silent mode, while soaking up a new language (Krashen, 1989). Again, if you've traveled to a country where you didn't speak the language, you'll empathize with the silent phase. Or if you've raised a baby, you know how they take in language for quite some time before they produce it. All the while, they are learning from your language modeling. When they do start to speak, it may be language to express basic needs and social language. Academic language—everything from vocabulary to forms and functions—must be explicitly taught.

Speaking is the foundation of communication. It is the most common way that we know what a student has learned. We hear them name story events in sequential order. We listen to them talk to a partner about their predictions. It is, in essence, the number-one way we evaluate and monitor progress at the beginning stages.

First, let's discuss the research on speaking, and then we'll review related activities and strategies.

The Research on Speaking

From talking (speaking before writing) to doing jigsaw activities (speaking while interacting), to decoding and comprehending (speaking while reading), to actively listening (which usually includes repeating back what someone said, so we're speaking), speaking helps us process and demonstrate what we know. Speaking, also known as *oral language*, is a crucial first step that almost always precedes students' ability to read and write. Extensive research supports the importance of speaking in learning English, or another new language. Speaking isn't just the first element of SWIRL; it's the most pivotal and overlapping of the five (Hopman & MacDonald, 2018).

Keep in mind that classroom speaking is accountable. The *Accountable Talk*® program, a registered trademark of the University of Pittsburgh, moves learning forward, ensures equitability, and supports "deep thinking, conceptual understanding, argument, and discussion" (Apodaca, DeMartino, & Bernstein-Danis, 2019). Accountable Talk, as outlined by Mikyung Kim Wolf, Amy C. Crosson, and Lauren B. Resnick (2004), has three aspects.

1. Accountability to the learning community
2. Accountability to accurate knowledge
3. Accountability to rigorous thinking

Finally, Accountable Talk encourages students to respond to each other, and helps them share and deepen their reasoning so that it can be heard and understood (Wolf et al., 2008).

Before they can have meaningful, rigorous, accountable conversations, students must acquire several skills.

- **Phonemic awareness:** This is the ability to recognize and produce the sounds and symbols that correlate with phonemes (letters and sounds). This awareness impacts rhyme, alliteration, onset and rime (word families), and the blending, segmenting, and manipulation of sounds. It is the primary building block of reading and writing.

- **Semantics:** This includes the vocabulary students need to be both expressive and receptive when speaking, writing, or communicating. The depth of vocabulary knowledge includes multiple-meaning words (homonyms), shades of meaning, figurative language, and relationships between words (synonyms, antonyms, and analogies).

- **Syntax:** Part of developing oral language skills is understanding *grammar*—the set of rules and structures that dictate how words and phrases make sentences (and sense), and how sentences combine to make paragraphs. This includes (but is not limited to) parts of speech, conjugations, and various sentence structures.

- **Morphology:** This refers to how words are broken into sounds and symbols. (Some consider this a subset of syntax or vocabulary [semantics].) For example, if one examined the word *bats*, a basic analysis would show there are four phonemes in it (/b/, /a/, /t/ and /s/). However, the word *bats* only has two morphemes (meaningful word parts). *Bat* is a baseball tool or a nocturnal animal, and *s* indicates there is more than one bat. Morphology also encompasses how words combine and build vocabulary (prefix, root, and suffix).

- **Pragmatics:** Some label this the *hidden curriculum*, because it refers to social norms of conversational turn taking, personal space, and socially acceptable behavior with peers and adults as it factors into myriad situations (classroom settings, the cafeteria, and presentations, for instance).

- **Discourse:** The critical skill that combines oral and written communication, also known as *discourse*, includes narrative storytelling, which follows a very specific format—beginning, middle, and end. Story elements such as characters, setting, conflict, plot, and resolution all fall under discourse. Discussing nonfiction, expository, or informational texts—persuasive, cause-and-effect, compare-and-contrast, and procedural—helps students go from point A (learning to read and discuss) to point B (reading to learn and discuss). Another great example of discourse is debate or Socratic seminar (see page 151). Students must speak in order to engage in discourse.

Speaking is a crucial part of learning English for several reasons. For example, consider vocabulary's importance in the scheme of learning as a whole. One study finds that "reading accuracy, as well as oral language skills, beyond just vocabulary predicts performance on [reading comprehension] outcome measures (Foorman, Herrara, Petscher, Mitchell, & Truckenmiller, 2015)" (Brooke, 2021, p. 6). The importance of the speaking part of learning English, and the circular nature of reading and vocabulary, becomes apparent here:

> Oral language proficiency (the ability to speak and understand the language) is the foundation on which academic language is built. Academic language found in texts—subject-specific vocabulary, complex syntax, rhetorical conventions—is particularly challenging for multilingual learners who have yet to master oral language proficiency. (Echevarría, 2021)

EL students are often at a disadvantage because they may lack exposure to fluent English language role models at home (Biemiller, 1999; Brooke, 2021). When it comes to your multilingual students, the research indicates that students learning English need "more instruction in oral English proficiency than their peers: things like vocabulary knowledge, listening comprehension, and syntax" (Schwartz, 2022). Yet, Hattie's (2012) research shows teacher voices are heard an average of 89 percent of the time in classrooms, at the expense of student voices.

If we want students' production of vocabulary and complex sentences to increase, we need to give them more airtime. Most teachers learn early on in their credentialing program about the 10/2 strategy. That is, for every ten minutes you talk and teach, give students two minutes to process information with a partner either through written reflection or discussion. Doing so "can help to promote student engagement in the class and encourages interaction between students and teachers" (Western Sydney University, n.d.). This strategy is commonly called *think-pair-share* or *turn-and-talk*. In essence, while this benefits all students, ELs may need more time to process information presented. Talking about it to a partner, either in their home language first or with someone who has a higher proficiency level and can support them, is one scaffolded way to help them make sense of the content.

So, what are you doing while they are talking? You don't just set them off to chat. As the teacher, you need to assess whether students are understanding the content. Circulate around the room during partner conversations, listen in, and ask or answer clarifying questions. Make notes. Overall, in terms of speaking skills, the "most important action you can take is to speak to your MLLs [multilingual learners] on a daily basis" says Wendi Pillars, a K–12 teacher for almost three decades in multiple countries (Ferlazzo, 2023). Do this while also giving them ample time to speak.

Activities and Strategies

The SWIRL method revolves around students' ability to say what they know, to ask about what they don't know, and to approximate, as well as your oral modeling of language for them. Speaking, by nature, is interactive, and it can also accompany writing, reading, and listening. Here is something else to consider: English learners will absorb, understand, and process information that they hear or read long before they start speaking the language. Once they do begin producing language, it is important to create varied and valuable opportunities for them to speak. As you assign tasks, do read-alouds, and analyze students' writing, prompt them to talk about the texts. Provide sentence frames and starters or stems, oral feedback, and celebrations of their efforts.

Speaking is not just a way to express oneself; it is also an opportunity to practice manipulating language. According to researchers, "Language learners improve more rapidly when they are able to practice what they've learned more often" (Kostadinovska-Stojchevska & Popovikj, 2019, p. 25). This is a marathon, not a sprint. Adopting that attitude might help *students* have patience with themselves, and you have patience with them.

Why will they need your help being patient with themselves? It's all about their affective filter, as discussed in the affective filter hypothesis (page 36). Students often feel embarrassed by their accents and mistakes. Or they feel deeply inhibited when trying out new English skills. Creating a safe space for all—one where risk taking is encouraged, even applauded—will allow them to lower their affective filter and, in turn, increase risk taking in an effort to improve their English language proficiency. According to Pillars, one way to create a lower affective filter for speaking tasks is to teach students "ways to advocate for themselves, how to ask for more information" (Ferlazzo, 2023).

In addition to empowering student voice, how you structure speaking time is important. Structured speaking activities and strategies, like those that follow in the rest of this chapter, hold students accountable and produce meaningful language during their conversations. Keep the language acquisition stages, outlined in chapter 2 (page 31), in mind when you digest the following strategies and activities. They are aimed at providing students ample opportunities to speak English.

Finally, consider the amount of time spent speaking compared to listening. Make sure there is a balance. Remain cognizant of the fact that listening is often inextricably tied to speaking. Writing, reading, and interacting (in response to something that students hear, read, or write) all go hand in hand. Also, self-assess your instructional time (or have a colleague observe and tally it) and note what percentage of time students are listening to you speak and what percentage of time they are speaking. Traditional teaching would have it weighted much more heavily on the former; however, the latter is more valuable in developing correct grammar, amplifying vocabulary, and prompting the desired productive struggle. At the very least, the ratio should be 50/50, but 70 percent speaking (student talk) and 30 percent listening (teacher talk) is better (Kostadinovska-Stojchevska & Popovikj, 2019).

This 70/30 ratio is backed up by research proving that it does the following (OnTESOL, 2021).

- It provides more opportunities for feedback.
- It allows more time for students to practice using English.
- It promotes fluency and improves confidence.
- It increases engagement.

How can you assess students' speaking skills? Become a fly on the wall! Circulate around the room and eavesdrop on their conversations. Take anecdotal records and offer feedback in real time.

SwIrL Purposeful Partnerships

Purposeful partnerships—pairing students for activities in a specific way for a strategic reason—give students more ownership. The pedagogical belief is that "learning is best when actual, genuine, practice time is allotted" (Sclafani, 2017, p. 5). You do not have to purposefully partner students for all speaking prompts. Sometimes, you can let students choose their partner to create balance and give them a sense of agency.

Pairing Students

Here are some options for pairing your students.

- One fluent English speaker and one English learner
- Two EL students at different proficiency levels
- Two EL students at similar or the same proficiency levels
- Triads with one beginner, one emergent speaker, and one bridging speaker
- Pairs or groups of students who speak the same home language

It is important to "engage students in discussions with heterogeneous groups so that students with lower vocabulary skills and limited background knowledge can benefit from hearing the discussions of their peers" (Brooke, 2021, p. 9). Partnering a fluent English speaker with a newcomer can allow them to teach each other. In some dual immersion programs, it's helpful to pair a Spanish speaker with an English speaker because these students serve as role models of their target language for each other.

You know your students best, so think about who should speak to whom. One study claims that the question of "how to best pair students in heterogeneous classes [depends] on the aim of the activity, and the dyadic relationship may be of greater significance than proficiency pairing" (Storch & Aldosari, 2013, p. 31). This means that students need to be able to work together—not just play around. Giving students choice sometimes is helpful in increasing their buy-in, but I caution you to ensure that students can be productive working together. They are usually fairly self-reflective about whom they can effectively work with. If they are not, the logical consequence is switching partners to teacher-selected pairs.

You can change these matches daily, weekly, or even every time you deliver a minilesson. Take notes about who works well together, and who does not, to inform future pairings. Additionally, it is important to let students know your expectations for their participation in the activities, since "students [are] sometimes working in a team setting for the first time in their school careers" (Sclafani, 2017, p. 5).

Structure this talk time so students can get to the discussion, not spend five minutes playing rock paper scissors to decide who goes first! You can tell them that the first person to speak is the one whose first initial comes first in the alphabet. Also, providing them with sentence frames, a specific written or oral task to complete, or a callback, such as repeating what their partner said, gives MLs an audience, purpose, and structure.

Many of these activities, including partnering students, cover both speaking and interacting. Table 4.1 (page 86) lists activities that fall into both categories and their possible groupings of students. These activities are detailed later in this book.

You might try parakeet partners after students speak to each other. Here, either with advance notice or on the fly, you ask a student to repeat what their partner said. If you give them a heads-up, they tend to listen more actively.

Table 4.1: Speaking and Interacting Activity Overlaps

Speaking and Interacting Activity	Number of Students
Think-pair-share	Two or three
Table talk	Between four and six
Along the lines	Whole class, divided in two
Fishbowl (inner-circle, outer-circle discussions)	Whole class, divided in two
Socratic seminar	Whole class
Oral presentations	Between one and four
Hot seat	One student seated and the rest of the class listening

Listening to Students When They Are Speaking

To teach students how to improve their speaking, we must "start with listening," says Pillars (Ferlazzo, 2023). When students are speaking, which should be most of the time, intently listen to them and their conversations. Model language if you hear mistakes or students are hesitating to speak. For example, if they are reluctant or unsure of what to say, point to the sentence frame and give an example. Or, better yet, have one of the students in the pair give their example. Ask and answer questions. Identify conversations that you found exemplary, and ask the pair's permission to be called on and share, which is paramount to keeping their affective filter low. If you get the go-ahead, call on those students when the whole class is back together, during the debrief.

It is important to model your expectations for the conversation, either with a volunteer or in a fishbowl demonstration, so that students understand they are to speak in complete sentences, use the key vocabulary, and stay on topic. Take notes, anecdotally, about your students' strengths and struggles when speaking English.

SwIrL Hand Up, Stand Up

For preK–12, this strategy helps match students who work at the same pace to begin their conversations when they are ready. Simply put, when a student is ready to meet with a partner, they put their hand up, identify someone else who has their hand up, and move to meet with that person. Moving around the room is quite effective and important for kinesthetic learners (and students who need to get out some energy). When their students are sitting on a rug, some preK–2 teachers invite them to connect their hands like a bridge to make it clear who the partners are.

Like all students, English learners need content, process, and product to be differentiated; however, they might also need lessons differentiated with regard to pacing. *Pacing* includes how fast you cover the curriculum, as well as how fast students finish an activity or task. Some students may finish earlier or later than others. Strategies like hand up, stand up help with managing the various paces at which students complete tasks. Hand up, stand up allows students to reflect on or share their ideas with a partner who finishes at the same time as them. This avoids having to constantly create partners, redirect off-task students, or receive the dreaded "I'm done. What do I do now?" This activity can also help you focus on supporting students as you circulate while they partner to discuss a topic or task.

Once a student has read a passage, completed a writing assignment, or thought of what they want to say in response to a question, they raise their hand. When they see another person with their hand up, both students stand up and find a space to talk with each other. You can continue that with partners putting their hands up when they are finished and looking for another ready pair to fold together as a quartet.

SWIRL Jigsaw

Jigsaw is a way to cut the cognitive demands of learning about various subtopics or responding to several sections of a text. Most effective at grades 3–12, a jigsaw involves dividing students into homogeneous groups (either by topic or by reading level), and assigning each group a particular section of a text or article in which they are meant to become experts. These group members read the text and discuss it, agreeing on the most salient points. Then, regroup the students heterogeneously, by subtopic, to teach each other about their area of expertise. Jigsaw groups can meet in the four corners of the classroom or at different tables.

Use this activity with students at expanding and bridging proficiency levels to have them read, talk, and write about a particular part of a subject. Jigsaw is helpful when you have a lot of text to get through.

Not only is a jigsaw academically helpful, but social psychologist Geoffrey Cohen explains that the activity helps strengthen peer relationships as well:

> It's in the kids' interests to cooperate.... It fosters equal status. If students are having trouble with the material, they can pick up little tips and tricks from their peers. All that combines to create a more congenial environment for kids. (Leonard, 2023)

Ideally, you allow students to choose what they learn about in a given unit—for example, which planet during a solar system unit. A planetary unit might look something like figure 4.1. After reading, researching, note taking, and discussing, and then regrouping into heterogeneous groups, one person from each of the homogeneous groups shares what they learned so the whole class now gets up to speed on the entire topic or text.

> *Read, discuss, and highlight three interesting facts about your planet.*
> - *Group 1: Pages 2–5 on Jupiter*
> - *Group 2: Pages 6–9 on Saturn*
> - *Group 3: Pages 10–14 on Venus*
> - *Group 4: Pages 15–18 on Mars*

Figure 4.1: Group assignments for a jigsaw.

Follow these steps.

1. Choose a topic. For example, say you want students to learn about the water cycle. Divide the class into four groups: (1) condensation, (2) evaporation, (3) precipitation, and (4) transpiration.

2. Assign each group a paragraph, article, or book to read about their part of the water cycle. They read the information, take notes, and discuss it with their expert group members.

3. The expert groups synthesize the information to teach it to other students. You may want to have a form to anchor students' discussion and note taking, such as that in figure 4.2.

4. Once they are in their heterogeneous family groups, have the students each take a turn relaying the important information about their expert group's part of the reading. You can have students do a gallery walk, instead of or in addition to this.

Figure 4.3 shows how you can make the expert and family groups.

SWIRL Sentence Frames, Starters, and Stems

From preK to twelfth grade (although most commonly used in preK–3), and from newcomer to developing EL, providing students with a skeleton they can use when speaking helps support their verbal expression. Sentence frames and starters are valuable scaffolds to ensure students speak in complete sentences, use specific vocabulary (*because*, *and*, *beginning*, *middle*, *end*, *infer*, and so on), and use proper grammar.

Name:	Date:
Expert Notes	**Jigsaw Group Reflections**
I am an expert on page _____.	We covered this topic:
Here are three things I learned. I will present these to my group.	
1.	Two things I learned from my group are:
2.	1.
3.	2.
On the back of this page, draw an illustration to help others understand more about your topic.	The most interesting thing I learned from an expert is:
	I still wonder this about our topic:

Figure 4.2: Jigsaw graphic organizer.

Visit **go.SolutionTree.com/EL** *for a free reproducible version of this figure.*

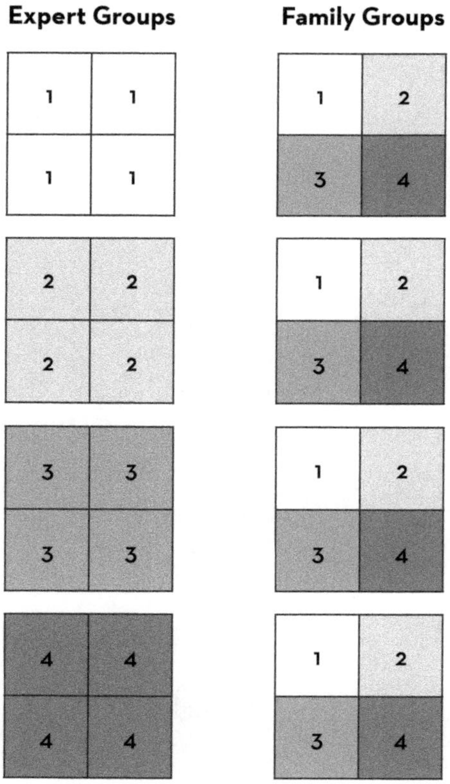

Expert Groups   **Family Groups**

1	1
1	1

1	2
3	4

2	2
2	2

1	2
3	4

3	3
3	3

1	2
3	4

4	4
4	4

1	2
3	4

Source: Adapted from Nickelsen & Dickson, 2022, p. 180.

Figure 4.3: Example of how to group students for jigsaw.

You can create these scaffolds in the following ways.

- **Sentence frames:** Most of the sentence is provided, and students fill in the blanks with vocabulary and verbiage. An example is, "A triangle has _____ sides." Another is, "The main character is _____, and they are trying to _____." Think academic Mad Libs®!

- **Sentence starters or stems:** These are phrases that help someone begin speaking. An example is, "My favorite part is _____." Another is, "In my opinion, _____."

When using frames, starting with what students know helps honor their background knowledge. For example, if you are reading aloud "The Three Little Pigs" (Halliwell-Phillipps, 1886), you could write the following sentence frames on the board or on a sentence strip. These are simple sentence starters you might use with students who are newcomers, entering ELs, or emerging ELs.

- I predict that _____ will happen next.
- My favorite part is when _____.

Here are more complex sentence frames specifically about "The Three Little Pigs" (Halliwell-Phillipps, 1886).

- I predict that the _____ will go to the _____'s house and _____.
- Since _____ builds a house with _____, that pig _____.

As mentioned, you can apply these strategies to topics other than literature. I've included some other examples of subject-specific sentence frames for topics like geometry and chemistry (Gonzalez, 2019). Visit https://tinyurl.com/59nsawfy for more examples of subject-specific sentence stems, and modify these according to your content needs.

Mathematics sentence frames follow.

- The square has _____ angles.
- The _____ has _____ angles.
- Based on the formula, I can infer that the _____ should be bigger and the _____ should be smaller.

History stems and frames follow.

- I anticipate _____ caused _____.

- I think _____ happened because _____.
- I think _____ because I know that _____.
- If _____, then _____.

Science stems and frames follow.

- One reason _____ may happen is because _____.
- Another reason that may occur is because _____.
- At first, I thought _____, but now I think _____ because _____.
- Based on the experiment, I can infer that the _____ will increase and the _____ will decrease.

Physical education stems follow.

- Pass the ball to _____.
- The rules of the game are _____, _____, and _____.
- _____ was out of bounds.

Visual and performing arts stems follow.

- Please pass the _____ (*color*) marker.
- _____ and _____ make _____ (*colors*).
- I need _____ (*materials*) to make _____.
- Where are the _____ (*scissors, glue,* and so on)?
- Your next line is _____.
- Move to stage _____ (*left* or *right*).
- What are the _____ of _____ (*song*)?

Write unit- or content-specific stems on a whiteboard, a SMART Board, or sentence strips. Hang frequently used stems like the following in the classroom so students can lean on them during conversations.

- Can you please repeat _____?
- I learned that _____.
- I noticed that _____.

- Can you explain _____ again?
- What if _____?
- How do you _____?
- What about _____?
- I agree/disagree with you because _____.
- I noticed that _____.
- I wonder if _____.

Professor and researcher Jana Echevarría (2016) argues that frames like these need to support students "in producing language that they wouldn't be able to produce on their own." Post anchor charts with sentence frames and stems around the classroom. Consider asking students for suggestions of frames they want to have as a visual reference.

SwIrL KWL T-Chart

Tapping into students' background knowledge, from prekindergarten to twelfth grade, is a way to teach from an asset-based (strengths-based) perspective. Every student, when they enter school, has some background knowledge to share. From newcomers all the way to students who are reaching English proficiency, students know a lot.

When you introduce academic vocabulary, check to see if students know the word, or root or base word, through doing activities like the Frayer model (page 44) or cognitive content dictionary (page 95), or by connecting Latin-based words to cognates (page 25). A widely used strategy to gather background knowledge is KWL. First introduced by reading and language professor Donna M. Ogle in 1986, KWL (*know, want to know, learned*) charts document and validate background knowledge since it plays a crucial role in students' verbal interpretation and reading comprehension. According to Ogle (1986), "To read well, we must access the knowledge we already have about the topic, or make it available appropriately so that comprehension can occur" (p. 565).

Before teaching a lesson or unit, follow these steps to complete a three-column KWL T-chart (What I Know in the first column, What I Want to Know in the second column, and What I Learned in the third column). Let students turn and talk first at every step. This scaffolds the learning and lowers their affective filter.

1. Ask what students already know about the topic, and have them write, on sticky notes or on the chart, what they know. For preK–grade 1 students and newcomers or emergent ELs, you may want to scribe their responses or share the pen. Remember to give them time to think independently and then turn and talk to a partner or table group before you record responses.

2. Ask what they want to know about the topic. Students are naturally curious. This step capitalizes on their wonderings and creates excitement, engagement, and buy-in for the topic.

3. Invite students to share aloud what else they want to know about the topic. Use question marks as you (or the students) record their questions on the chart. Then ask students to read each other's musings.

4. When the lesson, read-aloud, chant, or unit is complete, close it out by asking students what they learned and writing their new knowledge on the anchor chart. This codifies the learning, synthesizing what they have learned for better retention. Here, you can also see if any questions from the What I Want to Know column went unanswered. Some teachers add a fourth column with a *Q—New Questions* I Have.

A KWHLAQ chart expands on the KWL chart with additional columns to address the following questions.

- **H:** How will I learn it?
- **A:** How will I apply my knowledge?
- **Q:** What new questions do I have?

The KWHLAQ chart requires enhanced metacognition, real-world application, and critical thinking and problem-solving skills (Tolisano, 2015). It is most appropriate for grades 3–12 and those ELs at developing, expanding, bridging, and reaching proficiency levels. Figure 4.4 (page 94) is an example.

This next sample KWL, or KWHLAQ, lesson helps you discover what your students already know about a topic in order to build on their background knowledge. The lesson capitalizes on students' natural curiosity, and enables you to teach them basic facts and features of a topic while molding the unit around their questions.

What I Know	What I Want to Know	How I Will Learn	What I Learned	How I Will Apply Knowledge	New Questions I Have
World War II was started by Germany (Hitler and the Nazis).	Which groups of people did they target?	Read, research online, and take notes.	Over six million Jewish people were murdered, and also Romani, Black, gay, and disabled people, communists, and people who hid those groups of people were killed.	Research current anti-Semitism and how we can combat it.	How did Hitler come to power if he was so evil?

Figure 4.4: Example KWHLAQ chart.

These are the general steps to follow.

1. Draw a KWL chart on chart paper, or project a KWL chart for the class. (See the reproducible "KWL Chart," page 106.)

2. Check for background knowledge and what students want to know by following the previous KWL chart steps.

3. Sing songs, read poems, or incorporate some other engaging whole-class activity.

4. Ask students to identify powerful words (sharing the pen with students and having them come up and underline, highlight, or circle the words), and discuss this vocabulary as a class. Ask if they see any cognates, root or base words, or words they are already familiar with.

5. The next day, read a themed book aloud to the whole class, and model writing a poem about the topic using the words they learned the day before.

6. Offer other themed books for students to explore and, after they read, ask students to write a poem. This may take several days to complete. Have them read their poems to a partner or a small group.

7. On the third or fourth day, post the poems and do a gallery walk. Then, circle back to the KWL chart and ask volunteers to say what they learned. Record their responses in the What I Learned column, or give

students sticky notes and have them post those in the column. Again, encourage students to incorporate their new academic vocabulary.

For an example about octopi, consider these content objectives, both from the Next Generation Science Standards (NGSS Lead States, 2013).

- **4-LS1-1:** "Construct an argument that plants and animals have internal and external structures that function to support survival, growth, behavior, and reproduction."
- **4-LS1-2:** "Use a model to describe that animals receive different types of information through their senses, process the information in their brain, and respond to the information in different ways."

Language objectives follow.

- Discuss your argument about plants' and animals' internal and external structures with a partner, using the terms *survival*, *growth*, *behavior*, and *reproduction*.
- Draw and label a model of how animals receive different types of information through their senses, process the information in their brain, and respond to the information in different ways.

Then follow these steps for the unit.

1. Draw or project the KWL chart and check for background knowledge.
2. Play for and teach students the song "Octopi Have Tentacles" (The Levins, 2018).
3. Ask students to highlight powerful words.
4. The next day, read aloud the octopus page in *Teeth, Tentacles, and Tail Fins* (Reinhart, 2023), and model writing a poem based on that information.
5. Offer other octopus-themed books and, after students explore them, ask them to write their own poem, making sure to include academic vocabulary such as *tentacles*, *ocean*, and *suction cups*. When their poems are completed, host the gallery walk and circle back to the KWL chart.

SWIRL Cognitive Content Dictionary

This GLAD strategy helps students build oral academic vocabulary in grades K–12. Cognitive content dictionaries work for a range of proficiency levels, from newcomer to reaching. Ideally, they are displayed for the whole class to reference during a unit, as part of integrated ELD. (You can read more about academic vocabulary in chapter 7, page 161.) The dictionaries have elements of the research of Robert J. Marzano (2009), who devised six steps for vocabulary instruction.

1. Say and write the new word.
2. Have students describe it in their own words.
3. Ask students to illustrate (draw) a visual representation of the word.
4. Engage students in interactive writing and speaking activities to better understand the new word.
5. Have students turn and talk with partners, or their table group, about the new word.
6. Provide engaging games involving the new word.

Julia Simms and Robert J. Marzano (2019) urge teachers not to use the word's dictionary definition but, rather, to use the word in sentences; create or find pictures associated with the word; explain synonyms and antonyms of the word; and ask students for words they already know that relate to it, like cognates, base and root words, or extensions of the word. Finally, engage students in word games with new terms they've learned. For example, you might introduce the word *longitude*. Students might know the word *long*, and that it has to do with measurement. Some might know *latitude*. They can draw a picture of a map with coordinates.

We can't expect students to use advanced academic words if they don't know what the words mean or how to use them in context. A cognitive content dictionary provides a space for the class to predict the meaning of new words, find them in a passage or article, define them, and use them in a sentence. It is, in a nutshell, an open dictionary of academic, thematic vocabulary displayed on the classroom wall. See the reproducible "Cognitive Content Dictionary" (page 107) for a customizable version.

The dictionary is a fluid document that you build over time throughout a unit. You can record it on roll paper or chart paper and add a word or two each day. Here is how you introduce the concept.

1. Write a new academic vocabulary word in the cognitive content dictionary. Say the word out loud, and have students repeat the word with correct pronunciation.

2. Ask for a show of hands as to who is already familiar with the word. Tally the numbers of the following responses next to the word.
   - *F*—Is familiar with the word
   - *NF*—Is not familiar with the word
   - *H*—Has heard of the word
   - *KD*—Knows definition
3. Let students turn and talk about what they think the word means and then share their predictions with the whole class.
4. Dive into the text that contains that word, and see if students can derive the actual meaning.
5. Scribe that actual meaning.
6. Ask students to use the word in a sentence, and scribe that.
7. Draw or paste a picture as a visual representation of the word. For students in grades 3–12, you can add columns for antonyms and synonyms to the dictionary. See figure 4.5 (page 98).

Students should each have a small, reproducible version of the "Cognitive Content Dictionary" (page 107) to keep in a folder at their desk. This aids with team and individual tasks and differentiates for students who get distracted or cannot see the chart well from far away. Individual dictionaries allow them to more readily access the academic vocabulary.

SWIrl Paint Chip Vocabulary Strips

This strategy works best for grades 3–12 and is most appropriate for expanding, bridging, and reaching students. It teaches shades of meaning involving sophisticated vocabulary. First step? Grab some free paint chip strips at the local hardware store. You will use these strips to help students expand their vocabulary beyond basic terms to include synonyms and shades of meaning. Listing synonyms, ranked by difficulty, on the strips helps students build that skill. Model this for the whole class, and then group students in mixed English proficiency levels. Use this strategy to expand reading comprehension and writing skills. You can also use it to introduce academic vocabulary. Figure 4.6 (page 99) is an example.

Word	Prediction	Actual Meaning	Used in Sentence	Example or Nonexample*	Related Words We Know	Antonym and Synonym
Evaporation 11-H 10-N	A liquid that turns into a gas	The physical process in which water and other liquids become gasses	The lake evaporation made the air become humid.	Example: Lakes turning back into clouds Nonexample: Rain		
Condensation 2-H 19-N	When clouds are full of water	Change in state of matter from gas to liquid	The condensation from the shower steam gathered on the mirror.	Example: Clouds Nonexample: Rocks		
Precipitation 14-H 7-N	Rain that falls from the sky	Falling water caused by rain, snow, or hail	Yesterday, I saw precipitation when it was raining.	Example: Rain Nonexample: Leaves		

*This column can be drawings for K–2.

Figure 4.5: Cognitive content dictionary example.

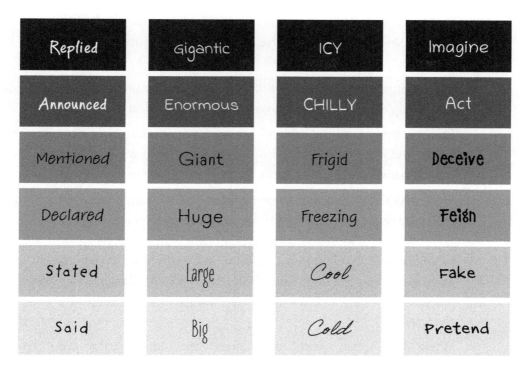

Figure 4.6: Paint chip vocabulary strip example.

Follow these steps.

1. Prior to class, write a different vocabulary word at the bottom of each paint strip. These should be the simplest forms of the words (*sad*, *angry*, and *happy*, for example).

2. Ask the class to define what a *synonym* is. They can give some examples aloud. Scribe their answers on an anchor chart. Tell them these are shades of meaning for the same word, each one more complex than the one below it.

3. Show the class a paint strip on which you've written a word at the bottom (lightest) color block. (In figure 4.6, it is the words *said*, *big*, *cold*, and *pretend*.)

4. Tell students, "I am going to build a more expansive vocabulary by adding a more *advanced*, or *complex*, synonym on each color." Tell them to think about a more sophisticated synonym for the vocabulary word. Give one example (in this case, *stated*).

5. Ask students to turn and talk about other words they've read or heard that they can use to mean essentially the same thing as the initial word

you shared with them. Then, ask students to share their words and explain their reasoning as to what order the words go in—from easier to harder.

6. Write a different word in each different color of the paint chip strip. (In this example, you might write *mentioned*, *announced*, and *replied*.)

7. Have students work in groups of three or four to brainstorm a synonym or two and write them on the strip. Have them write in pencil first, check their spelling, and then trace their writing in marker.

8. Once they record their one or two synonyms, have each group pass their strip to a nearby group. Or you can have each group complete their own full strip. If you do rotate the strips, you can use a signal to indicate that it's time to pass them to make this more structured. Perhaps reiterate one of the initial vocabulary words as a signal to swap strips: "When I say *declared*, team captains, pass your strip. Ready? *Declared*."

9. When all paint strips are filled out, display them on a board or word wall for students to reference. Invite students to do a gallery walk as they read the scaffolded vocabulary synonyms on the paint chips.

SwIRL Songs

The majority of students love to sing, especially students in grades preK–2. As content gets more complex, you can adapt songs for grades 3–5 as well. Setting content to songs (many are in the public domain) can be especially beneficial for students who are newcomers or entering, emerging, and developing ELs.

How many times can you remember being able to sing the lyrics to a song that you hadn't heard in years? Our brains store information easier when content is connected to music, a rhythm, or a beat (Kennedy Center, n.d.). Child psychiatry professor and practicing musician Kyle Pruett says, "Musical experience strengthens the capacity to be verbally competent" (Brown, 2012). Plus, music's effect on language development is visible in the brain, since "linking familiar songs to new information can also help imprint information on young minds" (Brown, 2012).

Multilingual learners and striving readers, in particular, benefit from hearing, reading, and singing content and curriculum set to familiar songs. Students can play instruments or just sing the lyrics to the rhythm or tune of a familiar song.

- For prekindergarten through grade 1, try nursery rhymes.

- For grades 2–4, try familiar public domain songs (such as "Three Blind Mice," "Take Me Out to the Ball Game," and "The Farmer in the Dell").
- For grades 5 and up, try popular music from different genres (pop, hip-hop, rap) or vetted TikTok or YouTube videos set to songs.

Each song is part of a lesson that incorporates best practice strategies such as inquiry charts (including KWL), pictorial input charts, T-charts, and cognitive content dictionaries. Integrating songs aligns well with STEM, Universal Design for Learning, and ELD in that it directly addresses those standards. It allows students to attain knowledge via multiple learning modalities, including auditory, musical, kinesthetic, visual, and linguistic. A reproducible of the song "Octopi Have Tentacles" (page 108), as well as two other songs ("Four Layers of the Rain Forest," page 109, and "Sweet Harriet," page 110), is available in this chapter. Visit **go.SolutionTree.com/EL** for a free downloadable version and links to the songs being performed.

SwIRL Trivia

Students in grades 3–12 enjoy showcasing their knowledge through games like *Jeopardy!*® Making learning into a game heightens engagement, increases agency, and lowers the affective filter (Krashen, 1982; Literacy Minnesota, 2017), and students love competing. This works as a review of material covered in a minilesson, article, or unit.

Follow these directions to play.

1. Divide the class into teams or groups.
2. Read a clue from the game board (like one found in figure 4.7, page 102) to the class.
3. Whoever buzzes in first (with the right answer, of course) should answer in the form of "What is *x*?" or "Who is *x*?" (You can find buzzers online, or you can use bells or other sounds.)
4. The game is done when all categories, including the bonus round, have been completed. Take note of any anecdotal or formative assessments you make during the game. Follow up in small groups with students who struggle with certain categories.

Universities	Presidents	Cities	Women	Illness	Famous Sayings
		200: The city where Ruth Bader Ginsburg was born			
400: Two of the Ivy League universities Ginsburg attended				400: The number of times Ginsburg survived cancer	
	600: This president appointed Ginsburg to the Supreme Court.				600: This is what Ginsburg said when she didn't agree with the other judges.
			800: This is another woman Supreme Court judge who is Latina.		

Figure 4.7: Sample trivia board clues.

Certain apps allow students to actually buzz in and let you turn over the square to reveal the answer (or clue, as the case is here). Some websites offer templates and software for creating your own trivia game.

- Factile (www.playfactile.com)
- JeopardyLabs (https://jeopardylabs.com)
- Super Teacher Tools (www.superteachertools.us/jeopardyx)

SwIrL Along the Lines

An early form of debate, along the lines offers two opposing opinions, one on either side of an imaginary line; students choose a side. This activity works best for grades 3–12 with students who are already developing, expanding, bridging, and reaching.

1. Make your statements and indicate where in the room students who have the first point of view and students who have the second point of view should stand. For example, say, "All students who think a dog is

the best pet to have, go to this side of the line. Go to the other side of the line if you think a cat is the best pet to have," or "Everyone who prefers rap music, move to this side. Those who prefer pop music, move to this side."

2. Give students one minute to silently choose a side and turn to face someone who is on the other side. If the lines are uneven, encourage students to make triads.

3. Pair up students so they can speak one-to-one, prompting each student to say why they chose that side of the room.

4. After two minutes of asserting reasons why their preference is better, one line moves down by one person so students form new conversation pairs.

5. Have students continue arguing their rationale until they've heard several people's reasoning. Ask a few volunteers to share their reasoning. You can also see if anyone's opinion was swayed during the along-the-lines debate.

SwirL Hot Seat

Students love being given a topic—one their peers chose or they pulled from a hat—and talking about it for one minute straight. Set a timer and prompt them to talk about the topic without stopping.

This old theater game, one of my third graders' favorites, works best with grades 3–12 and with students who are developing, expanding, bridging, and reaching. They can talk about a science or social studies topic, or about a particular musician, food, or amusement park, for example. The goal is to get students to keep talking for one minute. You'd be surprised how those who you normally can't get to stay quiet during lessons struggle to fill their minute when they are in the hot seat, or how your shy students blossom when given the spotlight. This activity makes some students nervous, which raises their affective filter. Let willing students go first and, eventually, all students are likely to volunteer. Invite only one to three students up to speak per day.

The rule is nobody in the audience can interrupt; however, they can ask questions, give compliments, or offer feedback (for grammar and pronunciation, for instance) once the minute is up. If a student offers constructive criticism, they must also offer a compliment.

SWIRL Process Grids

A GLAD process grid is used for a whole class of K–8 students at every proficiency level; however, when you group students for each category of the grid, you create heterogeneous language proficiency groupings so that newcomers and entering, emerging, and developing ELs can get support from their peers at higher proficiency levels.

While this mostly results in a reading and writing product, the speaking part of the process needed to create it is essential. When using a process grid, groups each research and report back on the features of a topic. This process leads to an end product (the process grid) and incorporates both expert groups (page 87) and a jigsaw, allowing all students to learn about various parts of the topic. Students read, take notes, and discuss the topic in order to complete the process grid with information about each subtopic. See the free reproducible "Process Grid" (page 111).

Follow these steps.

1. Walk students through the various categories in the process grid.

2. If time allows, ask for students' background knowledge (page 92).

3. As a whole class (K–2) or in small groups (3–8), organize students to research each subtopic. If you do the process grid in groups, students speak to each other while gathering information for the process grid. Then, each group presents that information to the whole class. Since each row of the grid includes several columns, every student in an expert group should speak about one of those areas. Encourage students to speak in English, but also to use their home language as needed.

4. As students share aloud information after reading and discussing, scribe their findings in the grid, or have them fill it in themselves with a specified color (in the upper grades).

5. If you choose to, and have time, reinforce the learning by having groups review their section with the class after it is filled in.

6. Add to the process grid as the unit continues and expert groups present to the whole class. While the main anchor chart is displayed on chart paper, each student also has their own standard paper copy of the process grid to fill out as the presentations take place.

Process grids work well with thematic teaching in social studies and science. For example, you might have process grids about various Native American tribes, different habitats, or genres of literature.

Conclusion

Let's circle back to our opening quote: "The person doing the speaking is doing the learning." This quote has been attributed to many people, including Jennifer York-Barr. At its core, it tells us that by verbally processing and articulating learning, students synthesize information and retain it. The activities covered in this chapter require students to speak about what they read and write. As they speak, they interact with and listen to peers and teachers.

One final note, I learned early on in my career that it is important to discern productive talk from off-topic, unproductive chitchat that distracts students from completing a task. That being said, we want students out of silent mode, off mute, and speaking as much as possible!

KWL Chart

What I Know	What I Want to Know	What I Learned

The SWIRL Method © 2025 Solution Tree Press • SolutionTree.com
Visit **go.SolutionTree.com/EL** to download this free reproducible.

Cognitive Content Dictionary

Word	Prediction	Actual Meaning	Used in Sentence	Image	Related Words We Know	Antonym and Synonym

The SWIRL Method © 2025 Solution Tree Press • SolutionTree.com
Visit **go.SolutionTree.com/EL** to download this free reproducible.

Octopi Have Tentacles

(Sung to the tune of "Mary Had a Little Lamb" by Sarah Josepha Hale, 1830)

An octopus has tentacles, tentacles, tentacles.
An octopus has tentacles—eight swirly, twirly limbs.

Each tentacle has suction cups, suction cups, suction cups,
which come in rows of one or two to catch prey as it swims.

It catches prey like fish and crabs, fish and crabs, fish and crabs,
and other tasty arthropods for a nightly snack.

It shoots ink as dark as night, dark as night, dark as night.
Enemies lose smell and sight when they try to attack.

Octopi use camouflage, camouflage, camouflage.
They can change both color and texture as they hide and seek.

They're super smart but have no spine, have no spine, have no spine.
They're invertebrates, which have no spine, but they have a real sharp beak.

Their beak's in the middle of the tentacles, tentacles, tentacles.
Octopi have tentacles—eight swirly, twirly limbs.

That's where the song begins.

Source: © 2016 by The Levins. Used with permission set to public domain song.
Adapted from Hale, S. J. (1830). Poems for our children. *Boston: Marsh, Capen & Lyon.*

Four Layers of the Rain Forest

(Sung to the tune of "Oh, My Darling Clementine" by Percy Montross, 1884)

In the tropics, at the equator
there's lots of sun and lots of rain.
That's where you find the rain forests
and the wildlife they sustain.

Chorus:
Oh the rain forest it consists of
different layers. There are four:
There's emergent, canopy,
understory, forest floor.

The first layer is called *emergent*
It is closest to the sky
Where the sun shines on the treetops
And the birds can safely fly.

(Chorus)

In the canopy there's a party
Most forest wildlife lives here
In the overlapping branches
a hundred feet up in the air.

(Chorus)

In the humid understory
It is dark but you will find
Monkeys, lizards, snakes, and jaguars—
countless insects of all kinds.

(Chorus)

It is damp and decomposing
Way down on the forest floor—
Filled with swamps and running rivers,
Herbaceous plants for herbivores.

(Chorus)

Source: © 2018 by The Levins. Used with permission. Adapted from Montross, P. (1884). Oh my darling Clementine. Accessed at https://americansongwriter.com/the-meaning-behind-the-cartoonish-yodeling-song-oh-my-darling-clementine on November 2, 2023.

Sweet Harriet

(Sung to the tune of "Swing Low, Sweet Chariot" by Wallace Willis, n.d.)

Chorus:
We love Sweet Harriet
Coming back to carry us home
Away from slavery
On the Underground Railroad.

Born a slave in Dorchester County,
but Maryland was not her home.
She escaped to Philadelphia
but came back to carry us home.

(Chorus)

Late at night, following the Dipper
Along a network of secretive homes,
Harriet never lost a passenger
to freedom along the unseen road.

(Chorus)

After the Fugitive Slave Act of 1850
Ms. Tubman led slaves further North
into Canada where she helped them
    find work
Harriet kept the train on course.

(Chorus)

On thirteen missions,
    some seventy people
Made their way to
    freedom's shore
They called Harriet Moses,
    because she led them
Through the waters to dignity's door.

(Chorus)

Harriet worked for the Union Army
as a cook, a nurse, a scout and a spy.
She guided the raid on the Combahee Ferry
Freeing seven hundred slaves by and by.

(Chorus)

When the Civil War ended, Harriet
    helped women
With voting rights until she got ill.
She was abolitionist and humanitarian;
soon you'll see her on the twenty-dollar bill.

(Chorus)

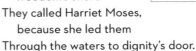

Source: © 2018 by The Levins. Used with permission. Adapted from Willis, W. (n.d.). Swing low, sweet chariot. *Accessed at https://americanart.si.edu/artwork/swing-low-sweet-chariot-12100 on November 2, 2023.*

Process Grid

Topic					

Topic					

The SWIRL Method © 2025 Solution Tree Press • SolutionTree.com
Visit **go.SolutionTree.com/EL** to download this free reproducible.

CHAPTER 5

Writing

*One child, one teacher, one book, one pen can change the world. . . .
When the whole world is silent, even one voice becomes powerful.*
—Malala Yousafzai

There is a direct line between speaking, reading, and writing. For students to succeed in grade school, college, and career, they need to be able to articulate their thoughts in writing. College entrance exams, certification tests, scientific hypotheses, legal briefs, and even poetry as a means of self-expression all demand that ELs be fluent writers.

When I was a literacy coach at a school with over 115 English learners (out of 332 students), I noticed that a lot of emphasis was put on teaching reading, but not as much time was dedicated to providing writing instruction. We know that reading and writing skills go hand in hand (Fink, 2017). They're so intertwined that they can be described this way:

> The relationship between reading and writing is a bit like that of the chicken and egg. Which came first is not as important as the fact that without one the other cannot exist. A child's literacy development is dependent on this interconnection between reading and writing. (K12 Reader, n.d.)

I especially saw that discrepancy when assessing students' writing. Whether it be because of spelling, grammar, or sentence variation, MLs consistently struggled to express themselves in writing. The third of our student population who were identified as English learners struggled the most in writing and reading comprehension portions of the reclassification test. There were some basic vocabulary and concept skills in which I noticed gaps (for example, naming the four seasons).

As you teach writing to EL students, keep in mind three important considerations to enhance your planning, execution, and assessment of writing assignments: (1) reading and writing are intertwined, (2) audience is an important motivating factor, and (3) foundational skills are essential, but so are voice and choice. Regarding audience, or MLs' purpose for writing, many students observe their family members writing in the home with a purpose: grocery lists, recipes, holiday cards, and so on. When students get to school, their audience is the teacher. They no longer see writing as integrated into their cultural context, their community, or the world at large. But you can create an audience and purpose for them by having students present their published writing to their parents, show it to other classes (big and little buddies), or enter writing contests.

What a teacher cultivates, grows. For example, I wanted my first-grade students to strengthen their writing skills and see themselves as authors. By the end of that school year, my students had published over one hundred books, which were prominently displayed in our classroom library. By far, the classroom library books that students checked out the most were the ones published by their peers. Fast-forward twenty-five years: several of those students have gone on to make their careers as writers, and most of them attended universities in a demanding academic field that required them to be fluent English writers.

How can you start instilling both a love of writing and the skills in mechanics (grammar and punctuation) and content (clarity, focus, organization, and structure) for students to become fluent writers?

- **Acknowledge that English is a difficult language with myriad exceptions to rules:** Take, for example, the fact that the words *blue*, *shoe*, *two*, and *do* all have the same ending sound but are not spelled alike. Add to that words like *they're*, *their*, and *there*, and you have a seriously confusing language. The majority of ELs in the United States speak Spanish, which is a phonetic language. That means words are spelled like they sound. English requires explicit instruction on foundational skills—the alphabet, concepts of print (directionality, book parts), phonological awareness, phonics, high-frequency words, and fluency. This extends to sound and symbol recognition, spelling of CVC words, and sound blends. Remember that languages like Arabic, Farsi, and Hebrew are written from right to left, so directionality is something that some ELs need to be taught. Other Asian languages are written with characters that represent phrases or concepts, not just letter sounds, and are read vertically. Take these crosslinguistic variations into account as you teach foundational skills to MLs.

- **Remember that just as students are more motivated when they get to choose what they read, they write more when they get to choose what they are writing about:** That is to say, a good portion of the time, you should allow them to choose their topic. You may introduce a genre or format—poem, research project, or five-paragraph essay, for example—but, for the most part, let students choose what topic they narrate or inform readers about. I usually start off the year by brainstorming a list of story ideas with students. I type it up, add a few blank spaces at the end for students to add more ideas, and staple a copy inside each student's writing folder.

First, we'll discuss the research on writing, and then we'll cover related activities and strategies.

The Research on Writing

SWIRLing helps students connect the various communication skills to become fluent speakers, writers, readers, and active listeners. Writing, in particular, allows students to communicate their knowledge, creativity, opinions, and theories to a broad audience. A word of caution, though: "Writing is the most challenging area in learning a second language. . . . Issues generally arise from incompetence in syntax, coherence, idea expansion, content selection, topic sentence, rhetorical conventions, mechanics, organization, lack of vocabulary, inappropriate use of vocabulary" (Fareed, Ashraf, & Bilal, 2016, p. 82).

Why is writing so important? In almost every career, articulating your ideas or research in writing is required. And because of SWIRL's interwoven nature, English language writing skills support "reading comprehension, vocabulary expansion, and oral fluency. . . . The skills gleaned from learning to write in another language transfer to all facets of life, making students more aware and more effective communicators in their native language(s)" (D'Argenio, 2022). Writing skills such as expressing a complete thought, staying on topic, and supporting your argument by citing textual evidence transfer between languages; however, certain rules, grammar functions, and exceptions in English require direct instruction.

Arizona State University's Steve Graham and fellow researchers Sharlene A. Kiuhara and Meade MacKay examined fifty-six studies on the benefits of *writing across the curriculum*, where students write more extensively than they might in more traditional, compartmentalized instruction, in topics including science, social studies, and mathematics (Graham, Kiuhara, & MacKay, 2020). Graham and colleagues (2020) found that writing across subject areas "reliably enhanced learning" in grades K–12 (p. 179). One reason for this may be that writing helps students recall information, connect different concepts, and solidify and synthesize information (Terada, 2021). After the COVID-19 pandemic, however, English learners' writing proficiency scores are alarming. According to WIDA assessment data (Poole & Sahakyan, 2024), every student demographic of grades 3–5, 6–8, and 9–12 experienced a decline in writing scores during the pandemic.

Activities and Strategies

The English Learners Success Forum (2020) provides guidelines for helping emergent multilinguals become confident writers, which include the following:

> Writing activities engage students in discussions of topics and prompts with peers and teacher throughout and as an integral part of the writing process.
>
> Writing activities are centered on specific shared texts so all students have shared content for orally communicating about disciplinary content, negotiating meaning collaboratively, gathering evidence from those texts, and other learning activities.
>
> Student materials ensure that students have many opportunities to communicate ideas to others and to consistently reflect on and use strategies to improve their communication ([metalinguistic awareness] strategies).
>
> Student materials provide opportunities for students to analyze, reflect on, and improve their own writing ([metalinguistic awareness]) using models, rubrics, and other reflection tools. (pp. 10, 13)

Before they start writing, students find it helpful to brainstorm or talk about what they will write. It is essential to provide students with independent think time, think-pair-share, or structured small-group opportunities and graphic organizers, anchor charts, or word banks to help them organize their thoughts. We give them think time since "students, particularly those at the beginner level, need ample time to think about the content before diving into the actual writing process" (D'Argenio, 2022). Also, co-constructing word banks that students can lean on as anchor charts when writing helps students refer to words they might need. If possible, allow students to write in their primary language and then share with you what they've written. This is a helpful scaffold, as teacher and consultant Tan Huynh (2022) writes:

> Often, MLs have ideas swirling in their minds but struggle to formulate them in English. To support these students, we can have them first brainstorm, organize, and outline in their heritage languages. Forcing students to write or speak only in English is like putting speed bumps in their way.

Allowing students to write in their home language shows that you value their assets—what they bring to the learning process—and is part of culturally responsive, culturally sustaining pedagogy. Omitting a heritage language and demanding that students write (or speak or read) only in English is not best practice. When we acknowledge that students come to school with a vast vocabulary and, often, rich oral traditions, we build on their knowledge, *adding* English, not subtracting their home language.

What if you don't speak your student's heritage language? Take heart. Research shows that "all teachers need to do is see students' multilingualism as an asset that extends learning and sustains students' connections to their communities" (Huynh, 2022). Pair entering- and emerging-level writers with older or more English language-proficient students to facilitate getting their creative ideas down on paper. For example, I used to buddy my second graders with fifth graders. Typically, teachers have reading buddies, but I found that my students had lots of creative stories to tell. They couldn't yet put those ideas on paper, so their older buddies helped scribe their stories.

Aside from the fact that writing skills are essential in every subject—from writing a hypothesis in science to writing a biography in social studies—being an articulate writer is a skill that opens doors to college, in students' careers, and in their personal lives. People need to understand someone's ideas when they communicate them in writing. Spelling or grammar mistakes on a résumé, or a lack of focus and organization in a cover letter, can prevent someone from even getting a job interview. Suffice it to say, writing skills are essential.

Writing, in the SWIRL model, should typically follow opportunities in a lesson for students to speak, interact, read, or listen. The main exception is when you ask students to write before they speak so they can gather their thoughts. That scaffold takes place mostly in grades 3–12. Writing and reading go hand in hand with tasks such as literature response journals, note taking, and text annotations. Writing and speaking overlap when students talk before writing in expert groups, on process grids, or with paint chip vocabulary strips. Students might write after listening to a lesson, video, or audio clip. Many writing activities involve listening and interacting—students partner to write joint essays or presentations, they read their writing to others for peer critique, or they turn and talk before they write.

SWiRL Word Families

Word families most benefit preK–2 students and entering, emerging, and developing ELs.

What can we do to facilitate English language acquisition when Latin-based languages, for example, are typically much more phonetic than English? The word for "table" in Spanish (*mesa*) is spelled just like it sounds—*me-sa*. But the silent *e* in *table* is just one example of why it's challenging for multilingual learners to acquire English. Referring back to the *blue, shoe, two,* and *do* example, a student who is new to English also does not intuitively know how to spell these various long /oo/ sounds.

To help them get them there, the strategy of word families, also known as *rhyming families*, is especially effective in English. Books with rhymes and rhyming families help because hearing the teacher's expression and the story's rhymes aloud teaches students about stressed and unstressed syllables (Fleta, 2017). Look at the following text from *Duck in the Truck* (Alborough, 2000) as an example of how rhyme helps students develop oral and written language. Underlining or highlighting the words that rhyme can help students become stronger spellers:

> These are the wheels finally gripping.
> This is the knot suddenly slipping.
> This is the truck with the engine on fast.
> Back on the track... UNSTUCK AT LAST!
> (Alborough, 2000, pp. 20-21)

A love of language naturally develops as students hear the rhymes and begin to predict what comes next.

One of my books, *My Mama Earth* (Katz, 2012), has the following lines:

> My Mama makes the hippos snore
> and mighty lions proudly _____. (pp. 8-9)

When I read this, I always pause to give listeners an opportunity to complete the sentence (called a *cloze*). They can predict, with the help of the illustrations' clues and context, that the missing word is *roar*. I usually prompt students to roar like a lion when they say the last word. Using cloze activities with narrative texts helps students improve their comprehension (Kusfitriyatna, Evenddy, & Utomo, 2021).

When students have mastered their basic letter sounds and names, I suggest shifting quickly to teaching rhyming families. Your students may recognize rhymes by hearing and saying them before they learn to read.

Aside from using popular rhyming books, such as those by Dr. Seuss, Anna Dewdney (author of the *Llama Llama* books), and Shel Silverstein as mentor texts, you can also design lessons that encourage students to come up with rhyming words in pairs or by table groups.

For grades 5–12 students, consider the following books, which are examples of novels in verse.

- *Booked* by Kwame Alexander (2016)
- *Crank* by Ellen Hopkins (2004)
- *Words With Wings* by Nikki Grimes (2022)

For middle and high school students, consider spoken word contests to get them to perform their writing. Visit the Poetry Foundation's website (https://tinyurl.com/2p9y96r6) for links to examples of spoken word projects.

For preK–2 students, a lesson with rhyming families might look like the following. Notice the gradual release of responsibility built into it.

1. Before class, prepare "houses" for different word families, such as *-at, -and, -up, -og, -ug,* and *-est*. The houses can simply be pieces of colored construction paper cut into the shapes of houses, with the family endings written on the attics.

2. Model a word-family brainstorm with a think-aloud (*I do*) at the rug, with the whole class, or in a small group. An example follows.

    > *Teacher: I'm going to visit the* -at *family. If I go through the alphabet in my mind, I think* b. B *plus* -at *equals* bat.
    >
    > *Students: Bat.*

3. In this case, add the letter *b* to the first line inside the house, and draw an image of a baseball bat, a flying bat, or both next to the word.

4. Ask students, "What comes next?" Then say the alphabet in order: "*A, b, c . . . C.* Hmm. If we add the letter *c* to *-at*, what word do we get? *C-at. Cat.*"

5. Write the letter *c* and draw a cat next to the word, as shown in figure 5.1. You can also share the pen and let students draw (*you do*).

6. After some prior practice with sound blends, if you feel like most students are ready, ask them if they know any two-letter sound blends that make a word ending in *-at*, such as *that*, *slat*, or *flat*.

7. Have students work in pairs (*two do*), in groups (*we do*), or individually (*I do*) to add words to other word families you've prepared on construction paper houses.

8. Give each group a chance to add a few words to a family, and then rotate the houses to the next groups. Have students write in pencil first as you circulate to edit spelling; then they can trace their writing in marker.

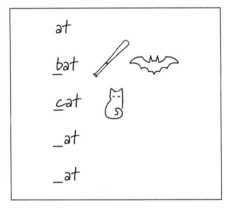

Figure 5.1: Working on word families.

Post the rhyming families as anchor charts, like the one shown in figure 5.2. As new words are discovered in texts, students should be able to identify the word families to which they belong and add them to the charts (*you do*). If you choose to, you may scaffold for emergent bilinguals by having them work in pairs (*two do*) before sending them off to work independently. The equivalent for dual immersion or bilingual teachers is working with Spanish syllables such as these: *ma, me, mi, mo, mu, pa, pe, pi, po,* and *pu*.

sWIRl Interactive Journaling

Interactive journaling works for all grades, but is best for grades 1–3 with entering, emerging, developing, expanding, and bridging students. The strategy involves writing questions to students in their journals to model correct spelling or clarify

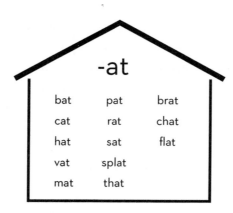

Figure 5.2: Word family anchor chart.

their writing. The teacher circulates in class and identifies errors that need correcting. When a student incorrectly writes something, the teacher responds with a question about what they wrote, correctly modeling the word. This methodology allows students to write freely and gives the teacher a chance to observe and model writing. An exchange might look like that in figure 5.3.

Figure 5.3: Interactive journaling example.

Let students know that you will underline misspelled words and circle incorrect words in a sentence. Try not to correct more than one or two words to keep the student's affective filter low. If you want to encourage them to express themselves and take risks in writing, allow students to use invented spelling in preK–1; however, redirect or correct invented spelling in grades 2 and beyond to prevent students from having spelling mistakes later in their academic careers (Arman, 2021).

Once, while visiting a high school class, I saw most students typing on devices as their teacher was circulating to read their writing and correct any mistakes. When we debriefed, I asked the teacher how she adjusts her instruction based on the skills she assesses, in real time, as areas where the students need more practice. She shared that her corrections largely focus on what is on the fluency test. In areas where the students are experiencing productive struggle, she does not correct them because that is how they will learn—from approximating (Y. May, personal communication, March 2022). Our pedagogical conversation deepened as we discussed why it is important to know that skill, even if students won't be tested on it when determining their fluency.

The point is for students to become fluent readers, writers, and speakers of the language, not just to pass the test. Writing is a life skill. It is key to college and career opportunities.

sWIRl Writers' Workshop

Writers' workshop, which best serves K–5 students at all English proficiency levels, is a dedicated time when students write and publish pieces in various genres, predominantly on topics of their choosing. Research indicates that it is important to involve English learners "in pair work or group work to develop their writing skills" (Srinivas, 2019, p. 5). Writers' workshop is an effective example of this kind of peer work. Its efficacy with ELs is well researched (American Institutes for Research, 2021; Masrul & Rasyidah, 2022).

Consider including units of study such as having students extrapolate on a small moment and expand it when writing. I set up my writers' workshop with the following five pillars to best meet the needs of all my students, especially ELs: (1) based on student choice, (2) driven by process, (3) differentiated, (4) celebratory, and (5) includes accountability.

Based on Student Choice

Just as students are more apt to read if they can choose books on subjects that they like, they are also more motivated to write if they can write about things that interest them. Start every year by doing a class brainstorm of ideas so students can never say, "I don't know what to write about." Type up that list—which likely includes everything from pets to planets to princesses—and print it and staple it inside each student's writers' workshop folder. Add a few lines at the bottom for them to record any new ideas they think of.

Of course, sometimes topics are assigned, such as when students are doing a report or writing to a prompt, but students should have the creative freedom to choose their topics about 80 percent of the time. Consider the following research findings:

> Letting students choose their topics and genres gives them a sense of ownership because they must look within to decide what they want to write about. They have a chance to showcase what they understand about a topic and research what they would like to learn. Both of these activities are strong motivators. And research shows that framing writing projects around personal interests encourages learners (Bennett, Lubben, & Hogarth, 2007; Gebre & Polman, 2020) helps them connect background knowledge to new information (Bruning, Schraw, & Norby, 2011) and fosters authenticity of learning (Gilje & Erstad, 2017). (Regional Educational Laboratory Program, 2021)

So many important factors surface when you give students choice about their writing topic: increased metacognition, a sense of ownership and agency, the building of background knowledge, motivation, cultural responsiveness, and authentic learning.

Driven by Process

Most days, writers' workshop starts with a minilesson on a particular skill pertaining to either mechanics (punctuation or grammar, for instance) or content (adding details or staying on topic, for example). Model by writing an example, or borrow a students' writing samples (but cover up the name).

List the stages of the writing process—brainstorming, prewriting, first draft writing, editing, revising, and publishing—on laminated posters with small illustrations or icons, and put those either vertically or horizontally across the whiteboard. Each poster should have space on it for students to sign their name, indicating what stage of the process they are in. This ensures some accountability in terms of noticing if they have not published or met with you in a while. Find time to do a quick check (of who might need a conference that day, what each student is writing about, or who is publishing) after the minilesson, before diving into independent writing time. That way, you can see where students are in their process. Some teachers write students' names on clothespins that they move along a continuum as the students progress through the writing process.

Differentiated

Meet one-on-one with each student at least every other week, if possible. During writers' workshop conferences, students read their stories to the teacher, and *the students hold the pen or pencil* to make corrections. This helps them self-correct, pronounce English words aloud, and learn to edit their own writing. I also ask students to circle any words they are not 100 percent sure of before we conference.

During this time, prompt students with questions like those in the reproducible "Writers' Workshop Conference Tool" (page 139).

- "What are you trying to say here?"
- "What sound do you hear at the beginning of this word?"
- "Where should the ending punctuation go?"

Take detailed anecdotal records. Knowing each student's English language proficiency level helps you decide if you are going to focus on leveraging rhyming families or multisyllabic words (for emerging and developing proficiencies), or revise content to add more details, humor, dialogue, and so on (bridging and reaching proficiency levels).

What you focus on during your conferences depends on the students' strengths and struggles that week, in that piece of writing, and their ability to clearly communicate their ideas. For example, consider the following.

- You can start by asking the student this simple question: "How's it going?"
- You can proceed with suggestions from *Every Child a Super Reader* (Allyn & Morrell, 2016): ask if they are struggling in any particular section, what they learned about themselves as a writer this week, or if they have any specific questions for you. Most of all, listen. Listen to them read their piece to you.
- You can focus on mechanics. For grammar, ask the student to read the story or essay once, all the way through. When the student reads it again, stop along the way. You might say, "This seems like a bit of a run-on sentence. I need to pause and take a breath. Where can we put a period and then a capital letter to start a new sentence?" For spelling errors, put a check mark or star above the letters they got right, and leave a blank space (or add a caret) for missing letters. For example, if the student writes *hamstr*, write *hamst_r*. Then, in English, say, "Every syllable needs a vowel. What do you hear in *ham-ster*?" Emphasize *-er*. Many times, the student can fill in that missing vowel on their own. If not, a phonics phone (figure 5.4, page 125) helps them discern each sound.

- You can focus on content (clarity, conciseness, and character development) or a combination of content and mechanics. When it comes to content corrections, you might stop and say, "I wonder if you can tell me what you're trying to say here. I'm a little confused." You might also ask them what additions or omissions might help improve the writing or what questions they think other readers might have.

You can keep anecdotal records of what you worked on with each student in the conferences on paper or with a program like ClassDojo (www.classdojo.com). These records help you know who needs to work on what specific skills.

For some EL students, it is helpful to use phonics phones, which are essentially two pieces of elbow pipe with a connector pipe, like those in figure 5.4. Glue those three pieces together or have a handy parent make the phones (they are also available to order online), and invite your students to hold one up to their ear when they get caught trying to spell a word. Let them whisper the word slowly and repeatedly to themselves. The phonics phone will amplify sounds for students so they hear sounds they have missed. Again, in my experience, nine times out of ten, they can self-correct their spelling by using the phonics phone.

Figure 5.4: Make and use a phonics phone.

A word of caution here: many schools follow Darlene M. Tangel and Benita A. Blachman's (1992) invented spelling pedagogy in grades K–3, which allows students to approximate words by writing whatever sounds they hear, not necessarily the correct ones. For example, a student may write the word *playground* as *plagrond*.

Invented spelling is fine in preK and kindergarten, and sometimes even into first grade, to encourage written expression and not squelch the creative process; however, in second grade and beyond, I find this is detrimental to English learners' progress. They can try to sound out a word but, if they are going to publish a piece for others to read, their spelling needs to be corrected (cooperatively with you as a learning experience) in a one-on-one conference. Writing is an academic skill. Spelling (especially in English, with all its exceptions to myriad rules) does not come as naturally as speaking. It must be taught. Word banks that go up on the wall, as anchors for students, must be spelled correctly.

If you teach in a dual immersion program, consider the following research:

> Associations between children's English code-related skills and invented spelling appear to work through Spanish code-related skills. In order to promote young dual language learners' English invented spelling skills, early childhood educators should seek to support children's English vocabulary and English and Spanish code-related emergent literacy skills. (Pendergast, Bingham, & Patton-Terry, 2015, p. 264)

In short, this works for Spanish speakers; since that language is phonemic, letting English learners write words as they sound correlates with their prior knowledge of how words work. All too often, little or no attention is placed on how literacy, particularly spelling, differs from Spanish to English.

In *180 Days: Two Teachers and the Quest to Engage and Empower Adolescents*, authors Kelly Gallagher and Penny Kittle (2018) discuss conferring (or conferencing) with older students. Their four goals are for students to do the following:

1. Develop confidence to generate ideas.
2. Use the writing process to develop those ideas.
3. Become independent and make their own decisions about what to do next in their writing.
4. View texts as mentors in the craft of writing. (p. 94)

Gallagher and Kittle (2018) go on to say that, when conferring with students in writing, it is important to do the following.

- Be fully present with students. Show you're giving them your full attention by leaning in and listening.
- After listening fully, say back to students what you heard. You might use prompts such as, "I heard this: . . . ," "I felt most interested when . . . ," and "The part where I got confused was when . . ." (Gallagher & Kittle, 2018; Graves, 1985).

- Cocreate steps with students for what they will do next.
- Give students space to make decisions.
- Use small-group writing conferences to build camaraderie around the skill of writing.

Gallagher and Kittle also caution teachers against avoiding personal narratives in favor of argumentative and informational writing assignments. They argue that a writer's voice is developed by sharing their own personal experiences. Journaling in notebooks, crafting poetry, and writing memoirs (or stories about small, expanded moments) yield the kind of language that "leaves us stunned in the wake of lovely sentences" (Gallagher & Kittle, 2018, p. 15).

Focus feedback on the task—a student's progress—instead of the achievement or the learner (Shute, 2008). Education professor and author Susan Brookhart (2017) encourages accompanying actionable feedback with a positive comment. Additionally, don't mark up a student's paper in front of them (Hattie, 2012). That can end the learning right there because actively seeing you mark a bunch of red corrections raises their affective filter. This is why students should be the ones using the pen during your conferences. It takes patience and practice, but students learn to hear your oral feedback, self-edit, and become more independent writers.

Celebratory

Every week or every other week, you can host an author's chair. During this activity, whoever is ready to read their story—meaning it is published—gets to sit in a special author's chair. I painted a wooden classroom chair white, and my students decorated it with letters and words.

A published piece is one that went through all phases of the writing process, including a conference with the teacher, and was edited for mechanics and content. Not all of students' pieces need to be published; however, I encouraged my students to publish as many stories as possible. We invited parents and, sometimes, other classes and the principal to hear our young authors read their stories. Remember, audience is important since "students benefit from opportunities to write for an actual audience" (Farr, 2020).

We also had a publishing party at the end of the school year, which families attended to hear their children read published stories to them. This mimicked real published authors' launch parties in bookstores and other venues, and it was celebratory. Writing can be quite a solitary process, so bringing others together to celebrate publication is part of the joy of writing. Ultimately, we want students to see themselves as authors.

Includes Accountability

In the speaking chapter, we talked about Accountable Talk (page 80); in writing, accountability is even more visible. You, as the teacher, can read and comment on students' writing to monitor their progress. Shared documents allow you to monitor writing and provide feedback, in real time, as students write; that works from about grade 3 to grade 12. In K–2, accountability might involve a classroom visual with displays of student work and writers' workshop conferencing with the teacher. You can, for example, staple students' final pieces in front of their rough drafts and brainstorms.

Showcase the whole writing process! Plastic sleeves from binders work great on a bulletin board so you can frequently update students' published writing. After years of trying to keep up with who had published what, I finally covered a bulletin board behind my desk with pieces of colored construction paper for every student. On each piece, I listed the titles of books that student had completed. That way, we could see who had published only one book versus five. I encouraged outliers to conference with me and get a nudge to publish more. That being said, students did not have to publish every piece of writing, just as adult authors have stories they start that never see the light of day.

SWIRL Peer Editing

Peer editing, or *critique groups*, is a social activity that encourages purposeful pairings, oral language, and metacognitive awareness of one's writing skills (Grant, 2019). It can start as early as second grade, when students have enough speaking and writing skills to effectively comment on each other's writing; however, peer editing is most effective in grades 3–12. Students at every proficiency level will benefit, with the caveat that it is best practice to make heterogeneous groups so the skill levels are balanced enough to allow for valuable, tangible, correct feedback.

Empowering and engaging students at the middle and high school levels includes peer conferencing, which mimics the critique or writer's groups that published authors participate in. Getting and giving constructive criticism is an essential skill to build as a writer. One recommendation is to have students focus on telling each other what really moved them in their peer's writing and where they think their peer's writing could grow (Gallagher & Kittle, 2018).

You can choose from several approaches to peer editing. The main construct is to have students partner up or meet in small groups, read each other's writing, correct it, and discuss what they noticed. What worked well, and what needs more work? This gives students a chance to find and fix errors—to make their writing stronger and clearer—before meeting with you.

Put students in groups, and have group members other than the author read the pieces aloud. This gives the authors an opportunity to hear their writing. The writers can take notes on each other's confusion, questions, suggestions, and compliments. It often takes some training, but students need to learn to listen to feedback without being defensive. They can ask for guidance in a particular area before the peer critique group begins. For example, they might ask for specific help on how and where to add more dialogue. Effective peer editing boosts English learners' ability to "self-edit and revise their future writing" (Ferlazzo, 2016).

When poetry and rhyme are involved, the author might benefit from listening to *where* their reader gets tripped up on the cadence or meter. As they listen to their piece be read aloud, they should take notes on the feedback that is given, and revise accordingly. Participants also have to be trained to speak one at a time. Because peer editing involves speaking, writing, interacting, reading, and listening, it is a stellar SWIRL example.

SWIRL Place Mat Note Taking

For students in grades 3–12 who are developing, expanding, bridging, and reaching, note taking is very valuable. However, note taking is a very specific skill that students must explicitly be taught. Highlighting, underlining, paraphrasing, and other forms of summarization and responsive writing are crucial for most tasks and career paths. Place mat note taking—an activity that involves the skills of speaking, writing, interacting, reading, and listening all rolled up in one lesson—has students take notes in a collaborative space and then negotiate the key points with their team, in writing. It is sort of a jigsaw, where students each read a section of an article and come together to discuss it. Alternatively, they can read the same article and write out the three most salient points in it.

The following steps are one possible approach. Prior to starting, however, you must teach note-taking minilessons that include the following three crucial elements: (1) culling the most important information, (2) putting it into your own words, and (3) organizing your notes so that they assist your learning and others can understand them. Model paraphrasing, highlighting, or underlining key phrases and researching outstanding questions. Drive home the need to avoid plagiarizing.

1. Place students into groups of three or four. Assign an article and ask each group to read it. Different students can read different sections (for a jigsaw), or all can read the same piece. In this example, on renewable energy forms, one student reads about solar energy, another reads about wind, a third focuses on hydropower, and a fourth covers geothermal energy.

2. Before students start reading, ask a specific, core question. In this example, it might be, "What is the most promising form of renewable energy?"

3. Give them some time to read, think, and write. After reading, students either use sticky notes or write directly on a blank, laminated place mat, in the section that faces them. See the reproducible "Note-Taking Place Mat" (page 140) for a free, customizable version that you can copy or download and print. You can color-code sticky notes to annotate texts in which students can't write directly.

4. Students discuss their written opinions with each other, educating the rest of the group on their topic. They can have a goal of coming to a consensus.

You can use this activity to do everything from comparing different versions of a story to debating a scientific, sociological, political, or historical topic.

SWiRL Poetry

From prekindergartners to twelfth graders, newcomers to students who are reaching, English learners benefit from poetry's "unusual sentences and structures [that they] normally will not find in prose" (Mittal, 2014, p. 21). Poetry also helps students learn to use vocabulary (especially descriptive, lyrical language), structure, tense, similes, metaphors, rhythms, and rhyme patterns, and connect to emotion, which can be motivational (Mittal, 2014; Ramirez-Espinola, 2023).

My fourth-grade teacher, Mrs. Schultz, exposed me and my classmates to various forms of poetry. She had us write all week and, on Thursdays, we got to go outside and sit on limestone boulders under a weeping willow tree. We read our poetry to other classes and entered it into contests. I became a writer through poetry.

Poetry—haiku, tankas, cinquains, acrostics, and so on—is conducive to social-emotional learning and culturally sustaining teaching. Often, poetry is an easy inroad for English learners. Alma Flor Ada and F. Isabel Campoy have several poetry collections for multilingual learners, including *Días y Días de Poesía: Developing*

Literacy Through Poetry and Folklore (Ada, 2008), *Yes! We Are Latinos: Poems and Prose About the Latino Experience* (Ada & Campoy, 2016), and *Mamá Goose* (Ada & Campoy, 2019).

Starting the year, at any grade level, with an *I am* poem or a name acrostic helps students express their identities and lets you get to know them. I used *I am* poems as part of a third-grade history unit studying the culture of Miwok people. The students and I visited Kule Loklo, a Miwok outdoor museum, and spent time in nature writing poems like the following one, which I wrote.

> *I am the gentle wind caressing the leaves.*
> *I am heron feathers floating in the breeze.*
> *I am a babbling creek, rolling over boulders.*
> *I am the screeching hawk with red-colored shoulders.*
> *I am the lightning striking in the sky.*
> *I am the thunderclap passing by.*
> *I am newborn fawns and full-racked bucks.*
> *I am a swan's curved neck near a mama duck.*
> *I am nature, and nature is me.*
> *I am as small as a ladybug and as tall as a tree.*

Name acrostics focus on adjectives that build ELs' descriptive vocabulary. An example I wrote follows; the first letter of each line spells my first name.

> **S**alsa and samba dancer
> **U**niversity of Michigan grad
> **S**peaks Spanish
> **A**rtistic
> **N**ewly rediscovered photography

A haiku is a simple, short poem form that hails from Japan. It has three lines, each with a specific number of syllables. Line one has five syllables, line two has seven, and line three also has five. Haiku are traditionally written about nature, but students can write them about food, people, buildings, books, or any other topic. An example follows.

> *Orange, red, falling leaves,*
> *Crisp, crunchy apples in pie.*
> *Autumn has arrived.*

A tanka is like an extension of a haiku. It has lines of 5/7/5/7/7 syllables. Here is an example.

> *Waves crashing on shore*
> *Leaving foam and scattered shells.*
> *A breeze blows sea foam.*
> *The high tide is going down*
> *Revealing starfish and crabs.*

Poetry allows students to express themselves in lyrical language. It is less prescriptive than, say, a five-paragraph essay. In the upper grades, it morphs into novels in verse and poetry slams.

From Pablo Neruda to Gabriela Mistral, there are hundreds of Latinx poets whose work students can read. As mentioned before, Nikki Grimes, Nikki Giovanni, and Kwame Alexander are three Black poets whose work resonates with many students and provides them with mirrors, windows, and sliding glass doors (page 169). Middle and high school students can analyze work by famous Middle Eastern poets such as Shams-ud-Din Muhammad Hafiz Shirazi, commonly known as Hafiz (1999, 2023), and Jalal al-Din Rumi, commonly known as Rumi (2004).

After you introduce and practice a poem in class, you can send it home with students to share with their families. Once students finish their own poems, you can publish a class poetry book. For example, if your elementary students are studying insects, each student can write a poem about a different bug, and then you can put them together in a class book. Or, with middle and high school students, you could make a wall display of their poems about justice, or have them deliver the poems in a poetry slam.

SWIRL Biographies

Typically, students are required to write a report about a historical figure somewhere between second and fifth grade. They might be required to research a historical figure and deliver an oral presentation dressed as that character. Biographies are an essential part of history curricula and are best suited as a task for students who are not English language newcomers or just emerging in their language proficiency, as this task requires a lot of research, synthesis, and complex speech. That said, you can pair newcomers with more fluent students for support as they write biographies.

Writing a biography offers important lessons, as doing so teaches students how to research, summarize, and write about someone else's life. Whether students do an author study or write someone's biography, there are hundreds of mentor texts for this writing assignment. Reports are another opportunity to be culturally sustaining. Encourage students to do a biography of either a family member or a famous person who has the same culture or heritage as they do.

I recommend the following framework of sections, or chapters, for a biography written by students in grades 3–12.

1. Childhood
2. College or young-adult years
3. Accomplishments
4. Hardships
5. Family life
6. Legacy

The following is a framework for such reports by grades K–2 students, which includes reading and research, writing, and, potentially, speaking as the students present their reports to the class or parents. You can hand out the reproducible "Writing a Biography" (page 141) for students to work in.

- The name of the person
- What makes them interesting
- What year they were born
- When they died
- Three interesting facts about the person

SWIRL Cooperative Strip Paragraphs

Cooperative strip paragraphs (Dunkin, n.d.) is a GLAD strategy that feeds off the process grid (page 104). The class cocreates a paragraph around a particular theme.

Follow these steps (Bechtel, 2001).

1. Create groups of four or six students. Assign each group a color. Provide them with colored markers or sentence strips of their color.

2. Display your class process grid (such as the example grid in figure 5.5, page 134) and model an example (such as the toucan) with the whole class. (See the reproducible "Process Grid," page 111.).

3. Each subject creates several subtopics. (For example, if the subject is rainforest animals, subtopics could include toucan, white-faced monkey, iguana, sloth, and so on.) Students use sentence strips to write down sentences or sentence fragments, based on the information in the process grid, like you see in figure 5.6 (page 135).

Animal	Rainforest Layer	Diet	Habitat	Size	Description
Toucan	Canopy	Omnivorous: fruits and berries, lizards, rodents, small birds, and insects	Neotropical rainforests from southern Mexico through Central and South America, up to northern Argentina	The largest toucan is the toco toucan (up to 24 inches long). The smallest toucan is the tawny-tufted toucanet (just 12.5 inches long). The toco toucan is the heaviest toucan (up to 1.9 pounds).	The toucan is a colorful, elusive bird whose body is black but whose colorful beak is green, blue, red, and orange and feathers are black and purple, with touches of white, yellow, and scarlet. The bellies of smaller toucans are yellow, with black or red bands. Toucanets have mostly green feathers (plumage) with blue markings. They have blue feet.
White-faced monkey					
Iguana					
Sloth					

Figure 5.5: A started process grid example.

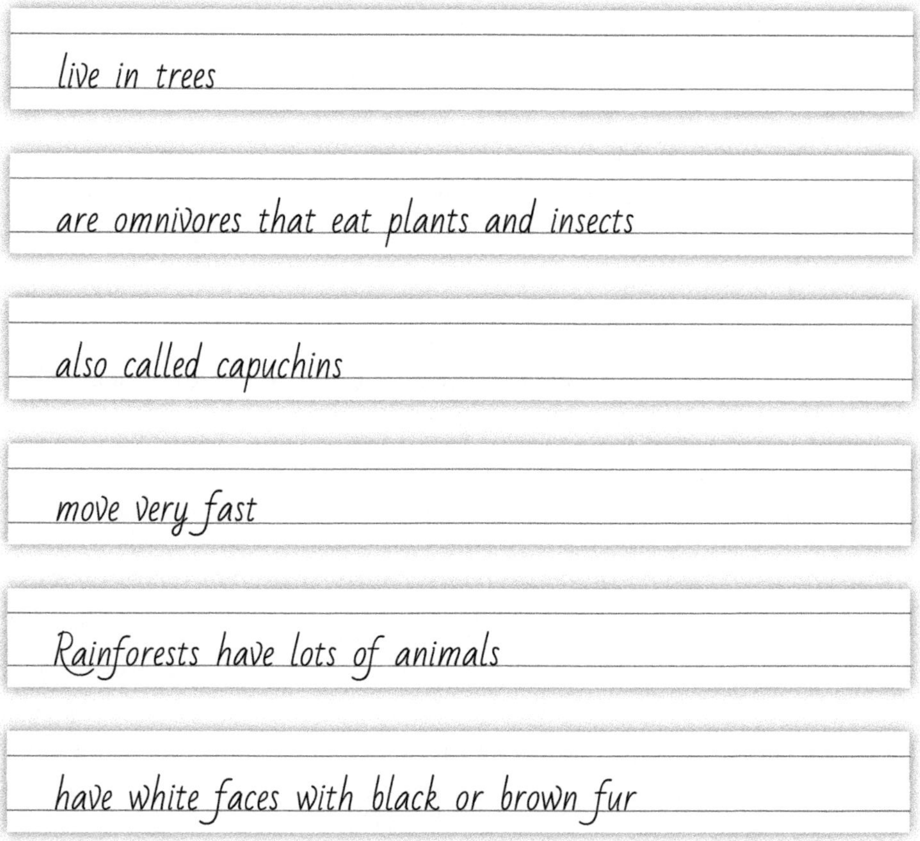

live in trees

are omnivores that eat plants and insects

also called capuchins

move very fast

Rainforests have lots of animals

have white faces with black or brown fur

Figure 5.6: Sentence strips when students begin.

4. Have cooperative groups put the information from their reading in the grid.
5. Create a topic sentence for one of the subtopics. Think aloud about how to use the information in each box for that topic to develop supporting detail sentences.
6. Give another topic sentence, and have each small group create a supporting detail sentence for it. Each group should write this sentence with their colored marker to identify it. Post the sentences in a pocket chart as a list. *Don't* put them in paragraph form yet.
7. Have the whole class read the sentences together. Then ask, "Are the sentences clear and do they make sense?" As a group, revise any that need to be changed. Remember to ask for permission to change a sentence, before just editing it. Use editing symbols, such as carets, to add words or dots to add periods. (Colorful dot stickers from the dollar

store are great visuals for students, who love adding them as periods.) Tear or cut a sentence strip wherever the sentence needs to continue on the next line.

8. Read the sentences aloud together. Then ask, "Does the order of the sentences make sense?" Rearrange any sentences that the class suggests shifting.

9. Read the sentences aloud together again. Then ask, "Can any of the sentences be combined?"

10. Together, read the sentences aloud. Rearrange the sentences from a list to a paragraph, like you see in figure 5.7.

11. Have students decide on punctuation, indenting, margins, and so on as needed. Cut or rip any of the sentence strips to make them form a paragraph.

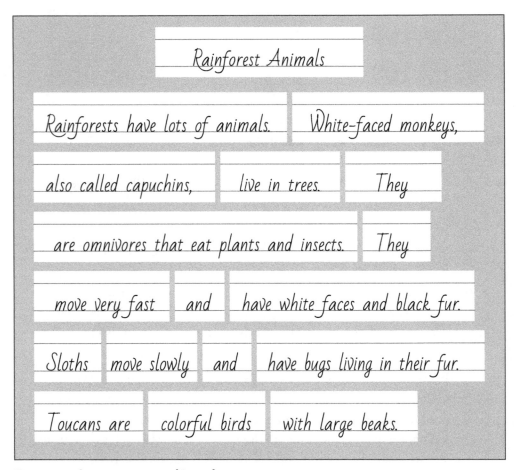

Figure 5.7: Sentences posted in order.

SWIRL Persuasive Essay Writing

It is important for English learners in grades 5–12, and students at developing, expanding, bridging, and reaching English proficiency levels (not entering or emerging), to have a solid model of what a persuasive essay contains. They need to know how to back up their arguments with facts. Writing essays that argue their opinions helps them learn how to do that.

For example, take the topic, *Should students be able to use their phones during school?* Students will have to research and find facts that support why it's safer for students to have phones to communicate with their families. They need to see a model of an assertion or thesis. When choosing topics and considering responses, be mindful of cultural differences (some newcomers to the United States may be unfamiliar with customs and pop culture) and socioeconomic statuses (some students may not have smartphones, for example).

Here are some possible persuasive essay topics (Staake, 2023).

- If I could change one school rule, it would be . . .
- The most important school subject is . . .
- The best holiday is . . .
- The very best food of all time is . . .
- The best music genre is . . .
- A book that everyone should read is . . .
- Is having school year-round a good idea?
- Should we stop giving final exams?
- Should every student have to participate in athletics?
- Should students be required to volunteer in their communities?

sWiRl Informational or Expository Writing

Since the release of the Common Core State Standards and their iterations, and the introduction of the Next Generation Science Standards, nonfiction texts are increasingly used in preK–12 classrooms. Prompt students at all proficiency levels to read and write informational texts. The advantage of this shift is that students have a natural curiosity and plenty of relevant knowledge about evergreen topics like animals, the ocean, planets, and geography. One potential challenge is that some of the language and vocabulary might be complicated for students with limited English proficiency. For example, newcomers—and those still entering, emerging, and developing on the WIDA proficiency scale—may need extra support to effectively read and write informational or expository texts.

The following scaffolds can help students.

- **Introducing academic vocabulary:** Tier two vocabulary words may not be seen or spoken in everyday language but are important for students' academic success. Highlight, and possibly create, word bank anchor charts featuring these academic vocabulary words. That way, students have exposure to these words prior to writing their expository or informational essay. See page 27 for more information about tiered vocabulary.

- **Leaning on cognates:** Cognates like *history/historia* and *planet/planeta* provide a springboard for students who speak Spanish. Cognates also work in French, Italian, and many other Latin-based languages, as well as Haitian Creole.

- **Breaking down compound words:** The word *extraterrestrial* is an example. *Extra* means "more" and *terra* means "earth," which could help students figure out that this word refers to something out of this world. Using Latin roots to break apart compound words and academic vocabulary gives students a tool to dissect words and figure out their meanings. For example, knowing that *contra* (which is also a cognate) means "against," students may deduce the meanings of *contrary* and *contraindicate*.

Conclusion

Writing is a very personal and cathartic form of expression. Many times, you will learn more about your students from their journals and stories than they are willing to share verbally, especially with the whole class. Lots of English learners do not speak out in class, but they will share personal anecdotes in their writing. For some, it can be a way to connect and reveal their home life or school concerns. Giving a lot of student choice, meeting one-on-one with students, holding them accountable, and celebrating their work are crucial. Using a gradual release of responsibility—I do, we do, two do, you do—empowers students and grants them agency. Peer critique groups help students improve their writing skills in a safe, supportive setting. Celebrating published essays, books, and poems gives multilingual learners a sense of pride and accomplishment in their writing.

Writers' Workshop Conference Tool

Name	
Question	**Response**
How is it going?	
What struggles are you having?	
What successes are you having?	
Have you used correct punctuation and spelling?	
How is the grammar?	
Does the story make sense?	
Does the story stay on topic?	
What more could you add?	
Does it feel like the story is in the right order?	
What are your goals for the next time we meet?	
Is there a balance of dialogue and description?	
Notes	

The SWIRL Method © 2025 Solution Tree Press • SolutionTree.com
Visit **go.SolutionTree.com/EL** to download this free reproducible.

Note-Taking Place Mat

As you read the assigned text, think about the posed question. After reading, write notes paraphrasing (in your own words) what you read. Only write in the section closest to you. You may write directly in your section or use sticky notes.

The SWIRL Method © 2025 Solution Tree Press • SolutionTree.com
Visit **go.SolutionTree.com/EL** to download this free reproducible.

Writing a Biography

When you are writing about someone else's life, you do research to find the following information. Take notes in the empty cells as you research and write.

Student's name	
Person's name	
What makes them interesting	
The year this person was born	
The year this person died (if they are no longer alive)	
Write a paragraph that reveals three interesting facts about the person.	

CHAPTER 6

Interacting

No significant learning can occur without a significant relationship.
—James Comer

Often, the *I* in *SWIRL* is overlooked, undervalued, or ignored altogether. Standards mention speaking, writing, reading, and listening as the main facets of language acquisition. Students want, and need, to talk to, collaborate with, debate, question, and critique *each other*. They need this practice of manipulating language not only as a whole class, but more often in pairs, triads, and small groups. Smaller groupings increase their risk taking and lower their affective filter (Vasquez, n.d.).

Human beings are social creatures, and children are no exception. In fact, peer interactions are motivating, low risk, and important for their social-emotional growth and language development (Pepler & Bierman, 2018). For that reason and many more, designing lessons that demand interaction between students is essential. The dialogical classroom—one that focuses on conversation as an integral part of education—positively impacts student learning (Alexander, 2004; Education Endowment Foundation, 2017; van der Wilt, Bouwer, & van der Veen, 2022). The needle moves in education when students start asking and answering more questions than teachers.

The essential features of the dialogical classroom follow (Alexander, 2020).

- Collective (learning/doing tasks together)
- Reciprocal (sharing ideas, actively listening to each other, considering other's opinions as alternative ideas)
- Supportive (discussion and exploration without fear of criticism or negative ramifications for making mistakes)

- Cumulative (building on each other's—and one's own—ideas)
- Purposeful (lessons are planned with clear goals and criteria for success articulated to each learner)

From think-pair-shares to place mat note-taking and jigsaws, all the way to the sophisticated practice of Socratic seminars, learners engage more in content, process, and product when they interact with each other (Jaggars et al., 2013). Research makes it clear why this interaction is crucial: "Verbal language is the most widespread mode of human communication, and an intrinsically social activity" and, in fact, research from various fields "clearly indicates that social interaction influences . . . language learning" (Verga & Kotz, 2013).

Consider the role that students' affective filter plays in their risk taking and success according to Stephen D. Krashen (1982; see page 36). Speaking in front of others, when learning an unfamiliar language, requires vulnerability. When students speak to a single peer or small group of peers, they are likely much less nervous, feel safer, and are more willing to take academic risks than if they have to share aloud in front of the whole class. When they do not feel judged, criticized, or made fun of, their affective filter is lower (Vasquez, n.d.). Additionally, ELs benefit from observing how their peers learn and solve problems (Colorín Colorado, 2018).

First, let's examine the research on interacting, and then we'll delve into related activities and strategies.

The Research on Interacting

The interacting portion of SWIRL helps students solve problems, gain insight, and leverage each other's language skills to complete complex tasks: "Peer learning can be a powerful tool in the classroom, particularly for [English learners]. Encouraging peer interaction and collaboration not only provides opportunities for language use and practice—it builds community in the classroom" (Colorín Colorado, 2021).

As you integrate more interaction into your lessons, recalculate the percentage of teacher talk time (the amount of time the teacher spends talking at the students), versus the amount of time students talk to each other or the teacher. Teacher talk should naturally decrease as active student participation increases. Take it even further by calculating how much structured time students spend speaking to each other (or with you) versus informally conversing. Researchers note that, "broadly speaking, availability of communicative interaction is necessary for second language acquisition and this results in observed changes in the brain" (Yusa, Kim, Koizumi, Sugiura, & Kawashima, 2017).

But shifting the ratio of teacher talk to student talk is not enough. Ask yourself the following questions when planning units, implementing them, and assessing learning and beyond.

- "What kinds of questions am I asking?"
- "How can I spark productive classroom discussions?"
- "How often do I allow students to process a portion of text by asking them a question or allowing students to pose their own questions?"

Often, it's helpful to put ourselves in our students' shoes. If you've traveled while learning a second language, you know that being forced to speak to others teaches you in a way that studying a textbook never can. Asking for directions, ordering at a restaurant, and renting a car all require you to listen, speak, and sometimes write or read, but mostly interact. You use physical cues—like holding up a glass and saying, "*Vaso*" ("glass" in Spanish).

Dialoguing with others is essential, since research suggests "social interaction is an important component of language learning," says Patricia Kuhl, codirector of the University of Washington's Institute for Learning and Brain Sciences (Taylor, 2018). Having to interact with others gives you a purpose and an audience. Sometimes, it meets survival needs, like eating and going to the bathroom. Research from various fields of study indicates the following:

> Social interaction influences human communication, and more specifically, language learning. . . . The necessity to consider sociality as a factor in L2 [second language] studies seem striking, as further suggested by the evidence that when new words are encoded in a social context, but not when they are learnt by translation, the pattern of activation in the retrieval phase is similar to the one observed for L1 words. (Verga & Kotz, 2013)

Without ample "planned opportunities for active processing" throughout lessons with new or critical information, "most novice learners will retain little" (Sahadeo-Turner & Marzano, 2015, p. 5). In short, vocabulary retention is stronger when social interaction is involved. Essentially, anyone who is acquiring a language needs to interact with others in order to process the vocabulary, content, and concepts. Interacting, as a means to language acquisition, is one part practice and another part processing.

Activities and Strategies

It is practically impossible to interact without speaking, writing, reading, or listening. If you are speaking, you are usually speaking to (or with) someone else, which means you are interacting.

This section contains some activities that involve interaction. For most of these strategies, you can arrange students in pairs, triads, or groups of four to six, or you can divide the class in half. Make sure to use both heterogeneous and homogeneous groups so students can speak in their home language, talk to peers at their same proficiency level, and learn from others at varying English proficiency levels.

Specific structures scaffold these interactions for the following purposes.

- **To circumvent social hour:** To give students agency and increase their enthusiasm about speaking through interaction, allow them to pick their partner most of the time—about 75 percent student-chosen partners and about 25 percent teacher-assigned partners. The caveat to this is that they have to be with someone they know they can work with, not just a friend they intend to play with during work time. Students quickly self-monitor once you change their partners, even one time, for fooling around. Then, they more responsibly select a partner with whom they can get the job done. Some social talk naturally takes place; however, the bulk of the conversation should be on task, using academic language.

- **To focus on objectives:** Including learning objectives and target-specific language for tasks throughout each week, unit, or lesson helps students stay accountable and on track. It also helps you assess if they understand the language forms and functions that you are teaching. Students have a place to start and a blueprint for arriving to their North Star of fluently interacting in English. Best practice dictates that teachers share a language objective and a content objective at the start of the lesson. (See chapter 3, page 49, for more about creating those objectives.) That language objective should be in student-friendly wording and posted someplace where everyone can refer to it throughout the lesson. To wrap up the lesson, the class self-assesses whether they, for example, used sequencing terms (*in the beginning, in the middle, at the end*) to retell a story in the correct order. A fist to five (having students show with their hands how well they understand on a scale of 0 to 5—fist, or zero fingers, being "I understand not at all" and five fingers being "I understand completely") is a quick way for you to read the room as students self-assess their achievement of the goal.

- **To ensure accountability:** Some students might be reticent to speak and interact, so this requires role assignments in groups or pairs (such as timekeeper, facilitator, notetaker, and clarifier; page 172) and a way to assess their progress (formally or informally). That accountability might be a product, a written response, or an active role necessary to complete the task.

The following list outlines components of quality student interactions. Keep these in mind as you design and implement the activities in this chapter (Billings & Mueller, n.d.).

- Interactions are sustained and reciprocal.
- Understandings are co-constructed (versus dominated by a single person).
- Interactions are related to disciplinary practices (such as asking and answering questions, comparing and contrasting, and so on).
- Interactions are academically rigorous.

Ask yourself the following questions when designing quality student interactions (Billings & Mueller, n.d.).

- Are guiding questions and prompts open ended?
- Do guiding questions and prompts ask students to engage in higher-order thinking about the topic (that is, synthesizing, hypothesizing, generalizing, and arguing)? (Refer to Bloom's [1956] taxonomy revised [Anderson & Krathwohl, 2001].)
- Do guiding questions or prompts encourage many perspectives or subtopics?
- Are tasks designed to create an equitable space in which every student participates and listens to peers?
- Are students allowed to pose questions to one another, respond directly to each other, and ask for elaboration or evidence?
- Is authority distributed among the students for them to reach consensus on the validity and value of ideas discussed?
- Does the activity invite rigorous engagement (that is, does it focus on central ideas, their interconnections, and analytic thinking)?
- Does the activity promote novel, critical, and extended thinking?

SwIrL Think-Pair-Share

Think-pair-share works for every grade, whether you are doing a read-aloud or teaching a new mathematics concept. At every proficiency level, preK–12, it is essential that students have the chance to think independently, pair up with a partner, and share their thoughts as part of interacting. Students need time to turn and talk to a partner to practice and process, as the "visible manifestations of active processing include talking, sharing, [and] explaining" (Sahadeo-Turner & Marzano, 2015, p. 5). Speaking to just one partner, as opposed to raising their hand and being seen and heard by the entire class, lowers a student's affective filter. Remember, a lower affective filter means lower inhibitions and a greater willingness to take risks (Krashen, 2019).

Building strong oral communication skills also means training students in nonverbal communication, such as eye contact, body language, nodding, and so on. I recommend modeling think-pair-share in a fishbowl. A *fishbowl* is where a pair or a small group of students sit in an inner circle in the middle of the room and the rest of the students sit around them, in an outer circle. Students in both circles face each other, making eye contact and actively listening. You also want to model the appropriate volume—speaking in an inside voice, for example—so your activity doesn't feel or sound unwieldy.

Think-pair-share takes place in preK–12, but possible configurations vary by grade level. For ELs in grades preK–2, you can have students do the following.

- Students turn to their table partner.
- Students find a partner who speaks the same language as them at home and make a bridge by locking hands.
- Students find their "sole mate" (someone who has the same shoe size as they do, or someone who has shoes similar to theirs).
- Students turn to the person on their right, on their left, across from them, and so on.
- Students find someone who is also wearing stripes (or a zipper, a hoodie, and so on).
- Students are assigned partners based on English language proficiency (heterogeneous or homogeneous pairings).

In grades 3–12, you might partner students by topic, interest, ability, or home language.

You may also want to revisit the idea of purposeful partnerships (page 84). Again, you can assign partners, or groups, by language level (entering, emerging, developing, expanding, bridging, or reaching) or by home language. Dual immersion teachers often pair a student whose home language is English with a student whose home or heritage language is the target language (Spanish or Chinese, for example).

When giving students a chance to turn and talk, supply them with either a sentence frame or a verbal prompt like the following examples.

- One thing I learned just now was _____.
- My favorite part of the story is _____ because _____.
- One question I still have about this topic is _____.
- If I could be one character from this book, I would be _____ because _____.

The think part of think-pair-share has students individually form their ideas and questions about a topic. Then, each person pairs up with a peer, which is a low-risk proposition. Finally, each person shares their ideas with their partner and, sometimes, other classmates. This activity increases participation by giving everyone a chance to talk, as opposed to just a few students who raise their hands and are called on or, much more stressful, who get called on to speak when they are not raising their hands. It focuses students' attention and allows teachers to assess comprehension and retention of the content.

It is vital that, as the teacher, you listen in on pairs' conversations about the topic, and that you then strategically ask certain pairs to share. Figure 6.1 has guidelines you can share with students before beginning the activity. Visit the Reading Rockets website (www.readingrockets.org/strategies/think-pair-share) for a video demonstrating how to set up think-pair-share in your classroom.

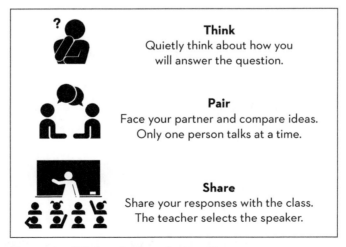

Figure 6.1: Think-pair-share instructions.

*Visit **go.SolutionTree.com/EL** for a free reproducible version of this figure.*

SwIrL Classroom Feud

This content review activity works best for grades 3–12 with students who are at developing, expanding, bridging, and reaching proficiency levels. Making language acquisition a game engages even the most reluctant of learners. Research shows gamification is "enjoyable, engaging, motivating, and fun" in classrooms with EL students (Dehghanzadeh, Fardanesh, Hatami, Talaee, & Noroozi, 2021, p. 934).

This game is similar to TV's *Family Feud*. Like the game show, you can survey students for answers to the questions, or use answers from the curriculum. Since classroom feud involves use of presentation slides, I encourage you to visit https://tinyurl.com/24fkmdc5 if you want a PowerPoint template. Follow these directions to play.

1. Make sure you have a slide deck with five or six questions (five or six slides per round, with one question per slide), two buzzers (bells, clickers, or whatever you have available that gets everyone's attention), and a way to keep score. Alternatively, students can write their answers on small whiteboards and raise them in the air for you to see.

2. Form two student teams. Have one student from each team face each other. They should have one hand on their team's buzzer and the other behind their back.

3. As the teacher, read a question from the game board. Whoever buzzes in first (with a right answer, of course) can play or pass to the other team. If certain students are not answering any of the questions correctly, you may want to pull a small group, later on, to reteach those students.

An example board appears in figure 6.2.

The main characters in *The Outsiders* are:

---

1. Ponyboy (41 points)
2. Johnny (32 points)
3. Dallas (15 points)
4. Darry (10 points)
5. Cherry (2 points)

Figure 6.2: Example classroom feud question and answers.

SwIRL Dice Discussions

In grades K–12, using giant dice to structure conversations is engaging, exciting, and differentiated by nature. Students at every proficiency level can participate but, for this activity, mix newcomers and emerging or entering students with those who have a more advanced level of English proficiency.

Interacting is easier when there are ready-made conversation topics. The sides of a die can offer topics that help students start talking to each other. Whether you use ready-made discussion dice (https://juniorlearning.com/products/discussion-dice), dry-erase cubes (often available at the dollar store), or plastic photo cubes with slips of paper in them, students roll the dice in this discussion game. The various sides might prompt students to answer questions and finish sentence starters such as the following.

- What was the book's setting, and why was it important?
- My favorite part of the book was when _____.
- The character I most identify with is _____ because _____.
- If I had to rewrite the ending, it would go like this: _____.
- One question I still have about this story is _____.
- Here's what happened at the beginning, in the middle, and at the end: _____.
- This book reminds me of _____.

You are a professional eavesdropper. Circulate around the room and listen in on conversations. Then, based on the conversations you overhear, gather data to inform your instruction. For example, what parts of the story are students still wondering about or confused by? Are students able to sequence the story? Interacting is learning! Students are discussing literature just like adults do.

SWIRL Socratic Seminar

Middle and high school students who have achieved an intermediate, advanced, or proficient level of English are ready for sophisticated discussion. A *Socratic seminar*, named for the Greek philosopher Socrates, is a pedagogical approach to processing and understanding information. In this method, the teacher creates a discussion, or *dialectic discourse*, around a specific text. Dialectic is like debate but is free of emotions and subjective rhetoric. Dialectic discussion is a motivational form of discussion based on an essential question. During a Socratic seminar, students thoughtfully dialogue with their peers. Divergent thinking is encouraged.

A Socratic seminar is defined as a "question-focused, student-led, and teacher-facilitated discussion, based on appropriate texts" whose purpose is "not the acquisition of knowledge via the expert; the aim is student understanding via active thinking out loud and probing of ideas by all students" (TeachThought Staff, n.d.). From a Socratic perspective, *critical thinking* is defined as "the application and analysis of information requiring clarity, logical consistency, and self-regulation" (Oyler & Romanelli, 2014, p. 144). Students ask questions and respond to attain a deeper understanding of complex concepts presented in the text.

Although students may have differing points of view, they seek answers via reasoned argumentation. I had the good fortune of observing a middle school teacher implementing a Socratic seminar. The students were running the show! Here is what I observed.

- Students were seated in a circle, facing each other.
- The teacher was part of that circle, not elevated or separated in any way.
- The students had a tremendous amount of agency in leading the discussion.
- The teacher was evaluating the students—taking notes and scoring them based on a rubric—as were all the students.
- The conversation included multiple references back to the text.
- It felt respectful, yet high stakes. (The students knew that a big part of their grade was based on how well they ran the discussion and responded to it.)

Follow these general steps for this kind of dialogue, keeping in mind that it takes practice to have a fully functioning Socratic seminar.

1. Decide, as a group, what the guidelines will be for the seminar. They might mirror the classroom norms in some ways. Examples include, "Cite evidence," "Don't interrupt," and "Share airtime." After one or two seminars, your class might want to revisit the guidelines as they learn more about the process.

2. Choose an appropriate piece of writing. (For beginning students, it might be poetry; for bridging students, it might be an argumentative or expository piece.)

3. Let students prepare by reading and annotating the piece of writing. How long this takes depends on the size and complexity of the writing.

4. Either the teacher or an assigned student asks an open-ended question. Questions are usually based on Benjamin Bloom's (1956) taxonomy revised (Anderson & Krathwohl, 2001), or Art Costa's (2008) three levels of questioning, which are as follows.
   - *Level 1*—Gathering information (complete, identify, define, and describe)
   - *Level 2*—Processing information (compare, contrast, analyze, and explain)
   - *Level 3*—Applying information (evaluate, judge, predict, and generalize)

5. Reflect and debrief. Ask students to do a written reflection on what they learned. Meet with groups of students who feel like they still need support in leading and participating in Socratic seminars.

Here are some of the kinds of questions that you or students might ask during a Socratic seminar, based on Costa's (2008) levels of questioning.

- **Level 1: Gathering**
    - What is the main idea?
    - Where in the story did _____?
    - When did _____ take place?
- **Level 2: Processing**
    - What would happen if _____?
    - Would you have done the same thing as _____?
    - What happens when _____?
- **Level 3: Applying**
    - What is most compelling to you in this _____, and why?
    - Could this story have really happened? Why or why not?
    - If you were there, would you _____?

Visit www.youtube.com/watch?v=e3IBLKYaK1E to see a high school–level Socratic seminar in action. Visit the following websites for lesson-planning resources.

- The National Paideia Center (https://paideia.org) has sample lesson plans across multiple subject areas as well as a library of texts.
- ReadWriteThink (https://tinyurl.com/mwjd6wcn) contains links to plans for different grade levels and subjects.
- Touchstones Discussion Project (https://touchstones.org) includes texts and lesson plans for all grade levels and disciplines.

SwIrL Swimming the Spectrum

I love this strategy! It asks students to identify their level of comfort with a new topic. Swimming the spectrum is a tool that allows students to self-assess their topic knowledge. It works well for grades 3–12 and for those at expanding and bridging levels of proficiency. It comes in handy when starting a unit so you can ascertain how much students already know on a topic, and create a forum in which they can share their background knowledge with each other. Students' self-assessment of their prior knowledge may not be exactly accurate; however, it is a solid measure of their self-confidence on that topic.

This strategy includes posting images like those in figure 6.3 on a wall of your classroom, and keeping a few questions in your pocket. You can ask those questions to prompt this activity when students get restless, since swimming the spectrum gets them out of their seats. Perhaps you pose the question, "How many of you feel like you know how to research and take notes?" Some students will self-identify as not feeling comfortable or confident in that skill. They will gravitate toward the "dipping their toe into the pool" at the end of the line. Students who feel like they know how to research and take notes but are not great at it might go toward the middle. Those who are whizzes at it will head to the diving board.

Figure 6.3: Swimming the spectrum images.

You can also use swimming the spectrum to determine students' background knowledge levels on topics like fossils. For elementary students, you can do this as an entry point into a new unit. Maybe you're about to study the life cycle of frogs, so students can line up based on how much they already know about frogs.

You can use this strategy in any classroom that has both fluent English speakers and English learners, or you can use this with multilingual learners to specifically work on conversation skills. Additionally, this approach benefits students academically and emotionally by making heterogeneous pairs. Curriculum designer Kara Wyman (2017) writes:

> Putting English learners in pairs or collaborative groups with students who are proficient or [fluent] speakers can help them learn from their peers' different backgrounds. These valuable partnerships can decrease fears and feelings of judgment, and give English learners a sense of belonging over time.

Follow these steps. The activity should take about twenty to thirty minutes.

1. Prepare a series of questions.

2. On one end of a long wall, post a picture like the leftmost image in figure 6.3 of a person dipping a toe into a pool.

3. At the midpoint of the wall, put an image of someone swimming.

4. At the opposite end of the wall from the toe-dipping picture, post a picture of someone diving off a diving board.

5. Give the class a particular topic (for example, how to take notes or how the government works).

6. Have students line up according to their own perceived depth of knowledge—from knowing very little (toe dipping) to being able write a speech about it (diving).

7. Fold the line in half, so the experts are talking to those who are new to the topic. Give the pairs conversation prompts, let them discuss them, and then, after posing a few questions, tell one side of the line to move down by one or two people.

8. Pose another, related question to the group. Indicate which side will go first.

9. Have students share their answers with their partners. Weave through the line and listen in on their (hopefully) robust conversations.

10. Ask one of the lines to move down a person again and pose another question. Repeat this a few times, taking maybe ten or fifteen minutes to have them do this.

SWIrL Four Corners

This activity, which works with any grade and proficiency level, allows students to discuss an area of interest, or rationalize an opinion. While students at all proficiency levels can participate, it is wise to make sure there is a mix of students from varying proficiency levels, as they gravitate toward one of the four corners.

Follow these steps.

1. Designate or label each corner of your space with a predetermined answer, topic, or article to read.
2. Ask the whole class a question. For example, you might pose the question, "Which is the best animal to have as a pet?" In each corner, post a piece of chart paper that says one of the following: *dog, cat, fish, bird*.
3. Tell students to choose an answer and move to that corner.
4. When in their corners, students might discuss why that pet is their favorite and decide, as a group, on the top three reasons that make it the best pet. Have them record those on the chart paper. The group can write on sticky notes or directly on the chart paper. Make your way around the room as the groups discuss. Look-fors and listen-fors include the following.
    - "It is best because . . ."
    - "This animal can . . . For example, . . ."
    - "Dogs are the best animals because they will fetch things and come when you call. Dogs protect you if bad people come to your house. Dogs are soft, loving, and happy all the time."
5. After ten or fifteen minutes, either pause the discussions and have each corner argue in favor of their pet, or have students do a gallery walk for about ten minutes (two minutes in each corner with time built in for transitioning) to read and respond to each other's posters.

You can also use four corners the following ways.

- **Jigsaw stations:** For instance, if you give students an article to read, divide it into sections (or chapters). Have students number off, and then send them to one of the four corners where they can discuss the content of that section with other students who have read it.

- **Scenario:** Read a scenario aloud. For example, you might present an article on the best sources of renewable energy and have high schoolers pick which they think is most promising and go to that corner to read that part of the article. For elementary school students, you might read an article about how different people have saved various types of animals (think Jane Goodall with chimps). Students can choose a corner based on interest or opinion. In one professional learning experience I attended, the facilitator's scenario was about a blown tire. She asked what each of us would do if we had a flat tire: (1) call a family member or friend, (2) call a tow truck, (3) change it ourselves, or (4) wave someone down to help us. We learned a lot from that activity. In a room of about thirty adults, only one knew how to change a tire! Many of us vowed to have someone teach us soon.

SWIRL Snowball

This activity, which works best in grades 2–12 and with students with developing to bridging proficiency levels, allows students to anonymously exchange ideas, and prompts interaction and conversation. It works best with pop culture or personal experiences students might be reticent to share with the whole class (for example, a time they were scared or embarrassed).

1. Give each student a piece of paper. You can have a question preprinted on the papers or have students write an answer to a prompt. For example, you might ask students to write their favorite musician's name and a little about that person or their music.
2. Have students crumple up the paper and toss it across the room.
3. Everyone grabs a different "snowball," unfolds it, and reads it.
4. Students guess or ask who wrote the message, find that person in the classroom, and talk with them about the topic (in this example, about the musician). Start a song to cue students to mill about. Then, stop the song when it's time for them to find the person who wrote that answer as a partner. Prompt them to chat about what they wrote and why.

As an alternative, have each student read the message aloud, and have the class guess who wrote it. However, having students find another student to talk to often results in productive language—especially when it's about pop culture.

SwIRl Memory

Memory works well with K–5 students who are emerging to expanding in proficiency. Developing visual memory is very helpful for English learners and "can lead to improvements in reading motivation and achievements" (Almekhlafy & Alqahtani, 2020).

Visual memory can be described as:

> the ability to create a mental image of an object, place or form in the mind's eye. . . . Visual memory enables [us] to see printed letters and words and to decode them visually. Reading requires [us] to assemble words and phrases into a visual image and once this occurs through the mind's eye, your child recognizes words, creates meaning and reading comprehension occurs naturally. (Driscoll, 2018)

That is when someone recognizes words and makes meaning. Teachers refer to it as *one-to-one correspondence*—the moment we see the light bulb go on when a student starts decoding.

Follow these steps.

1. Students first must get a chance to study the content that they need to memorize. So, prior to playing memory, they should review the content, preferably multiple times.

2. Also prior to playing, create enough cards for each group. Each word card should have a corresponding card with a matching image or definition card. You can match scientific words with their definition, mathematics problems with their answer, or vocabulary with a picture of the item or action. (You can print the cards on paper and cut them up.)

3. Break students into groups of four to six. If you have fewer students than allows for this, you can have them play in pairs.

4. In groups or pairs, students flip all the cards upside down and shuffle them around, ultimately arranging them in rows.

5. Student A flips over two cards at a time, hoping for a match (a word with its definition, a problem with its answer, or vocabulary with its image). If there is a match, student A takes another turn. Student B does the same when student A stops getting matches. To increase language proficiency, prompt students to say or read aloud their matching cards.

The player with the most matches at the end of the game wins. Memory usually lasts twenty to thirty minutes, depending on the number of cards and students' ages. For an extension of this game, you can have students make their own memory cards. This can help students because the "unique, complex, spatial and tactile information associated with writing by hand on physical paper is likely what leads to improved memory" (University of Tokyo, 2021).

SwIrL Salute

This game, for grades 3–8 students who are of expanding and bridging proficiencies, requires three players. Salute is something students can play to review addition and subtraction or multiplication and division. The best time to use this activity is prior to an assessment, as a review.

1. Split students into triads and have them decide who will be sergeant, who will be soldier, and who will be scorekeeper.

2. Two of the three players split a deck of cards between themselves, placing the cards facedown. A regular card deck works fine. Just remove the jokers, jacks, queens, kings, and aces.

3. When the sergeant says, "Salute," both players flip a card up toward their forehead. They cannot see the card. They are holding it up for others to see.

4. The third player responds. Here is an example of students playing multiplication salute. Student A holds up a 9 and student B holds up a 7. Student C says, "Sixty-three." Now, each of the other two students can see one number from the equation on the other person's forehead, and they know the quotient. They then need to divide to figure out the answer. Ideally, they know that $9 \times 7 = 63$. Student A knows that 7 goes into 63 nine times, and that they must be holding up a 9 card.

5. The first player in the trio to correctly name the number above their own head gets a point. They can play this game during center time for twenty to thirty minutes, switching roles throughout.

SwIrL Who Am I?

This game is similar to salute, but with nouns. It works best with vocabulary building or character analysis from a recently read story. It is ideal for grades K–5 and with students who are at emerging to bridging proficiency levels.

1. Prior to playing, create enough cards for each student to have two or three different cards. You'll also need either tape or enough headbands for every student as well.

2. Pass out a facedown card to each student. Either the student tapes a word (or picture) to their forehead, or someone else tapes it to their back. *Students should not see what is on their card.*

3. Have the students mill about and ask each other questions to try to identify who, or what, they are. If you are studying the rainforest, for example, you could provide cards naming animals or insects. A student might ask other students, "Do I live on the ground or in the trees?" "Am I furry?" "What do I eat?" and "Do I have a tail?" When a student thinks they have figured out who they are, they go up to the teacher (or a student assigned the role of facilitator) and ask, "Am I _____?" If they are right, they get a point. As a group, the milling about and guessing can take about fifteen minutes.

You can play this game with famous figures in history, the periodic table of elements, or Greek gods.

Conclusion

Having EL students study and perform vocabulary drills doesn't provide the kind of social interaction they need to learn a new language (Altavilla, 2020). It may feel like students are getting individualized attention and assessments with technology; however, in those cases, what is missing for English learners is the opportunity to interact and use the language in an engaging and meaningful way, which is crucial to their learning.

Student interaction increases multilingual learners' engagement, enthusiasm, and achievement, and here is why: "Encouraging peer interaction and collaboration not only provides opportunities for language use and practice—it builds community in the classroom" (Colorín Colorado, 2021). You are the creator of that community!

CHAPTER 7

Reading

I have always imagined that paradise will be a kind of library.
—Jorge Luis Borges

Reading is a portal to another world. It is through reading that students learn about new topics and gain empathy for others, which teaches them appropriate social behaviors (Chiaet, 2013). Reading spirals into writing—responses, reports, summaries, and poetry. We love to talk about books with friends, which involves speaking, interacting, and listening. Newcomers, and those at entering and emerging levels, might straddle both *learning to read* and *reading to learn* in the upper grades. Typically, this transition takes place around third grade.

During my early years of teaching in the classroom, there was a movement back toward whole language and away from phonics. We were focused on helping young students develop a love of literacy, not on teaching sight words and giving spelling tests. Then, the idea of *balanced literacy* evolved, and neither phonics nor whole language was demonized or favored. The pendulum has, once again, swung back toward phonics and phonemic awareness with the approach now commonly known as the *science of reading*—a "vast, interdisciplinary body of scientifically-based research about reading and issues related to reading and writing"; that research involves explicitly teaching phonics so that students can learn to sound out words (The Reading League, n.d.).

I do not argue the benefits or disadvantages of one method or the other; however, I will address how these opposing approaches impact EL students. Studies show marked growth from using the science of reading with English speakers (Council of the Great City Schools, 2023; Pearson, Palincsar, Biancarosa, & Berman, 2020; The Reading League, 2023; Schwartz, 2022), but some skeptics call into question its appropriateness for emergent multilingual learners (Stavely, 2024). There is no equivalent curriculum in other languages, such as Spanish, arguing that the science of reading fails to account for crosslinguistic connections that value and build on students' home languages.

For example, incorrectly applying the science of reading by solely focusing on phonics may be detrimental to ELs' developing oral fluency and making crucial connections between English and their home language. In March 2023, members of The Reading League and the National Committee for Effective Literacy held a summit to discuss the early literacy needs of English learners and how those align (or do not) with the science of reading. From that meeting, a joint statement was drafted by experts in the fields of reading science and English learner/emergent bilingual (EL/EB) education. In part, it reads, "Using this body of scientific research, including the researching on teaching emerging bilingual learners, we can uplift practices that support students in developing their language proficiency in language, reading, and writing—in English and in students' home languages" (The Reading League & National Committee for Effective Literacy, 2023, p. 3).

Since then, much debate about the science of reading in relation to emergent multilingual learners continues. In a nutshell, the research supporting the science of reading indicates a need to return to a phonics- and phonemic awareness–focused, systematic approach to teaching letters and their corresponding sounds; it also recommends teaching fluency and comprehension (National Center on Improving Literacy, 2022). There is no Spanish version of the science of reading that would enable a student to learn to read in their primary language first, nor is there any plan to transition readers from Spanish reading to English phonemic awareness. Multilingual learners require supported phonics instruction with crosslinguistic connections, cognates, or the formal integration of home language.

One part of the shift, for educators and students, is moving away from leveled books and letting students choose what they want to read. Much research proves that student choice and leveled texts lead to increased engagement and achievement (Marzano & Pickering, n.d.). My assessment of the movement toward the science of reading is that it happened as a reaction to the "pandemic slide," during which many students lost one to two years of quality in-person instruction.

We don't have to choose one approach or the other. Learning to love literature through book clubs, guided reading, reports, research, and so on is as important to a student's long-term academic success as learning phonics is. Then again, you can't enjoy literature if you can't decode it. Whether you ascribe to the science of reading or are using leveled texts, all educators agree that reading is a fundamental skill that every student needs to master.

First, we'll discuss the research on reading, and then we'll review related activities and strategies.

The Research on Reading

Students must process and understand what they read. Whether they read for pleasure or for new information, they almost always find it helpful to speak and write about the text, listen to others' thoughts and literary analysis, and interact with peers around what they have read. No matter what career path students take, they will need to know how to read.

In the first few years of school, students are learning to read. Around third grade, they begin reading to learn. Across all curricular areas—including science, mathematics, and social studies—being a fluent reader is essential to understanding content and completing assignments. Furthermore, being able to read fluently is key to college and career readiness.

The essential elements to teaching reading follow (National Reading Panel, 2000).

- **Phonemic awareness:** Knowing that letters make sounds, and which letters make which sounds, is fundamental in learning to read. For ELs, some common confusions surface. For example, the letter *e* in English is pronounced the way the letter *i* is said in Spanish. MLs who use characters (in Mandarin, for instance) need to learn the entire sound and symbol system in English. All students must understand one-to-one correspondence in order to read.

- **Phonics:** Beyond the letter sounds and names, sound blends and decoding multisyllabic words are also part of phonics. The good news is that once someone masters phonics, they usually do not have to learn it again. (The exception is students who have dyslexia or dysgraphia and need reminders.)

- **Fluency:** As someone learns to read, they may be stilted in their pronunciation, speed, or intonation—each element of which impacts their overall fluency. Encouraging MLs to approximate, correct, and monitor their own fluency is crucial. Feeling like their accent impacts their fluency is just one common challenge multilingual learners may face. It is important to create a safe space where students can approximate pronunciation and hear words modeled before they repeat them.

- **Vocabulary:** Expanding vocabulary to include more academic language, including complex, content-specific terms, builds a student's toolbox for expression. Pulling apart compound words in complex texts with ELs helps students make meaning (Richardson, 2023).

- **Accuracy:** When students are first learning to read, and even after they are fairly fluent, they may mispronounce, omit, or substitute words. Analyzing their miscues can help identify what particular sounds, sound blends, or word families trip up a student most often. You are looking for 90 percent accuracy on assessments in order to know that the text is at the right level for that student (Northwest Evaluation Association, 2023).

- **Comprehension:** Being able to decode a text does not necessarily mean someone can comprehend it. Asking comprehension questions allows you to ascertain if students understand what they read. One pedagogical debate with regard to English learners is whether their ability to summarize what they read in their home language should count as comprehension. In my professional opinion, if an EL student reads the text in English, is asked comprehension questions in English, and correctly responds in their home language, that counts as comprehension. They understood the text in English, but just don't yet have the vocabulary to answer in English. However, the long-term goal is that students be able to answer those questions in English as well.

Studies on instruction in reading's five components—(1) phonemic awareness, (2) phonics, (3) fluency, (4) vocabulary, and (5) text comprehension—have shown that all have "'clear benefits' for [ELs]" (Schwartz, 2022). Elements of dissecting reading passages include cause and effect, compare and contrast, explain and describe, and persuasion, just to name a few.

There are language demands that multilingual learners must master to complete initial, intermediate, and culminating tasks. Setting clear language objectives for lessons or units helps ELs access text and measure their progress in anchor or supporting tasks.

English learner expert Jana Echevarría (2021) states:

> It can't be assumed that because multilingual students need foundational literacy skills that they'll learn just like their English-speaking peers. While the skills are the same and transfer across languages, learning how to read in a language you're still acquiring is distinctly different from

learning in your home language, a language whose syntax, everyday vocabulary, and usage is familiar.

Oral language fluency, along with cultural relevance, student choice, and an asset-based approach, impacts teaching reading to someone who is just learning a language. As noted, instruction is most effective when it is "tailored to [ELs'] specific needs and unique founts of knowledge" (Schwartz, 2022).

Many English learners often struggle with comprehension and fluency, even once they've mastered decoding. Research shows that ELs' struggles with comprehension are due to three main factors (August & Shanahan, 2006).

1. **ELs are less likely to have the background knowledge needed to understand texts.**

2. **ELs need to read at a text level comparable to their oral proficiency, as it factors into their comprehension.** Echevarría (2021) further notes that academic vocabulary is especially difficult for multilingual learners who are not yet proficient in oral language.

3. **ELs often need more repetition and exposure to new vocabulary and increased access to anchor charts, visuals, multimedia, and song in order to learn and retain literacy skills.** AnkiApp (www.ankiapp.com) generates flash cards that help make learning new words fun for multilingual learners. Tapping into background knowledge, lived experiences, and home language (for example, using cognates as a springboard) makes reading more meaningful and relevant.

Another consideration in sheltered English immersion, dual language, or bilingual classrooms is that many families may not be literate in their primary language. There are a limited number of teachers who are fluent in the primary language (or languages) of their students and able to teach literacy skills in that language. I spent my entire career educating my students to become bilingual and biliterate. When possible, the best-case scenario is for children to learn to read in their home language first and then transfer those skills to reading in English. In fact, "young children who were exposed to age-appropriate books and literature in their native language developed stronger pre-literacy skills than children who were only exposed to books in their second language" (Association for Childhood Education International, 2003). Researchers reiterate that being literate in a person's primary language positively impacts their literacy achievement in English (Thomas & Collier, 1997).

In terms of phonemic awareness, ELs need to learn the sounds and names of letters in English. They then need explicit, repeated practice with the sounds that are difficult, confusing, or both. As I mentioned, the letter *i* in Spanish is pronounced like the *e* in English. The *b* and *v* are very similar in Spanish and other languages. MLs need a lot of practice with these letters.

Programs like Lexia's (n.d.) Language Essentials for Teachers of Reading and Spelling (LETRS®) train teachers and literacy specialists in the science of reading. Louisa Moats, an authority in the field of literacy, developed and leads LETRS, which teaches written language, phonological awareness, phonics, vocabulary, fluency, and comprehension.

Another program that focuses on reading and writing fundamentals was developed by Carol Dissen at the University of Oregon's Center on Teaching and Learning. Enhanced Core Reading Instruction (ECRI) is a multitiered program that features a series of teaching routines designed to increase the efficiency and effectiveness of reading instruction in K–2. It is a supplemental program that aligns with core reading programs. ECRI also involves sequential lessons and strategies that focus on phonemic awareness, reading fluency, accuracy, and spelling. It teaches sounds, blending, sight words, and irregular words with cards, dictation, and decodable texts.

ECRI demonstrates strong evidence of effectiveness under the Every Student Succeeds Act for improving student reading outcomes. One ECRI efficacy study shows it increases progress toward reading proficiency compared to more standard Tier 2 interventions (Fien et al., 2015). I will say, though, when I observed ECRI lessons in action, I saw a lot of uniform, unidirectional, and read-on-demand strategies. Perhaps my aversion to the strategies stems from the tapping on a clipboard (or clicking of a dog-training clicker) to prompt students to choral read. I prefer leaning in to listen to each student read during small-group guided reading instruction and coaching them individually. The science of reading definitely falls on the opposite end of the spectrum from students learning to love reading through exposure to quality, complex texts.

Whatever your approach to teaching reading, MLs need explicit instruction to practice and master skills like summarizing, analyzing, comparing, and contrasting. These skills all play into ELs' and MLs' overall comprehension and meaning making. Teaching these skills is not an end point; practicing with accessible texts enables proficiency. Once students experience success with these skills, they will apply them to more complex texts.

I don't think any educator will argue with the fact that reading is an essential skill for students; however, SWIRL helps students process, write about, talk through, and comprehend texts. Specific scaffolds are put in place for multilingual learners to experience the most success possible.

Now, we're going to delve into various reading strategies, interventions, and scaffolds to support MLs in reading.

Activities and Strategies

Reading makes SWIRL a spiral, interlocking the various forms of communication through anchor texts. Students respond to what they've read in writing and through speaking. As they interact with peers and the teacher, they listen, write, or perhaps reread a passage.

In this section, you learn about many strategies to support MLs in reading. How do you decide when to use which strategy? It's simple: do what your students need, based on their English proficiency levels and the demands of the text. Does the text have a barrage of multisyllabic or multiple-meaning words, for example? That is when you may want to pull apart compound words, leverage cognates, or check context clues. This list is not exhaustive; rather, it is a starting point for you and your colleagues to discuss reading strategies as they pertain to MLs. Feel free to add to this toolbox and create a treasure trove of reading scaffolds.

According to a study of eighth graders, when students are allowed to choose what they read instead of being assigned texts, it results in "increased reading volume, a reduction in students failing the state test, changes in peer relationships, self-regulation, and conceptions of self" (Ivey & Johnston, 2015, p. 297). One meta-analysis concludes that the most powerful factors in increasing reading motivation and comprehension are access to lots of books and the choice about what to read (Guthrie & Humenick, 2004). Obviously, there will be a certain percentage of teacher or district decisions when it comes to "core literature," dictating which texts students will read. But some part of every instructional day should allow for student choice in reading.

The following strategies, covered in previous chapters, apply to the reading part of SWIRL: cognitive content dictionary (page 95) and cooperative strip paragraphs (page 133). There inherently is overlap in SWIRL activities.

SWiRL Academic Vocabulary

At every grade level, students need exposure to, and increased familiarity with, general and discipline-specific academic vocabulary, since "reading researchers have consistently found strong correlations between student performance on vocabulary and reading comprehension assessments" (Lawrence, Knoph, McIlraith, Kulesz, & Francis, 2021, p. 669).

An expectation that newcomers understand and master academic vocabulary must be tempered, or put off temporarily. Newcomers first need proficiency in basic interpersonal communication skills. For example, before they can talk about whether animals are omnivores, herbivores, or carnivores, they need to be able to say, "I am hungry" or "I would like an apple, please." Once they are communicating at the emerging and entering stages of language acquisition, and especially when they are developing, expanding, bridging, and reaching, gradually increase the cognitive load in terms of frequency and difficulty of academic vocabulary.

Some 70 to 80 percent of reading comprehension is attributed to one's vocabulary knowledge (Bromley, 2007). Reading is not just about books. It comes in many forms—from brochures to grocery lists to essays and online stories.

SWIRL Anchor Charts

If our ultimate goal is to have fluent readers who understand what they are reading, logic follows that amplifying academic vocabulary is beneficial. One way to do this is by using anchor charts.

The following anchor chart types are examples of ways to teach academic vocabulary: chants, poems, and songs. Anchor charts may hang in your classroom just during one lesson, one week, or a monthlong thematic unit. Some anchor charts may stay up all year (like anchor charts of cognates or compound words).

Chants

One of the most well-known Guided Language Acquisition Design (GLAD) chants for ELD is the "Here, There, Everywhere" chant. This is very repetitive—and students *love* the predictability and patterns. They can feel successful with that formula to draw on. Figure 7.1 shows an example chant that works similarly.

Poems

As discussed in chapter 5 (page 113), about writing, poetry offers the chance for students to play with language, recognize rhymes, complete cloze sentences, and discover the wonder of words. I learned to write through poetry. Including haiku, tankas, novels in verse, cinquains, limericks, and spoken word is essential to EL students learning to love language. And the funnier, the better! Humor draws in even the most reluctant readers. Shel Silverstein is one of the funniest poets for K–3 students, and more serious poems like Maya Angelou's (1994) "Still I Rise" can be exemplar texts for students in grades 4–8.

> Birds here, birds there,
> Birds, birds everywhere!
> Colorful birds flying,
> Loud birds chirping,
> Small birds feeding,
> And large birds walking.
> Birds floating in the sky,
> Birds resting on a nest,
> Birds hiding in the brush,
> And birds ducking underwater.
> Birds here, birds there,
> Birds, birds everywhere!

Figure 7.1: Example chant.

Songs

In chapter 4 (page 79), about speaking, I cover content and concepts set to music. It is important to remember that when students sing a song, they are reading the lyrics. Research shows that retention is higher when concepts are set to music (Fabiny, 2015). Listening to and performing music reactivates areas of the brain associated with memory, reasoning, speech, emotion, and reward.

Two studies—one in the United States and the other in Japan—found that music doesn't just help us retrieve stored memories; it also helps us lay down new ones (Fabiny, 2015). Again, think of the last time you heard a song that you hadn't heard in a while. The lyrics came flooding back to you, right? Songs can improve ELs' listening and pronunciation skills. Through the use of songs, you can teach vocabulary and sentence structures. But, perhaps most important, and least quantifiable, songs bring out joy.

swIRL Mirrors, Windows, and Sliding Glass Doors

There is a call in the authorial community for diverse writers to publish books in which the youth who read them see themselves reflected. It is important that these readers' cultural lived experiences be accurately represented. Students need books in which they can see themselves reflected (books that act as mirrors), learn about cultures other than their own (books that act as windows), and escape into an imaginary world (books that act as sliding glass doors; Bishop, 1990). View student

Akhand Dugar's (TEDx Talks, 2020) and children's and young adult author Grace Lin's (TEDx Talks, 2016) speeches to learn more about this topic.

These videos originated with children's literature researcher Rudine Sims Bishop's (1990) observations about literature, which are important:

> Books are sometimes windows, offering views of worlds that may be real or imagined, familiar or strange. These windows are also sliding glass doors, and readers have only to walk through in imagination to become part of whatever world has been created or recreated by the author. When lighting conditions are just right, however, a window can also be a mirror. Literature transforms human experience and reflects it back to us and, in that reflection we can see our own lives and experiences as part of the larger human experience. Reading, then, becomes a means of self-affirmation, and readers often seek their mirrors in books. (p. ix)

Although the idea of being able to see oneself in books as mirrors, and learn about other cultures in books as windows, is not new, it still holds true and merits emphasis.

English learners, while they may or may not have been born in the predominantly English-speaking country, almost always experience cultural practices and speak a heritage language at home. It is essential that classroom libraries reflect students' customs, ethnic backgrounds, and traditions. Books like those in the following list provide stories for students to see themselves, and their families, in a positive light. In the wake of increased book banning (PEN International, 2024), families can let educators know what books they don't want their child to read, but let's *not* deny students the opportunity to see themselves in literature and to learn about people who are different than they are.

Here is an inexhaustive list of exemplar multicultural books that can be mirrors, windows, and sliding glass doors.

- *Across a Hundred Mountains* by Reyna Grande (2006)
- *Bright Brown Baby* by Andrea Davis Pinkney (2021)
- *Brown Girl Dreaming* and *The Day You Begin* by Jacqueline Woodson (2016, 2018)
- *Eyes That Kiss in the Corners* by Joanna Ho (2021)
- *Hair Love* by Matthew A. Cherry (2019)
- *Last Stop on Market Street* by Matt de la Peña (2015)

- *Paletero Man* by Lucky Diaz and Micah Player (2022)
- *Strong Girls in History* by Susan B. Katz (2022)
- *Sulwe* by Lupita Nyong'o (2019)
- *Too Many Tamales* by Gary Soto (1993)
- *We Are Water Protectors* by Carole Lindstrom (2020)

Visit the Pragmatic Mom website (http://tinyurl.com/42k6tcu7) for more titles.

SWIRL Making Connections

You can prompt students in any grade to make connections with a text. Newcomers may struggle with this strategy, but beyond that, every student should be making connections to text in the ways outlined in this section.

Few instructional strategies in my thirty years of teaching transformed my classroom the way that the making connections strategy did. The book *Mosaic of Thought: The Power of Comprehension Strategy Instruction* (Keene & Zimmermann, 2007) covers many reading strategies, but this one is among the most salient. It involves explicitly teaching students to make the following connections.

- Text-to-text ("How are these two books similar or different?")
- Text-to-self ("How does this book remind me of my life?")
- Text-to-world ("What in this book is like what is going on in the world?")
- Text-to-media ("How is this book like or unlike a movie or TV show?")

Making connections is an especially important skill for English learners, as they benefit from building on prior knowledge and being able to connect their own life, or the world around them, to what they are reading.

In my classroom, after explicitly teaching each of these connections through sentence stems, modeling, and whole-class and small-group lessons, I color coded. My third graders used small color-coded sticky notes to flag where they made a connection. For example, a yellow note meant they made a text-to-text connection on that page. They would write the title of the book that they were comparing it to, and how it was like that text, on the note. This way, as students read independently, I could circulate around the room and immediately take note of who was making which types of connections. My questioning of the reader's life became instantly targeted and purposeful.

Consider the difference between walking around your room to ask students what a book is about and being able to come up to a student and say (based on their sticky note), "I see that you made a text-to-self connection on page 43. How does the character's shyness remind you of yourself?"

Similarly, as you are doing a read-aloud or shared reading, students can hold their thumb and pointer finger, formed in the shape of the letter C, to their chest to indicate that they are connecting to the text. If you choose to, you can pause and ask the student to share what type of connection they made to the text.

As adult readers, we naturally make these kinds of connections when we read; however, young children, and even teenagers whose first language is something other than English, need to be explicitly taught how to make connections. *Think-alouds*, in which you model for students how to make these connections, are helpful for teaching this meaning-making strategy. Examples include the following.

- "Wow! This part really reminds me of when we got my dog, Ginger, a new doghouse. I just made a text-to-self connection."
- "I think that *Star Wars* is similar in its plot to *Harry Potter* in that there is an orphan who is famous in another land. What type of connection am I making?" (Students should be able to identify that as a text-to-media [text-to-movie] connection.)

SwIRL Roles for Book Clubs

Once students are reading independently—likely grades 3 and up—at developing, expanding, bridging, and reaching levels, they can meet as a group to discuss a book. If you put students in book clubs or jigsaw-like groups of five or six students, it is important that they have roles assigned to them so they have agency and accountability. Possible roles are explained here, and each gives students a purpose to participate actively in the discussion.

- The **encourager**'s role is to pull more information out of a reluctant speaker. For example, an encourager might enthusiastically say, "That's so interesting! Can you say more about that?" or just "Great point, Sam!" Think of the role as a motivator.
- The **timekeeper** not only monitors the minutes on each topic, question, or task but also points out if the group is going off on tangents.
- The **notetaker** records important or interesting parts of the discussion and shares them with the reporter after.

- The **reporter** shares out the information, or opinions gathered in the group, to the whole class. Sometimes, that is done by several members of the group, but the reporter is the default presenter if it is just one person's responsibility. They might share the group's main takeaways or questions with the whole class after groups have discussed for about twenty or thirty minutes.

- The **clarifier** can ask questions of the teacher or other groups to gain clarity if the group is confused about a task. They can also prompt a student to point to evidence of their opinion.

- The **facilitator** ensures the flow of conversation is smooth and resolves any disputes that may arise. They act as the "teacher" in the group for that period of time. Facilitators might call on people or read the questions aloud. They also make sure that all students get a chance to speak and that nobody is dominating the conversation.

- The **voice monitor** oversees making sure the group uses quiet voices so that other groups can hear each other.

- A **materials manager** distributes the timer, dice, and other tools to the group and gathers and returns them to their designated spots after the lesson or discussion ends.

You don't have to use all these roles if your book clubs are smaller. Timekeeper, notetaker, reporter, facilitator, and clarifier are the most crucial. Displaying the roles on name badges (like those you wear at conferences) helps students remain clear on who is taking what role. The badges also clarify for observers, such as you, students' families, or your principal, who is doing what. Figure 7.2 (page 174) shows role cards that you can share with students.

SWIRL Rime Magic©

Sharon Zinke developed an intervention called Rime Magic, published by Scholastic, in which I was trained as a literacy coach. I used this program as an intervention with K–5 students, who were predominately English learners, and saw more students' reading fluency improve than with any other intervention I've used. While it is mainly implemented in K–5, Rime Magic specifically targets any striving reader (developing and beyond ELs) whose word recognition grade equivalent is below the third-grade level.

Rime Magic is a phonics and fluency accelerator used just five to ten minutes alongside any phonics or reading program to get much faster results. Rather than

Encourager This person motivates other people in the group to speak and gives positive feedback. If you're the encourager, try the following phrases. • "Let's give _____ a chance to talk." • "Can you please talk a little louder so we can hear you?" • "That idea has some good evidence behind it!" • "Thank you for sharing your ideas."	**Timekeeper** This person helps keep people focused during their discussion. They keep an eye on how much time they have left, let group members know, and encourage the group to keep a good pace to ensure all topics are covered. If you're the timekeeper, try the following phrases. • "Let's stick to the topic we were given." • "We have _____ minutes left." • "Let's find a resolution and discuss the next topic."	**Notetaker** This person records the group's important points and final decisions. If you're the notetaker, try the following phrases. • "I'm writing down what _____ said." • "It seems important to share that point with the class. Do you agree?" • "How should we phrase that?"
Clarifier or Facilitator This person is the discussion leader. If you're the clarifier, try the following phrases. • "_____, what are your thoughts about this topic?" • "I think what you are saying is _____. Is that right?" • "What questions do you all have?"	**Materials Manager** This person hands out the tools to the group and puts them back in their places after the discussion. If you're the materials manager, try the following phrases. • "I'll take your dice. Thank you." • "How many total cards do we have?" • "Has everyone given me their form?	**Reporter** This person presents the main points (usually to the whole class) after the group discussion. Together, the reporter and the notetaker make sure important points are written down so the reporter can use the notes while sharing. If you're the reporter, try the following phrases. • "What is the most important part of our discussion to share?" • "Our group decided that _____." • "The main thing our group wants to get across is that _____."

Sources: Adapted from Nickelsen & Dickson, 2022; Twinkl, n.d.

Figure 7.2: Possible student roles for participating in a discussion.

asking students to make their way through each word letter by letter, Rime Magic teaches students to go straight to the *rime* (new way of referring to word family or phonogram). Let's take the word *middle* as an example. Many students know that it starts with an *m*, and they might hear the letter *l* at the end, but they need to be able to recognize the rime (the key part of the word) *-id* to easily decipher the word.

Rime Magic is based on onset/rime research (Calfee, 1977; Goswami & Bryant, 1990; Liberman, Shankweiler, Fischer, & Carter, 1974; Treiman, 1983, 1985) and is different from traditional instruction in that it focuses on the middle chunks in words. Historically, teachers at the learn-to-read grades of K–2 spend a lot of time on beginning and ending sounds. Rime Magic has students learn to recognize the middle chunks (rimes) like *-id*, *-an*, *-om*, *ank*, and so on. Rather than asking students to memorize letters and sounds in a particular published sequence, Rime Magic is daily immersion in a whole array of phonics elements each day for five minutes. As they are immersed in highly engaging sessions, each student becomes proficient with the structure of words in their own time, when they are ready. Students who have fallen behind catch up quickly and elementary students get a solid foundation before third grade. Rime Magic allows an easy and engaging transition to word recognition for English learners.

Visit **go.SolutionTree.com/EL** for a link to a video of Sharon implementing a Rime Magic lesson; www.rimemagic.com to purchase the Rime Magic kit; and www.youtube.com/@shayrime to watch videos of Sharon using the materials with students.

sWiRL Including Informational, Nonfiction, and Complex Texts

Informational and nonfiction texts enhance accessibility because many students are naturally curious about the world around them. But, on the flip side, these texts often contain difficult words, phrases, diagrams, and so on.

Four key components constitute a complex text (Richardson, 2023).

1. **Purpose (for informational texts) or levels of meaning (for literary texts):** Why an author wrote an informational text, the text's topic, and its intended effect on the reader are its *purpose*. *Levels of meaning* are how readers can interpret a literary text, including themes and metaphors.

2. **Structure:** The ways an author connects ideas, processes, and events is *structure*. Structure encompasses a text in its entirety, and more granularly, as well as visually with graphics and typeface.

3. **Language conventionality and clarity:** A text's vocabulary and sentence structures equate to its *language conventionality*. How dense or concrete the author has made a text, as well as style choices (including voice and tone), is the *language clarity*.

4. **Knowledge demands:** The type and the amount of knowledge that are required of a reader to fully access a text are the *knowledge demands*. Knowledge types can be general or specific to disciplines, cultures, and regions.

A Stanford University research paper on text complexity as it relates to English learners states:

> Texts through the third grade are meant to teach children how to read, so they are composed using simple sentence patterns, decodable words and selected high-frequency words that are meant to be learned by sight, and they are accompanied by pictures that support an understanding of what the texts are about. Since the texts have minimal responsibility in bearing the meaning, they tend to lack the richness, depth and complexity found [in more complex texts]. From the fourth grade on, however, the texts themselves have a new purpose: children are supposed to have completed the process of "learning to read," and are ready to begin "reading to learn," as the saying goes. (Fillmore & Fillmore, 2021, p. 2)

The only way that the learning-to-read phase's text complexity can be a successful experience for ELs is if they get access to literature with complex text features such as bolded words, captions, subheadings, varied sentence structure, compound or scientific words, and idioms. But, typically, texts for English learners are watered down or simplified in such a way that strips the text of these features, thus denying ELs the opportunity to dissect and interact with complex texts (Fillmore & Fillmore, 2021). A sidenote here, referring back to the science of reading, is that many books being used in conjunction are almost reminiscent of the old *Dick and Jane* books. Simple, repetitive patterns, while predictable, do not motivate students to fall in love with reading.

If you begin with a close read of just *one* single sentence, with teacher support, ELs are able to pull apart the clauses and extract the meaning from this complex text (Fillmore & Fillmore, 2021). Figure 7.3 shows how that looks, with comments and questions in the margin of Mary Shelley's (1818) *Frankenstein; Or, The Modern Prometheus*, a complex text.

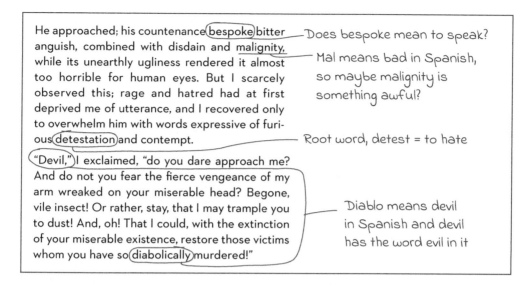

Source: *Adapted from Shelley, 1818.*

Figure 7.3: Example comments and questions in the margin of a complex text.

While the Stanford researchers have not yet completed a formal study on the effectiveness of a close read on a single sentence of complex text, anecdotal evidence suggests that the approach works. Consider this: teachers and leaders at the schools who tried out this EL strategy moved to using it for all students. They based this decision on the increasing numbers of ELs passing the state English language arts proficiency exam, and on the fact that ELs actually outperformed non-EL students in that yearly test (Fillmore & Fillmore, 2021)!

SWiRL Compound, Root, and Base Words

As students in grades 3–12 at the expanding, bridging, and reaching levels tackle more complex texts, especially nonfiction ones, it is important to explicitly teach word analysis strategies. Students need to learn how to tease apart compound words in order to extract meaning. While compound words do exist in languages like Spanish (*palabras compuestas*), they are far more common in English. For example, *abrelatas* in Spanish unpacks as "open" (*abre*) plus "cans" (*latas*)—can opener.

When an EL sees a compound word in a text, they may feel overwhelmed. Teach them how to divide the word to extract its meaning. Here is one example, with the word *firefighter*, of how you may approach it.

1. When students see the compound word, ask, "What two words do you hear in the word *firefighter*?"
2. Invite a volunteer to draw a slash between the two words.

3. Write the words separately.
4. Ask what each word means and say, with emphasis on the words, "So, a *firefighter* is someone who *fights fires*."

One study proved that knowing the meaning and use of eighty-two specific roots and affixes (twenty-seven root words, thirty-two prefixes, and twenty-three suffixes) unlocks access to over one hundred thousand English words (McEwan, n.d.). Visit https://tinyurl.com/4ejxrcrc or simply search online for a list of common Greek and Latin roots to share with students.

Root and base words, like much of what this chapter presents, apply to content areas beyond English language arts. For example, knowing Latin and Greek roots is very useful in mathematics, science, and social studies. If students come across the words *microscope* and *telescope*, for instance, teach them that the Greek root word *scope* means "viewing instrument" and that it can stand alone or be combined with other Greek root words to create the words *microscope* (*micro* is "small"; *scope* is "viewing instrument") and *telescope* (*tele* is "far off"; *scope* is "viewing instrument").

In tandem with root words, teaching MLs the meanings of prefixes and suffixes is paramount to their success. Common prefixes include *un-* and *re-* and suffixes include *-ing* and *-ed*. Knowing how the meanings of these affixes change the root or base word gives students the key to unlock the code we call the English language. It becomes decipherable and they can infer meaning more often when they know the way a prefix, a suffix, or a combination thereof impacts a word. Prefixes, suffixes, and root or base words are good anchor chart foci. Also, several prefixes and suffixes have cognates in Spanish, such as *con-* (*contrast/contraste*), *sub-* (*submarine/submarino*), and *-able/-ible* (*sustainable/sostenible*).

SwiRL Pronunciation, Accuracy, and Fluency

The ability to accurately decode a word when reading it is an essential skill. The accuracy with which students crack the code allows them to become more fluent. Accuracy includes the correct pronunciation with the emphasis on the right syllable, letter, or word.

Pronunciation

English learners may struggle more than their peers with how to pronounce certain sound blends. Intonation and inflection in Asian languages can be quite different from English intonation and inflection. In fact, the inflection and emphasis of a word can change the meaning in many Asian languages. Similarly, *I read* (present tense) and *I read* (past tense) mean different things. How is a newcomer to distinguish those? On top of that, the color *red* is pronounced like the past-tense *read*! And *red* in Spanish means "net"! English pronunciation is super confusing.

Common Spanish examples include the following.

- The *th* blend does not exist in Spanish. You have to actually teach students to put their tongue between their teeth in order to make the *th* sound. They need to practice *th* words repeatedly in order to improve their fluency, confidence, and comprehension. Think of how often *the, that, those, these, them,* and other *th* words come up in everyday reading.

- Spanish-speaking students tend to say "Espanish" or "eschool" because the Spanish words *Español* and *escuela* lead them to believe those words should be pronounced that way. You need to teach that the sound in English is different.

- The *-ed* sound at the end of past-tense verbs can be pronounced like a *-t*, or a *-d*, but many ELs say it as a separate syllable, like *mark-ed*, when it is pronounced *markt*. This has to be explicitly taught, as conjugations are nonexistent in many Asian languages and are quite different in the Latin-based languages.

Aside from correctly saying letter sounds and blends, pronunciation heavily impacts students' accuracy.

Accuracy

Fluency and accuracy are two sides of the same coin. For English learners, it is essential to explicitly teach certain sounds and pronunciations in order to improve their accuracy. Reading accurately is part of being English language proficient. Teachers must mix the following strategies to support students in reading accurately.

- Stop and pronounce the word correctly for them as a model, or play audio of the word. (Many online reading programs, such as i-Ready, have a button students can click on that pronounces the word for them as a model.)

- Ask them to try to sound out the word.

- Ask another student in the group to help them pronounce it.

Chunking the text also allows students to slow down and read more carefully. The standard acceptable accuracy goal for reading a text is 95 to 98 percent of the words correct and comprehended (Betts, 1946). That is a just-right text for a student, one with which they are having productive struggle. Assess and reassess using literacy tools.

Fluency

Fluency for English learners includes skills like intonation and inflection for punctuation. In Spanish, for example, there are question marks and exclamation marks at the beginnings of sentences. Those give the reader a clue to raise their voice with inflection; however, in English, we only put those punctuation marks at the ends of sentences. So, Spanish-speaking ELs need to learn how to scan ahead in order to correctly read the sentence.

Repeated read-alouds increase oral fluency (Padeliadu & Giazitzidou, 2018). Interventions such as the following include repeated readings for ELs.

- Curriculum Associates' i-Ready
- Helping Early Literacy with Practice Strategies® (HELPS)
- Scholastic's Short Reads
- Rime Magic

For first through sixth graders, average reading rates range between 80 and 185 words per minute. Middle and high school students tend to read between 195 and 204 words per minute (Lastiri, 2021). It can be helpful to record students reading and have them listen to themselves—especially as a formative assessment at the beginning, middle, and end of the school year. This is something that really marks their progress and is useful during parent-teacher conferences as well.

SWiRL Checking Comprehension

As students develop fluency and accuracy, and their English language proficiency level increases beyond entering or newcomer, you also need to check that they understand what they are reading. That includes knowing story elements (such as characters, setting, problem, and resolution), making predictions, and sequencing.

You can scaffold this for English learners in the following ways.

- **Host a picture walk before reading:** In this strategy, you simply flip through the book and ask students to tell you what is going on, based on the pictures. This is important because a precursor skill to reading is being able to "fake read" and make up a story that matches the pictures on the page. It also teaches ELs to use picture clues to figure out what is going on in a book. While the science of reading discourages "three-cueing"—using (1) semantic cues, which focus on gaining meaning from context and sentence-level cues; (2) syntactic cues, which involve the grammatical features of the language; and (3) grapho-phonic cues, which deal with spelling patterns with the use of pictures—I believe that this is still a very valuable and natural tool for students who predominantly read picture books.

- **Preview key vocabulary:** Whether you do it in a pocket chart, on a SMART Board, or on a sheet of paper, pulling out key vocabulary ahead of time that you think will be difficult for students is crucial. It sets them up for success.
- **Make predictions:** Stopping along the way to ask students to predict what might happen next helps ELs develop the cognitive skills needed to comprehend text.
- **Dissect story elements:** After reading a book, have students dissect the where and when (setting), who (characters), why (plot and problem), and how (solutions). One fun way to do this is through a flip book like that shown in figure 7.4.
- **Sequence:** Have students delineate what happened at the beginning, middle, and end of a text. The flip book works for this as well.

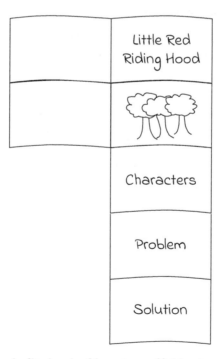

Figure 7.4: Example flip book of how to scaffold using story elements.

You can stop and check for comprehension when infusing idioms, delineating story elements, or asking students to make predictions in a literacy lesson. Online programs like i-Ready (www.curriculumassociates.com) can help you monitor accuracy and comprehension.

SWiRL Idioms

From newcomers to bridging ELs, idioms (or sayings that aren't literal) confuse and amuse students.

Take a look at these common English idioms.

- "Break a leg."
- "Hit the sack" or "Hit the hay."
- "Bite the bullet."
- "You hit the nail on the head."
- "You're barking up the wrong tree."
- "They're a fish out of water."
- "They're beating around the bush."

Many of the preceding idioms do exist in, or translate to, other languages. Some do not, though. For example, in English, people say, "That's the straw that broke the camel's back" or "That's the last nail in the coffin." In Spanish, people say, *"Clavar el último clavo al ataúd"* (more or less also "Put the last nail in the coffin"). Many of these sayings might be open to misinterpretation if a newcomer or emergent ML hears them. Here are a few ways you can have fun teaching these to English learners.

1. Illustrate the literal meaning and the figurative meaning of an idiom.
2. Research the genesis or origin story of the phrase. Let's look at an example.

   > *"Break a leg": In theaters, long ago, actors lined up to perform. If they weren't in the scene, they had to stay behind the "leg line," which also meant they wouldn't get paid. If you were to tell an actor to "break a leg," you were wishing them good luck and the opportunity to cross the leg line, perform, and get paid.*

3. Have students pick an idiom and write its definition and a sample sentence (see figure 7.5).

> **A FISH OUT OF WATER**
>
> **Meaning:**
> Someone in an uncomfortable position or situation
>
> ---
>
> **Example:**
> It was Allison's first day at her new school, and she felt like a fish out of water.

Figure 7.5: Defining an idiom and writing a sample sentence.

SWIRL Homonyms and Homophones

Once students are emerging English learners, they will come across words that look and sound the same but mean different things. Direct minilessons on homonyms usually start around second or third grade and can stretch into fifth grade with complex vocabulary.

The English language is challenging for many reasons: it is not always phonetic; there are irregularities and exceptions to almost every rule (*i* before *e* except after *c*, for example); and there are hundreds of *homonyms*, or multiple-meaning words that sound the same and are spelled the same. These words can confuse even English language proficient students.

Take, for instance, these homonyms for the word *beat*.

- To beat an egg (to whip it)
- To beat a drum (to pound or play it)
- To beat someone in a game (to win it)
- The beat of your heart (the heart's pulsation)
- Being beat (being very tired)
- To beat someone (to hit them hard and badly bruise them)

It is important to point out the words that might have multiple meanings either as you come upon them in text or as part of a dedicated, evolving T-chart or graph.

Here are some other examples (Spelling City, n.d.):

- I *left* my phone on the *left* side of the room.
- The baseball *pitcher* asked for a *pitcher* of water.
- The committee *chair* sat in the center *chair*.
- The *crane* flew above the construction *crane*.

- While they are at the *play*, I'm going to *play* with the dog.
- She will *park* the car so we can walk in the *park*.

It is especially important that ELs learn to use context clues—like "park the car" or "construction crane." Using highlighters or pens to underline context clue words is a strategy that will help ELs distinguish between homonyms.

Homophones are words that sound the same but are spelled differently and mean different things (for example, *knew* and *new* or *meat* and *meet*). Doing some mini-lessons on these, cocreating a growing anchor chart, and pointing out homophones in texts are all strategies that will benefit MLs' reading skills.

Conclusion

Many educators would argue that reading is the most important skill, as it is foundational across all curricular areas. An English learner's ability to read fluently and accurately—and to comprehend what they've read—is the key to academic success. They need to know how to fluently read and fully understand fiction, informational texts, mathematics story problems, scientific theories, historical graphs, poetry, and so on.

The influx of immigrants from countries whose languages don't share the same alphabet, directionality, or sound and symbol system means that we have to honor and acknowledge the connections and disconnections with phonemes, directionality, and meaning. While teaching the needed foundational skills—like the science of reading does—is essential to unlock students' access to content, inspiring a love of reading in students is also fundamental.

Teaching reading involves many nuances and intricacies. It is a process, and it takes time, especially for English learners as they are gradually acquiring oral vocabulary in a language, while trying to learn to read. In-depth meaning making and comprehension cannot fully take place until students are fluent, accurate readers.

In closing, I want to leave you with a personal vignette. My Aunt Judy was a teacher. When I started my career in education, I asked her if she had any suggestions or words of advice. Without hesitation, she said, "Read to them every day. Sometimes twice." She taught second and fifth grade, and I kept that lesson close to my heart as I taught hundreds of students over my thirty years. Even older students enjoy being read aloud to and having a quiet, dedicated, and sacred space and time to read independently.

Creating a space where reading becomes joyful—and can serve as an escape from other circumstances—is invaluable. Words open up worlds, and it is our job and privilege to provide texts that can transport students into fantasy, fiction, fables, and the natural world.

CHAPTER 8

Listening

The art of conversation lies in listening.
—Malcom Forbes

Listening may appear to be the most passive of the five SWIRL method elements; however, a study shows that, while 65 percent of people are primarily visual learners, 30 percent are auditory learners, and 5 percent are kinesthetic learners (Buşan, 2014). Originally labeled as learning styles, *visual*, *auditory*, and *kinesthetic* refer to each person's preferred method for taking in, retaining, and demonstrating information. Do you learn from listening to podcasts or TEDx Talks, or do you need to read words, take notes, or see a visual representation to remember (Fleming & Mills, 1992; Gardner, 1983, 2011)?

We do learn a lot from listening to our computers, phones, TVs, friends and family, teachers, podcasts, lectures, and more. But listening is often the most solitary of learning paths and the hardest for a teacher to evaluate. How can you know what is going on in a student's brain and if they are, in fact, retaining what they hear? They need to show what they know by speaking, writing, or interacting.

And much of what the preceding chapters cover inherently requires students to have listening skills—barring a hearing issue, students listen when their teacher speaks, and they listen to their peers. Students also listen to themselves as they read and respond to text, participate in conversations, sing songs, recite chants, hear shared reading, and share ideas in group work. All these tasks require learners to attentively tune into others. That might include listening to a peer, the teacher, a video, or a song to process and make meaning of content. (Students with hearing issues may inevitably rely more on visuals or kinesthetic movements to adequately process oral language. Many teachers also use microphone systems to support students who are hard of hearing or have ADHD.)

When it comes to listening skills, keep gradual release of responsibility (page 72) in mind, as it aims to slowly, methodically hand over the onus of learning to the students. Gradual release is especially important when students are listening, as they need to learn to understand, process, and respond to oral directions and information in order to make meaning of texts and the world around them. The gradual release of responsibility (I do, we do, two do, you do), as it applies to listening, is outlined in the following steps (Fisher & Frey, 2021).

1. **I do:** The teacher models the strategy for students. You might do a think-aloud. As a class, listen to a section of audio and then talk about your inferences or interpretations of the information—for example, "I hear the character expressing fear of the unknown. I wonder what the next step will be, given how afraid he is." Or, you might write a sentence correctly or read aloud with fluency and intonation. You are modeling fluent English.

2. **We do:** This part, sometimes called *we do together*, is done by the students and teacher in collaboration. Have students point to evidence in a story, share their thinking, or annotate a text after listening to it read aloud. A cocreated graphic organizer can be helpful during this step.

3. **Two do:** Students work in pairs and listen to each other. They can think, write, share, and collaborate in these discussions. This part of gradual release lowers students' affective filter and increases their willingness to take risks. It sets them up for success because they can lean on a partner before being asked to do a task on their own.

4. **You do:** Students build up to being able to listen and respond independently. They should be able to, for example, identify the rhyming words in a poem or song, annotate a section of a novel, or write a short response to what they read in a book, heard on audio, or saw in a video.

Students need a lot of accountability in this area, as it is often hard to determine whether they are understanding what they are hearing—or if they're listening at all.

First, let's discuss the research on listening, and then we'll review related activities and strategies.

The Research on Listening

Listening is a crucial part of practice in EL instruction for the following reasons.

- Listening is often referred to as the key to teaching ELs how to speak (Ferlazzo, 2023). In fact, about 40 to 50 percent of our time is spent listening (Owen-Hill, 2024). Circling back to chapter 2 (page 31) on language acquisition, like a baby learning its first language, a student might often listen silently for a while before they begin producing language. That does not mean they are not learning! Once a child starts speaking, there is a tipping point when they go from predominantly listening to speaking more to socialize, exchange information, and gather more insight.

- It is through listening that a learner receives language they can understand and make sense of (comprehensible input), which is key when learning a second language (Krashen, Lee, & Lao, 2018).

- Some learners tend to process text better when listening to it than when reading it. Students who prefer auditory learning favor listening to new information. They retain and remember information better when they receive it via sound or speech than when it's written or when they read it. Examples include lectures, songs, discussions, audiobooks, and video with audio (SimpleK12 Staff, 2023).

- Listening allows students to take in and process information before having to write, speak, or read about the topic.

- Repeatedly listening to vocabulary and grammar helps students learn pronunciation, expand their vocabulary, and note patterns in grammatical structures.

- Extensive listening and extensive reading are so intertwined that their relationship is referred to as the *buy-one-get-one-free effect* (U.S. Department of Education, 2020). Extensive listening (for example, to read-alouds) builds stamina, enables a deeper understanding of language (Simon & Simon, 2024), and increases a student's ability to understand language in big chunks as well as make meaning from context.

After decades of research on language acquisition, Stephen D. Krashen and Beniko Mason (2022) have concluded that there is only one way that language acquisition happens: "when we understand what we hear and what we read" (p. 1). Providing *optimal, comprehensible input* means that students can understand instruction and that it is deeply engaging, with much input (Krashen & Mason, 2022).

Activities and Strategies

While I was learning Spanish in high school, there was a language lab during which my classmates and I would listen to a recorded voice say, *"Listo, vamos a empezar."* ("Ready, we're going to begin.") We were required to answer questions based on what we heard. But, when I moved to Costa Rica and listened to the radio, or heard a friend tell a joke at a party, that language lab practice didn't quite cut it. It didn't prepare me to comprehend double entendres or figure out words in context in Spanish. You know how a foreign language always sounds so much faster than your mother tongue? For that reason, and many others, ELs need audio chunked in sound bites. They need to listen for a little, turn and talk or write about what they heard, ask questions to clarify, and then listen to another sound bite.

Students listen all day long—to their parents, teachers, peers, and bus drivers; to audiobooks, TikTok videos, and songs. They naturally want to sing, draw, chant, and so on. Everything from content set to songs to total physical response, and even fist to five, helps determine if students actually understood what they heard. Accountability and repetition are the name of the game with listening. The simple partner barrier game, where partners sit across from each other with a folder blocking their view of each other's paper, is a fascinating assessment of how well they are understanding what they are hearing. If one student says, "Draw a red square," does the other student know how to do that? You will see it on paper.

Keep in mind that listening strategies should be relegated to only 25 to 30 percent of instructional time (OnTESOL, 2021). Remember, you want students to SWIRL: speak, write, interact, and read—not just listen.

As you employ the activities and strategies in this chapter, as well as others in this book, remember the following.

- **Ensure talking and listening doesn't become social hour:** Make sure students are with a productive partner, and keep tabs on the conversations by circulating around the room and listening in. Are they staying on topic? Are they using academic vocabulary? Are both students in a pair or all students in a small group speaking?

- **Help students know where to start:** They need to know what their North Star is. What is their learning target? What is the task required of them? For example, their task might be to listen to a story being read aloud and then sequence the events of the story using the phrases *in the beginning*, *in the middle*, and *at the end*.

- **Ensure accountability:** This might be in the form of a poster, presentation, written response, or oral language exchange that students are required to produce as a final product to demonstrate that they understood what they heard. Keeping anecdotal records of students' language production in response to comprehensible input will help you monitor, adjust, and target instruction.

An additional strategy for listening, of course, is integrating songs, chants, and poetry slams (pages 100 and 168). Learning content to music increases retention and engagement because "music engages a diverse network of brain regions and circuits, including sensory-motor processing, cognitive, memory, and emotional components" (Zaatar, Alhakim, Enayeh, & Tamer, 2024). Setting content to song helps students remember it and makes it entertaining. Visit www.youtube.com/watch?v=O9MR0D_jnu8 to see the accompanying hand motions for a chant. Listening activities can also become center or group activities where students practice academic vocabulary. When I first started teaching, my school had a listening center in which students listened to books on tape; now this often happens via online reading programs.

Here are some other activities and strategies that integrate or enhance listening and listening skills. As you employ them, keep in mind specific structures to scaffold these interactions, many of which are similar to those for speaking.

SwIrL Active Listening and Body Language

All students, at every EL proficiency level, need to employ active listening techniques. That doesn't mean they can't occasionally lie down on the rug or stand up and meet a partner (like with hand up, stand up; page 86), but when they are listening, they should be on task, not talking to someone else or tuning out the speaker altogether.

Consider that as you enter any classroom, you will often find students chattering away. Listening is a social skill that people use every day. However, while most students absorb a lot of content through listening, they must learn specific skills to be able to process and retain knowledge. Body language is an inextricable part of active listening, and according to research, "non-verbal signs are of great significance for [EL] learners and [EL] teachers as they help cover the communication gap in the form of gestures, eye-gaze, facial expressions, and body language" (Saleem, Rana, & Bashir, 2022, p. 39). Body language is a crucial part of how you convey feedback and respect, and it also helps you determine ELs' level of engagement in conversations and their content processing. Their body language helps you gauge where they are in the learning process.

In addition to modeling body language that helps facilitate listening, you will have to give behavioral examples. Table 8.1 provides examples of body language that is conducive and not conducive to listening.

Table 8.1: Body Language That Is and Is Not Conducive to Active Listening

Conducive Body Language	Inconducive Body Language
Nodding to indicate understanding	Glancing around
Leaning toward the speaker	Looking at your phone or around the room
Maintaining eye contact (if culturally and neurologically applicable)	Not facing the speaker
	Not reacting to conversation
Making attentive facial expressions, like smiling	Fidgeting
	Interrupting
Facing the speaker	Folding your arms
Gesturing (such as pointing to an object when naming it)	

Source: Adapted from Everyday Speech, n.d.; Yang, 2017.

You must keep in mind the nuances of cultural differences in relation to body language since many ELs' immediate or extended families hail from other countries. Doing a bit of basic research can help. My own mother taught art for thirty-five years in the Metro Detroit area. Many Japanese families gravitated to Detroit for the auto industry. At first, my mom thought it was disrespectful that boys from Japan would not look at her when she was giving directions. She soon came to realize that, in Japanese culture, maintaining constant eye contact with an elder is a sign of disrespect (Chebbouba, 2023).

That is one example of how being culturally sustaining and sensitive can inform our expectations for active listening. In other cultures, gesturing with one's hands to express emotions, or tell a story, is part of the process. Getting to know your MLs means embracing and encouraging their culture while also demonstrating expectations that people might have of them if they engage in a conversation in a formal setting (the workplace, an interview, or a lecture, for instance).

Similarly, neurodiverse students may not make eye contact easily or often. Students on the spectrum might flap their hands or need to squeeze an object. The traditional "hands in your lap" expectation might go against the grain of differentiating for these learners. No student who experiences this kind of special need should be forced to make eye contact.

Activating schemata and backchanneling are two methods you can use to teach active listening skills. The following list includes ways to show a speaker you are listening through these methods.

1. **Activating schemata:** What prior experiences (*schemata*) do your ELs have of what it looks like to be an active listener? Students are mostly asked to passively listen from preschool age on. To get feedback from them, and confirm whether they are listening to what is happening in class, ask them to identify the nonverbal cues that show someone is listening—keeping one's eyes on the speaker, closing one's mouth, leaning in, and nodding are examples. Most students can identify what active listening sounds, looks, and feels like based on their prior school experiences. Many teachers make a corresponding T-chart as an anchor at the start of the school year and refer back to it periodically. This chart may include visual icons, such as an eye with the What Active Listening Looks Like column and an ear with the What Active Listening Sounds Like column. Many teachers add a third column with a heart and the header What Active Listening Feels Like. In response, students often say, "Safe, respectful, calm, fair."

2. **Backchanneling:** Being an active listener means not only seeming attentive, but also actively engaging in conversation and responding to the speaker. That can mean asking clarifying questions to learn more, adding to what they say, or commenting in agreement or disagreement. Showing interest takes the form of backchanneling and reacting through nonverbal cues—body language—like nodding, leaning in, smiling, and making eye contact. Here are some phrases students should know for backchanneling (Everyday Speech, n.d.).

    - "Wow!"
    - "Could you say that again?"
    - "No way!"
    - "What do you mean by that?"
    - "If I understand correctly, you mean . . ."
    - "Yeah?"
    - "I'm sorry, I didn't hear you."
    - "Could you say more about that?"
    - "I hear what you're saying, and I'd like to add . . ."

Just as important as teaching active listening and body language to students, you must notice students' body language and correct them. That feedback provides "information by watching the students' expressions in their eyes, on their faces and noticing their actions" so you can "adjust and organize" your instruction (Yang, 2017, p. 1333).

SWIRL Story as Input

For all grades, stories are the lifeline of human experience. We crave hearing stories—ghost stories by the campfire, stories of struggle and triumph from our friends or family, and stories in books and movies. Again, while all EL levels benefit from this strategy, try to combine students of varying EL proficiency levels so they can support each other.

Most children, even teens, love to be read to. Read-alouds boost EL students' confidence around pronunciation and can help them memorize words (Ninsuwan, 2015), but they need scaffolds for comprehension, aiding them in understanding potentially difficult phrases and words (Krashen, Mason, & Smith, 2018). This scaffolding may include the following techniques.

- **Using sentence frames:** The goal of this strategy is twofold. First, sentence frames give students a starting point so producing language doesn't feel so overwhelming. In short, we start the sentence for them, and ask them to finish it (for example, "One reason the main character ran away was _____" or "This story took place in _____"). Second, we want students to learn to speak in complete sentences, so a sentence frame helps scaffold that language objective from day one. See page 88 for more about sentence frames.

- **Previewing vocabulary:** Before reading aloud a text—fiction or nonfiction—identify words that you think may be unfamiliar or difficult for students to decode or comprehend. Share these words with students prior to reading the text and either (1) cocreate a cognitive content dictionary (page 95) on chart paper where students guess what the words mean and how to use them in a sentence, or (2) model how to say the words and give students the definitions. The focus is on making the text more comprehensible, not on mastering the vocabulary words themselves.

- **Doing a picture walk:** For students in K–2, or newcomers and entering ELs, showing just the text's pictures and asking what is happening helps defuse any anxiety about decoding words. Picture walks are a natural way for early readers to make sense of the text.

- **Using cognates:** There are thousands of cognates from Latin-based languages to English; students can uncover meaning by listening to how words in their home language vocabulary and in English sound similar. For example, the word *history* is very similar to the word *historia* in Spanish. Viewing students' home language as an asset, a springboard of sorts, allows them to utilize their prior knowledge in deciphering English. See chapter 1 (page 13) for more about cognates.

Listening to stories is a pathway to speaking, reading for pleasure, and overall language and literacy growth. For multilingual learners, it is a gateway to language development. Hearing words pronounced correctly, and sentences read fluently, models for them how to become a reader who comprehends and applies what they learn.

Figure 8.1 features example read-aloud instructions broken into steps before, during, and after reading.

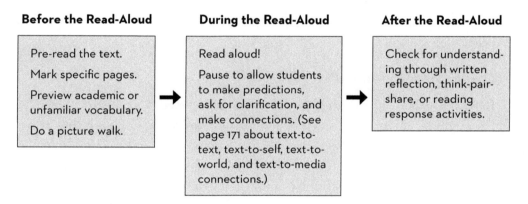

Figure 8.1: Read-aloud instructions.

Before the Read-Aloud

Pre-read the text to yourself, preferably aloud. If you've ever stumbled over words while doing a cold read-aloud, you know that this is a crucial part of the process. Mark pages (with sticky notes, for example) where you want to pause and ask students to make predictions. You may cover up words at the end of sentences that rhyme. That creates a cloze activity, which has students fill in what word they think fits. Figure 8.2 (page 196) shows two pages in *My Mama Earth* (Katz, 2012) with a cloze you can create by putting a sticky note over the last word, *roar*.

Source: © 2012 by Katz. Used with permission.

Figure 8.2: A cloze incorporated into a book.

Also, identify academic, or potentially challenging, vocabulary that you want to preview with students.

During the Read-Aloud

Read aloud! Start by showing the cover and asking students to predict what the book might be about. You can choose to do a picture walk, or chunk the text by pausing periodically (every few pages) for predictions, to check for connections and understanding. Allow students to turn and talk about the text. Many teachers guide their students to show a C with their thumb and pointer finger placed at their chest when they have a text-to-text, text-to-self, text-to-world, or text-to-media connection (page 171).

Read with inflection, intonation, and fluency. Students love it when teachers use character voices to indicate who is speaking. Remember that you may be the only model of a fluent English reader in a student's world.

After the Read-Aloud

Check for understanding. Revisit the text and ensure that students can make meaning from it. Cocreate graphic organizers on which students or you document story elements like the characters (who), setting (where and when), problem and plot (what and why), resolution (how), and sequencing of events. Record cognates, new words, or important academic vocabulary. Have students create a class list of any words or idioms they did not know. (Idioms such as "green with envy," for example, may be confusing.)

It is important that students listen to other students read, too. Pairing English learners of different proficiency levels to read to each other encourages them to help their peers through productive struggles. This enables you to circulate around the room and listen to students as they are reading. If you're privy to a student who needs help cueing another student, instead of helping the student striving to read, you should model for the "student teacher" to cover up part of the word—say, if it's a compound or multisyllabic word. Show them how to prompt the student to say what sound the word begins with and to name words that have the same ending. Or, per Rime Magic (page 173), ask them what the middle chunk is so they can push through the word more easily.

sWirL Chunked Audio and Video for Processing

In all grades, audio and video segments help students acquire information. Some English language assessments even have a section that is completely based on having students listen to an audio clip and respond to comprehension questions about it. While the actual test asks that teachers play the audio in its entirety, students must be given time to process it in chunks in preparation for this task.

Think about the first (or last) time you listened to a radio segment, or a TV show, in a foreign language. Again, it typically feels like people speaking another language are speaking very fast, perhaps without pausing between words. But, if you are able to press pause and process what they are saying, it helps you make meaning of the content. You can break up a five-minute piece so students listen to a minute at a time and then process, discuss, or respond in writing to, what they heard.

Studies prove that more fluent speakers are "able to speak faster and with less hesitation due to the effective use of chunks" (Towell et al., 2019, p. 7). Idioms such as, "I'll be there in a jiffy," are also better digested in chunks. Visit http://tinyurl.com/ynzh7tjz for sample audio from WIDA.

SwIrL Partner and Group Conversations

All English learners, at every proficiency level, need to listen to each other in structured partner and group conversations throughout the day, every day.

You can structure partner and group conversations to facilitate active listening (Singer, 2018). Best practice dictates that students switch partners and groups often, and are able to choose their partners or groups as much as possible. The caveat is that you may want to purposefully partner students based on English proficiency or home language to give them a model of a stronger English speaker or make them more comfortable in springboarding off their home language. You might also group students at the same or similar language proficiency levels when you are differentiating the difficulty of a task.

When students are talking, your job is to listen in. Become a professional eavesdropper, and take some anecdotal records while you're at it! Some teachers strategically rotate between pairs or table groups. This is an opportunity to record formative assessments on their speaking and listening skills. Document their strengths and challenges to inform your instruction, and identify any potential language objectives that you need to reteach. Note their skills in the following areas.

- Academic vocabulary (word choice)
- Inferring
- Analyzing
- Synthesizing
- Building on an idea
- Using evidence to support their opinions
- Speaking with correct grammar
- Asking and answering questions

Partner conversations can take the following forms.

- **Think-pair-share:** Pair students of varying English language levels, similar proficiency levels, or the same home language. When reading a text or explaining a new concept, pause and ask students to think about your question, pair up with their partner, and then share their thoughts with each other. Finally, ask a few students to report out to the whole class what they said or what their partner said.
- **Think-write-pair-share:** This mimics the preceding process, adding an element of written reflection before speaking. Older or more advanced English speakers may respond to literature in this way. You might also ask for a written piece as a response to watching a video or listening to an audio clip.
- **Clock partners:** Students sign up on each other's clock partner sheet. You say, for example, "Find your three o'clock partner. Discuss your favorite character and why that character is your favorite." Typically, they might speak to their clock partner for two or three minutes, and

then you can give another oral prompt and ask them to find, say, their six o'clock partner. For older students, and subject-specific connections, you can label the clock times with parts of speech (*noun*), scientific terms (*ventricle*), or famous historical events (*D-Day*). You might say, "Meet your left ventricle partner and decide what the heart's main function is." You can use the reproducible "Clock Partners" (page 202) for this activity.

Group conversations can take the following forms.

- **Fishbowl (see page 148):** This strategy provides a structure in which students can watch and listen to a model of the task they will be asked to perform. In the center of a whole-class circle, have either a pair, a group, or half of the class sit and model. The rest of the class listens, observes, reflects, discusses, and takes notes with a specific purpose. Select students you know will successfully model the activity to be in the center of the fishbowl; however, try not to always pick the same students.

- **Active observation:** You can do this in tandem with the fishbowl, making the outer-circle observers play an active role. They might take notes on what the speakers are saying, tally who is speaking more, or say things like, "Can you clarify?" or "Please say more about . . ." The idea is to give students who are listening some agency, input, and a focused task.

- **Sentence frames or stems (see page 88):** When students are meeting in partners or small groups to discuss a text or topic, you can provide some sentence stems to prompt the conversation and help them use language in a more formal, academic way.

Refer back to the Purposeful Partnerships section (page 84) in chapter 4 for more partnering options.

swirL Narrative Input

Best used in K–8 with students at every English proficiency level, narrative input is a visual retelling of a story, or an expository explanation of a concept. The rationale for narrative input is that it tips its hat to students who come from cultures where a tradition of oral storytelling is prevalent. It is also a way of teaching the narrative genre. You can highlight the skill of sequencing while giving a visual introduction to the story the students will be reading.

Using a large anchor chart, teachers tell a story while adhering pictures to the chart. Each picture conveys a crucial component of the story. Teachers often place the words of the story on the back of the picture cards to remember them and be able to recite them fluently. Visit https://tinyurl.com/bdf79ctt to watch a narrative input of *Click, Clack, Moo: Cows That Type* (Cronin, 2000)—one of my all-time favorite books.

Keep in mind that, during the narrative input, you follow these steps.

1. Have students sit close to you, either on the rug or near the board, so they can see the chart.
2. Use a colorful background and story cards with pictures on the front and the words on the back.
3. Do a first read-through, in which you tell the story with fluency, voices, and gestures.
4. Ensure that the narrative incorporates academic vocabulary.
5. Offer a reflection or turn-and-talk question at the end of the story for students to process it.

As a follow-up, the next day, retell the story while the students add word cards or speech bubbles to the background. That is a collaborative class retelling of the story.

SwIrL Total Physical Response

Particularly helpful for preK–2 students and newcomers at any grade, total physical response is a fast way for students to show that they understand what you are saying by doing something concrete you direct them to do. This strategy is an oldie but a goodie for this reason: "Linking language with actions drives it deep into our memory" (Kawasaki, 2020). In total physical response, the teacher gives a direction using gestures (pointing, clapping, or tapping, for example). Students respond by doing the action you ask for. For example, you might say, "Bring me the crayons." You might hold a crayon in the air and then gesture with a "come here" wave of your hand. Model the action so students mimic it. Simon Says is the best example of total physical response.

Here are some other possible total physical response commands.

- "Open your book to page _____."
- "Stand up if you _____."
- "Sit down if you _____."

- "Point to the person to your left (or right)."
- "Put your finger on _____ word."
- "Show a thumbs-up (or thumbs-down)."
- "Display fist to five to indicate your level of understanding."
- "Point to the window (or door, anchor chart, and so on)."
- "Act out a word (via charades)."

When my twin nephews were toddlers, their nanny spoke only Spanish to them. So, I spoke to them in Spanish a lot as well. (They asked for *agua* or *leche* before they learned *water* or *milk*.) At one point, I broke my elbow in a biking accident. When I went over to their house, I asked my three-year-old nephew, "Please bring me the yellow pillow," in Spanish. He understood and brought the yellow pillow to rest my elbow on. (His compassionate, three-year-old self brought another pillow for himself and mimicked me by putting his elbow up on a pillow, too.) He could not say that sentence yet, nor could he have read it or written it. But he knew—through listening—exactly what I was saying and showed me that by bringing me the yellow pillow. I'm happy to say that the twins, as of the publication of this book, are in advanced Spanish classes as juniors in high school. I believe this early language learning gave them a strong base for Spanish language development.

Conclusion

Since listening may be the most passive of the five SWIRL skills, it is paramount that we check for understanding, give students opportunities to turn and talk, and chunk audio input so that it is comprehensible. From songs to chants to stories, students' active listening can take the form of fishbowls, purposeful partnerships, Socratic seminars, or an array of other structures that engage students and give them both agency and accountability.

Students must listen to other students read. Pairing English learners of different proficiency levels to listen to each other read encourages them to collaboratively push through productive struggles. It also enables you to circulate around the room and listen to students reading.

Begin by making sure that you know your students, including what their home language is and what level of proficiency they have in that home language. Encourage them to share their cultures and customs and to view their home languages as assets.

Clock Partners

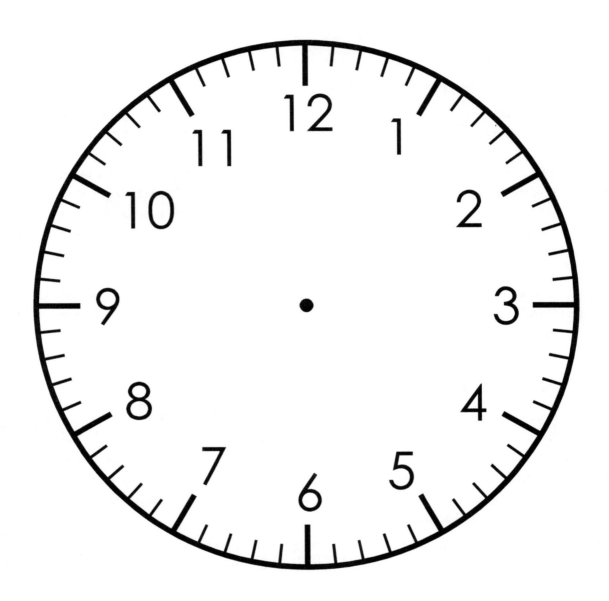

EPILOGUE

Learning another language is not only learning different words for the same things, but learning another way to think about things.

—Flora Lewis

Congratulations! You just took in dozens of strategies to support your multilingual learners. Hopefully, you tried some out along the way. Every class is different, as is every EL student. You might have just a few ELs from Bulgaria and Serbia, or half your class might be from Mexico and Central America. If you teach middle or high school, you might have all long-term ELs, or you might have a few newcomers. If you teach kindergarten, you might have many newcomers or students who were born in this country but whose parents have only ever spoken another language to them at home.

This is—*you are*—their introduction to and main model of the English language. The very best way to ensure they learn English is to give them a plethora of opportunities to SWIRL—speak, write, interact, read, and listen—every single day.

The key to SWIRL is to mix it up. None of these skills is more important than the others. Students need to SWIRL, with all five elements, for the magic to happen.

1. **Speaking:** Multilingual learners need a lot of opportunities to talk, discuss, debate, present, role-play, and complete team tasks collaboratively. Focus here on their development of oral language proficiency—accuracy, fluency, and comprehension.

2. **Writing:** Give students lots of low- and no-pressure chances to get their ideas down on paper. When students are summarizing, sequencing, drafting essays, writing reports, creating poetry, and journaling, emphasize grammar, academic vocabulary, clarity, and organization. Conference with them one-on-one and have peers critique each other's

writing beforehand. Provide an audience and a purpose, and celebrate their published work through author's chairs or spoken-word or poetry slams.

3. **Interacting:** The *I* in the middle of *SWIRL* helps us remember that interacting is the bridge between all other learning activities. Keeping a ratio of 70 percent student talk and 30 percent teacher talk is ideal (Kostadinovska-Stojchevska & Popovikj, 2019). If you're unsure what your percentages are, ask a peer to time a lesson or two. Collaborating with partners, in small groups, on team tasks, and during fishbowls, book clubs, and Socratic seminars emulates the real world and workforce the students will eventually join.

4. **Reading:** Whether books, articles, short stories, poems, chants, or students' own writing, reading is key. Giving students choice in what they read is paramount. Stocking your classroom library with diverse books that serve as mirrors, windows, and sliding glass doors increases engagement and achievement as students see themselves in, and learn about others through, literature. Phonics, oral language, and home language are the building blocks for becoming a voracious reader.

5. **Listening:** Ideally, your students are listening while you and others are speaking—but don't assume that. As the facilitator of English language acquisition, you can create ways for ELs to respond, ask questions, and demonstrate that they are listening and they understand the content, assignment, or ideas expressed in audio clips, videos, turn-and-talks, and class discussions. Focus on developing students' comprehension of spoken English and their ability to respond appropriately.

Keep in mind that language acquisition is not a finite skill. It develops over time, usually taking students three to seven years to achieve fluency, and is not necessarily linear (IRIS Center, 2011a). Some students might learn to read fluently before writing. Others will seemingly be fluent speakers; however, their writing and reading comprehension may not match that proficiency level.

Our North Star is to create fluent, confident, articulate multilingual students who can speak, write, interact with, read, and listen to English (and another language or two) in order to succeed in school and beyond. SWIRL is a mix of best practices for all multilingual learners. When you integrate SWIRL into your lessons, students feel a greater sense of agency and engage in more active ways. That is not to say there won't still be some quite passive reading on a computer or listening to a story;

however, when those more passive activities combine with other SWIRL elements, students get opportunities to practice all facets of learning a new language.

Please be patient with your students and yourself. English is a difficult language with many exceptions to rules, and learning any language is a roller coaster of challenges and triumphs. Give students brain breaks and celebrate their successes along the way. Invite students to add to co-constructed word banks of cognates, new vocabulary words, and idioms.

I sincerely hope *The SWIRL Method* helps you become a more effective, compassionate, culturally responsive and sustaining, attuned, energetic, impactful, and empathic educator. Along the way, acknowledge their grows and celebrate their glows. May it make your students fluent in English, in addition to fluent in their home languages

REFERENCES AND RESOURCES

Aberli, J. (2019, March 7). *Student choice is the key to turning students into readers* [Blog post]. Accessed at www.literacyworldwide.org/blog/literacy-now/2019/03/07/student-choice-is-the-key-to-turning-students-into-readers on July 17, 2023.

Ada, A. F. (2008). *Días y días de poesía: Developing literacy through poetry and folklore.* Des Moines, IA: Hampton-Brown Books.

Ada, A. F., & Campoy, F. I. (2016). *Yes! We are Latinos: Poems and prose about the Latino experience* (D. Diaz, Illus.). Watertown, MA: Charlesbridge.

Ada, A. F., & Campoy, F. I. (2019). *Mamá goose* (M. Suárez, Illus.). New York: Little, Brown Books for Young Readers.

Alborough, J. (2000). *Duck in the truck.* New York: HarperCollins.

Alexander, K. (2016). *Booked.* Boston: Houghton Mifflin Harcourt.

Alexander, R. (2004). *Towards dialogic thinking: Rethinking classroom talk.* New Orleans, LA: Diálogos.

Alexander, R. (2020). *A dialogic teaching companion.* New York: Routledge.

Allyn, P., & Morrell, E. (2016). *Every child a super reader: Seven strengths to open a world of possible.* New York: Scholastic.

Almekhlafy, S. S. A., & Alqahtani, A. A. J. (2020). The visual memory development technique: A remedial and pre-reading activity to enhance EFL learners' motivation. *Heliyon, 6*(3), Article e03627.

Alowais, A. (2021). The effects of leveled reading on second language learners. *International Journal of Research in Education and Science, 7*(4), 1281–1299.

Altavilla, J. (2020, April 27). *How technology affects instruction for English learners.* Accessed at https://kappanonline.org/how-technology-affects-instruction-english-learners-altavilla on September 2, 2024.

Althen, G. (2003). *American ways: A guide for foreigners in the United States* (2nd ed.). Yarmouth, ME: Intercultural Press.

American University School of Education. (2020, May 20). *Disproportionality in special education: Impact on student performance and how administrators can help* [Blog post]. Accessed at https://soeonline.american.edu/blog/disproportionality-special-education on February 26, 2024.

Anderson, L. W., & Krathwohl, D. R. (Eds.). (2001). *A taxonomy for learning, teaching, and assessing: A revision of Bloom's taxonomy of educational objectives.* Boston: Allyn & Bacon.

Andrade, H. L., Du, Y., & Mycek, K. (2010). Rubric-referenced self-assessment and middle school students' writing. *Assessment in Education: Principles, Policy and Practice, 17*(2), 199–214.

Angelou, M. (1994). *The complete collected poems of Maya Angelou.* New York: Random House.

Apodaca, R., DeMartino, S., & Bernstein-Danis, T. (2019, April 25). *Engaging in meaningful Accountable Talk: Discussions with emergent multilingual students.* Accessed at www.ifl-news.pitt.edu/2019/04/engaging-in-meaningful-accountable-talk-discussions-with-emergent-multilingual-students on September 3, 2024.

Arman, N. M. (2021). *The impact of interactive journaling on seventh-grade students' writing self-efficacy, writing performance, and attitudes towards writing* [Doctoral dissertation, University of South Carolina]. Scholar Commons. https://scholarcommons.sc.edu/etd/6317

Ashwell, T., & Elam, J. R. (2017). How accurately can the Google Web Speech API recognize and transcribe Japanese L2 English learners' oral production? *JALT CALL Journal, 13*(1), 59–76.

Association for Childhood Education International. (2003). Native language books boost kindergarteners' literacy development. *Facts in Action.*

Atwell, N. (1998). *In the middle: New understandings about writing, reading, and learning* (2nd ed.). Portsmouth, NH: Heinemann.

August, D., & Shanahan, T. (Eds.). (2006). *Developing literacy in second-language learners: Report of the National Literacy Panel on Language-Minority Children and Youth.* Mahwah, NJ: Erlbaum.

Australian Curriculum, Assessment and Reporting Authority. (2015, June). *English as an additional language or dialect teacher resource: EAL/D learning progression—Foundation to year 10.* Accessed at https://docs.acara.edu.au/resources/EALD_Learning_Progression.pdf on September 2, 2024.

AVID. (n.d.). *Three-story house: Costa's levels of questioning.* Accessed at https://wpvip.edutopia.org/wp-content/uploads/2022/10/Costa27s-information.pdf on July 20, 2023.

Bateman, K. D. (2018). *Moving to learn: Improving attention in the classroom setting for elementary school children* [Doctoral dissertation]. Boston University Libraries OpenBU. Accessed at https://hdl.handle.net/2144/27556 on October 29, 2024.

Bechtel, M. (2001). *Bringing it all together: Language and literacy in the multilingual classroom.* Carlsbad, CA: Dominie Press.

Beck, I. L., McKeown, M. G., & Kucan, L. (2002). *Bringing words to life: Robust vocabulary instruction*. New York: Guilford Press.

Beeman, K., & Urow, C. (2012). *A third way, the third space: Immersion educators and bridging between languages*. Accessed at https://carla.umn.edu/conferences/past/immersion2012/handouts/UrowBeeman_ThirdWay_Handout_Oct2012.pdf on September 24, 2024.

Bennett, J., Lubben, F., & Hogarth, S. (2007). Bringing science to life: A synthesis of the research evidence on the effects of context-based and STS approaches to science teaching. *Science Education, 91*(3), 347–370.

Berkeley Unified School District. (n.d.). *BUSD grade level academic vocabulary*. Berkeley, CA: Author. Accessed at www.berkeleyschools.net/wp-content/uploads/2013/05/BUSD_Academic_Vocabulary.pdf on December 18, 2023.

Betts, E. (1946). *Foundations of reading instruction*. Boston: American Book Company.

Bialik, K., Scheller, A., & Walker, K. (2018, October 25). *6 facts about English language learners in U.S. public schools*. Accessed at www.pewresearch.org/short-reads/2018/10/25/6-facts-about-english-language-learners-in-u-s-public-schools on October 4, 2024.

Biemiller, A. (1999). *Language and reading success*. Newton Upper Falls, MA: Brookline Books.

Billings, E., & Mueller, P. (n.d.). *Quality student interactions: Why are they crucial to language learning and how can we support them?* Albany, NY: Office of Bilingual Education and World Languages. Accessed at www.nysed.gov/sites/default/files/programs/bilingual-ed/quality_student_interactions-2.pdf on September 9, 2024.

Billings, E., & Walqui, A. (n.d.). *De-mystifying complex texts: What are "complex" texts and how can we ensure ELLs/MLLs can access them?* Albany, NY: Office of Bilingual Education and World Languages. Accessed at www.nysed.gov/sites/default/files/programs/bilingual-ed/de-mystifying_complex_texts-2.pdf on January 6, 2024.

Bintz, W. P. (2011). Teaching vocabulary across the curriculum. *Middle School Journal, 42*(4), 44–53.

Bishop, R. S. (1990). Mirrors, windows, and sliding glass doors. *Perspectives: Choosing and Using Books for the Classroom, 6*(3), ix–xi.

Black, P., Harrison, C., Lee, C., Marshall, B., & Wiliam, D. (2004). Working inside the black box: Assessment for learning in the classroom. *Phi Delta Kappan, 86*(1), 8–21.

Bloom, B. S. (Ed.). (1956). *Taxonomy of educational objectives: The classification of educational goals; Handbook I: Cognitive domain*. New York: McKay.

Bor, D. (2012). *The ravenous brain: How the new science of consciousness explains our insatiable search for meaning*. New York: Basic Books.

Brechtel, M. (2001). *Bringing it all together: Language and literacy in the multilingual classroom* (Rev. ed.). Carlsbad, CA: Dominie Press.

Breiseth, L. (n.d.). *Why reading to your kids in your home language will help them become better readers.* Accessed at www.colorincolorado.org/article/why-reading-your-kids-your-home-language-will-help-them-become-better-readers on September 2, 2023.

Breton-Guillen, B. E. (2020). *Best practices for bilingual learners in virtual classrooms* [Unpublished master's thesis]. Western Oregon University.

British Columbia Ministry of Education. (2017). *Province of British Columbia: English language learning (ELL) standards.* Victoria, British Columbia, Canada: Author. Accessed at www2.gov.bc.ca/assets/gov/education/kindergarten-to-grade-12/teach/pdfs/ell/ell-standards-full.pdf on September 1, 2024.

Bromley, K. (2007). Nine things every teacher should know about words and vocabulary instruction. *Journal of Adolescent and Adult Literacy, 50*(7), 528–537.

Brooke, E. (2021). *The critical role of oral language in reading instruction and assessment.* Concord, MA: Lexia. Accessed at www.lexialearning.com/user_area/content_media/raw/The-Critical-Role-of-Oral-Language-in-Reading-Instruction-and-Assessment.pdf on November 5, 2023.

Brookhart, S. M. (2017). *How to give effective feedback to your students* (2nd ed.). Alexandria, VA: ASCD.

Brookhart, S. M., & Moss, C. M. (2014). Learning targets on parade. *Educational Leadership, 72*(2), 28–33.

Brown, L. L. (2012, May 7). *The benefits of music education.* Accessed at www.pbs.org/parents/thrive/the-benefits-of-music-education on September 18, 2024.

Bruner, J. S. (1967). *Studies in cognitive growth.* New York: Vintage Books.

Bruner, J. S. (1975). The ontogenesis of speech acts. *Journal of Child Language, 2*(1), 1–19.

Bruning, R. H., Schraw, G. J., & Norby, M. M. (2011). *Cognitive psychology and instruction* (5th ed.). Boston: Pearson.

Buch, E. R., Claudino, L., Quentin, R., Bönstrup, M., & Cohen, L. G. (2021). Consolidation of human skill linked to waking hippocampo-neocortical replay. *Cell Reports, 35,* 109193. https://doi.org/10.1016/j.celrep.2021.109193

Buffum, A., Mattos, M., & Malone, J. (2018). *Taking action: A handbook for RTI at Work.* Bloomington, IN: Solution Tree Press.

Bușan, A.-M. (2014). Learning styles of medical students: Implications in education. *Current Health Sciences Journal, 40*(2), 104–110.

Butrón, V., & McGregor, M. (2016, Spring). Teaching tip: Cognates are everywhere! Introducing cognates to language learners. *ITBE Link.* Accessed at www.itbe.org/v_newsletters/article_56124917.htm on June 19, 2023.

Calderón, M. (2007). *Teaching reading to English language learners, grades 6–12: A framework for improving achievement in the content areas.* Thousand Oaks, CA: Corwin.

Calderón, M., August, D., Durán, D., Madden, N., Slavin, R., & Gil, M. (2003). *Spanish to English transitional reading: Teacher's manual.* Baltimore: The Success for All Foundation.

Calderón, M., Slavin, R., & Sánchez, M. (2011). Effective instruction for English learners. *The Future of Children, 21*(1), 103–127.

Calfee, R. (1977). Assessment of individual reading skills: Basic research and practical applications. In A. S. Reber & D. L. Scarborough (Eds.), *Toward a psychology of reading* (pp. 289–323). New York: Erlbaum.

California Department of Education. (n.d.a). *California English Language Development Test.* Accessed at www.cde.ca.gov/re/pr/celdt.asp on March 22, 2023.

California Department of Education. (n.d.b). *Culturally relevant pedagogy.* Accessed at www.cde.ca.gov/pd/ee/culturalrelevantpedagogy.asp on August 11, 2023.

California Department of Education. (n.d.c). *Multilingual education FAQs.* Accessed at www.cde.ca.gov/sp/ml/mlfaq.asp on September 1, 2024.

California Department of Education. (n.d.d). *NGSS for California public schools, K–12.* Accessed at www.cde.ca.gov/pd/ca/sc/ngssstandards.asp on March 18, 2024.

California Department of Education. (2014). *California English language development standards: Kindergarten through grade 12.* Sacramento, CA: Author. Accessed at www.cde.ca.gov/sp/ml/documents/eldstndspublication14.pdf on September 1, 2024.

California Department of Education. (2024, November 5). *Dual language immersion (DLI) program.* Accessed at www.cde.ca.gov/sp/ml/edgedli.asp on November 19, 2024.

Cambridge University Press. (2019, July). *Learning language in chunks.* Cambridge, England: Author. Accessed at www.cambridge.org/elt/blog/wp-content/uploads/2019/10/Learning-Language-in-Chunks.pdf on January 6, 2024.

Canagarajah, S. (2011). Translanguaging in the classroom: Emerging issues for research and pedagogy. *Applied Linguistics Review, 2,* 1–28.

Center for Applied Linguistics. (2016). *Annual report: 2015–2016.* Accessed at www.cal.org/wp-content/uploads/2022/05/CAL-Annual-Report-2015-16.pdf on October 16, 2024.

Chebbouba, S. (2023, February 21). *Japanese body language: A guide to nonverbal communication in Japan.* Accessed at https://arigatojapan.co.jp/japanese-body-language-nonverbal-communication-japan on September 6, 2024.

Cherry, K. (2023). *Understanding body language and facial expression.* Accessed at www.verywellmind.com/understand-body-language-and-facial-expressions-4147228 on October 20, 2024.

Cherry, M. A. (2019). *Hair love* (V. Harrison, Illus.). New York: Kokila.

Chiaet, J. (2013, October 4). Novel finding: Reading literary fiction improves empathy. *Scientific American.* Accessed at www.scientificamerican.com/article/novel-finding-reading-literary-fiction-improves-empathy on September 5, 2024.

Cho, Y., Kim, D., & Jeong, S. (2019). Evidence-based reading interventions for English language learners: A multilevel meta-analysis. *Heliyon, 7*(9), e07985.

Cho, K., & Krashen, S. D. (1994). Acquisition of vocabulary from the *Sweet Valley Kids* series: Adult ESL acquisition. *Journal of Reading, 37*(8), 662–667.

Chomsky, N. (1965). *Aspects of the theory of syntax*. Cambridge, MA: MIT Press.

Chomsky, N. (1968). *Language and mind*. New York: Harcourt, Brace & World.

Chomsky, N. (1975). *The logical structure of linguistic theory*. New York: Plenum Press.

Chomsky, N. (2000). *New horizons in the study of language and mind*. New York: Cambridge University Press.

Clay, M. M. (2000). *Running records for classroom teachers*. Portsmouth, NH: Heinemann.

Cole, J. (1992). *The Magic School Bus on the ocean floor* (B. Degen, Illus.). New York: Scholastic.

Colorín Colorado. (n.d.a.). *Sentence frames and sentence starters*. Accessed at www.colorincolorado.org/teaching-ells/ell-classroom-strategy-library/sentence-frames on December 4, 2024.

Colorín Colorado. (n.d.b). *What are BICS and CALP?* Accessed at www.colorincolorado.org/faq/what-are-bics-and-calp on September 18, 2024.

Colorín Colorado. (2018). *Cooperative learning strategies*. Accessed at www.colorincolorado.org/article/cooperative-learning-strategies on October 20, 2024.

Colorín Colorado. (2021). *6 strategies to help ELLs succeed in peer learning and collaboration*. Accessed at www.colorincolorado.org/article/6-strategies-help-ells-succeed-peer-learning-and-collaboration on September 7, 2024.

Colorín Colorado. (2023). *How to create a welcoming classroom environment for ELLs*. Accessed at www.colorincolorado.org/article/how-create-welcoming-classroom-environment on October 20, 2024.

Coniam, D. (1999). Voice recognition software accuracy with second language speakers of English. *System, 27*(1), 49–64.

Constantino, R., Lee, S.-Y., Cho, K.-S., & Krashen, S. D. (1997). Free voluntary reading as a predictor of TOEFL scores. *Applied Language Learning, 8*(1), 111–118.

Conzemius, A. E., & O'Neill, J. (2014). *The handbook for SMART school teams: Revitalizing best practices for collaboration* (2nd ed.). Bloomington, IN: Solution Tree Press.

Costa, A. L. (Ed.). (2008). *Developing minds: A resource book for teaching thinking* (3rd ed.). Alexandria, VA: ASCD.

Council of the Great City Schools. (2023). *A framework for foundational literacy skills instruction for English learners: Instructional practice and materials considerations*. Accessed at www.cgcs.org/cms/lib/DC00001581/Centricity/domain/35/publication%20docs/CGCS_Foundational%20Literacy%20Skills_Pub_v12.pdf on October 29, 2024.

Creese, A., & Blackledge, A. (2010). Translanguaging in the bilingual classroom: A pedagogy for learning and teaching? *The Modern Language Journal, 94*(1), 103–115.

Cronin, D. (2000). *Click, clack, moo: Cows that type* (B. Lewin, Illus.). New York: Simon & Schuster Books for Young Readers.

Crumlish, L. (2024, March 16). *The 5 stages of second language acquisition.* Accessed at https://bilingualkidspot.com/2018/09/19/5-stages-of-second-language-acquisition on December 18, 2023.

Cummins, J. (1984). *Bilingualism and special education: Issues in assessment and pedagogy.* San Diego, CA: College-Hill Press.

Cummins, J., & Swain, M. (1986). *Bilingualism in education: Aspects of theory, research, and practice.* New York: Longman.

D'Argenio, L. (2022, August 19). *Teaching writing to ESL/EFL students: Tips and activities for any level.* Accessed at https://bridge.edu/tefl/blog/teaching-writing-esl-students on September 18, 2024.

Dehghanzadeh, H., Fardanesh, H., Hatami, J., Talaee, E., & Noroozi, O. (2021). Using gamification to support learning English as a second language: A systematic review. *Computer Assisted Language Learning, 34*(7), 934–957. https://doi.org/10.1080/09588221.2019.1648298

de la Peña, M. (2015). *Last stop on Market Street* (C. Robinson, Illus.). New York: G. P. Putnam's Sons.

Derwing, T. M., Munro, M. J., & Carbonaro, M. (2000). Does popular speech recognition software work with ESL speech? *TESOL Quarterly, 34*(3), 592–603.

DeSalle, N., & Reed, D. K. (2021, October 26). *Learning English with your children and teens: Focus on language development during shared reading* [Blog post]. Accessed at https://irrc.education.uiowa.edu/blog/2021/10/learning-english-your-children-and-teens-focus-language-development-during-shared on November 8, 2023.

Diaz, L. (2022). *Paletero man!* (M. Player, Illus.; C. Tafolla, Trans.). New York: Harper.

Doran, G. T. (1981). There's a S.M.A.R.T. way to write management's goals and objectives. *Management Review, 70*(11), 35–36.

Dougherty, J. (2021). Translanguaging in action: Pedagogy that elevates. *ORTESOL Journal, 38*, 19–32.

Driscoll, L. (2018, July 30). *Visual memory—where 80% of learning happens.* Accessed at https://lorrainedriscoll.com/visual-memory-where-80-of-learning-happens on July 14, 2023.

Duchastel, P. (1979). Learning objectives and the organization of prose. *Journal of Educational Psychology, 71*(1), 100–106. https://doi.org/10.1037/0022-0663.71.1.100

Dunkin, S. (n.d.). *GLAD Corner: Deepen your use of the cooperative strip paragraph.* Accessed at https://ntcprojectglad.com/2020/04/30/glad-corner-deepen-your-use-of-the-cooperative-strip-paragraph on November 9, 2023.

Dutro, S. (2016). *Busting myths about integrated and dedicated English language development.* Vista, CA: E.L. Achieve. Accessed at https://drive.google.com/file/d/1gTbR2e929ReTIuYpHIDisBGqM-jstwz3/view on May 15, 2024.

Dutro, S., & Kinsella, K. (2010). English language development: Issues and implementation at grades 6–12. In F. Ong & V. Aguila (Eds.), *Improving education for English learners: Research-based approaches* (pp. 151–208). Sacramento, CA: California Department of Education.

Dutro, S., Levy, E., & Moore, D. W. (2011). Equipping adolescent English learners for academic achievement: An interview with Susana Dutro and Ellen Levy. *Journal of Adolescent and Adult Literacy, 55*(4), 339–342.

Dutro, S., & Moran, C. (2003). Rethinking English language instruction: An architectural approach. In G. C. Garcia (Ed.), *English learners: Reaching the highest level of English literacy* (pp. 227–258). Newark, DE: International Reading Association.

Dutro, S., Núñez, R. M., & Helman, L. (2016). Explicit language instruction: A key to academic success for English learners. In L. Helman (Ed.), *Literacy development with English learners: Research-based instruction in grades K–6* (2nd ed., pp. 43–77). New York: Guilford Press.

Echevarría, J. (2016, March 30). *Are language frames good for English learners?* [Blog post]. Accessed at www.janaechevarria.com/?p=191 on September 18, 2024.

Echevarría, J. (2021, November 30). *How does the science of reading apply to teaching multilingual learners?* [Blog post]. Accessed at www.janaechevarria.com/?p=2833 on May 15, 2024.

Echevarría, J., Vogt, M. E., & Short, D. (2017). *Making content comprehensible for English learners: The SIOP model* (5th ed.). Boston: Pearson.

Edelman, E. R., Amirazizi, S. A., Feinberg, D. K., Quirk, M., Scheller, J., Pagán, C. R., et al. (2022). A comparison of integrated and designated ELD models on second and third graders' oral English language proficiency. *TESOL Journal, 13*(3), Article e659.

Education Endowment Foundation. (2017, July). *Dialogic teaching: Evaluation report and executive summary.* London: Author. Accessed at https://d2tic4wvo1iusb.cloudfront.net/production/documents/projects/Dialogic_Teaching_Evaluation_Report.pdf?v=1689187525 on July 12, 2023.

Edutopia. (2018, November 16). *Scaffolding discussion skills with a Socratic circle* [Video file]. Accessed at www.youtube.com/watch?v=e3IBLKYaK1E on May 4, 2023.

E.L. Achieve. (n.d.). *Systematic ELD.* Accessed at www.elachieve.org/systematic-eld on December 18, 2023.

Ellis, N. (2003). Constructions, chunking, and connectionism: The emergence of second language structure. In C. J. Doughty, & M. Long (Eds.), *The handbook of second language acquisition* (pp. 63–103). Malden, MA: Blackwell.

English Learners Success Forum. (2020). *Guidelines for improving English language arts materials for English learners.* Albuquerque, NM: Author. Accessed at https://cdn.prod.website-files.com/5b43fc97fcf4773f14ee92f3/5e73a4231ef80672d63be713_ELSF%20ELA%20Guidelines.pdf on September 5, 2024.

ESL Kids Games. (2020, January). *ESL warmer: Draw me something.* Accessed at www.eslkidsgames.com/2020/01/esl-warmer-draw-me-something.html on January 6, 2024.

Everyday Speech. (n.d.). *Understanding the power of body language: A comprehensive lesson.* Accessed at https://everydayspeech.com/sel-implementation/understanding-the-power-of-body-language-a-comprehensive-lesson on October 16, 2024

Fabiny, A. (2015, February 14). *Music can boost memory and mood.* Accessed at www.health.harvard.edu/mind-and-mood/music-can-boost-memory-and-mood on July 2, 2023.

Fareed, M., Ashraf, A., & Bilal, M. (2016). ESL learners' writing skills: Problems, factors and suggestions. *Journal of Education and Social Sciences, 4*(2), 81–92.

Farr, T. (2020). *Teaching students to write with a reader in mind.* Accessed at https://medium.com/teaching-ela/teaching-students-to-write-with-a-reader-in-mind-aae2e3c46da4 on October 20, 2024.

Ferlazzo, L. (2016, March 30). *Peer review, Common Core, and ELLs* [Blog post]. Accessed at www.edutopia.org/blog/collaborative-peer-review-core-ells-larry-ferlazzo-katie-hull-sypnieski on January 6, 2024.

Ferlazzo, L. (2023, April 27). Listening is the key to teaching English-learners how to speak [Blog post]. *Education Week.* Accessed at www.edweek.org/teaching-learning/opinion-listening-is-the-key-to-teaching-english-learners-how-to-speak/2023/04 on September 9, 2024.

Fien, H., Smith, J. L. M., Smolkowski, K., Baker, S. K., Nelson, N. J., & Chaparro, E. (2015). An examination of the efficacy of a multitiered intervention on early reading outcomes for first grade students at-risk for reading difficulties. *Journal of Learning Disabilities, 48*, 602–621.

Fillmore, L. W. (1989). Teachability and second language acquisition. In M. L. Rice & R. L. Schiefelbusch (Eds.), *The teachability of language* (pp. 311–332). Baltimore: Brookes.

Fillmore, L. W., & Fillmore, C. J. (2021, December). *What does text complexity mean for English learners and language minority students?* Stanford, CA: Stanford University. Accessed at https://ul.stanford.edu/sites/default/files/resource/2021-12/06-LWF%20CJF%20Text%20Complexity%20FINAL_0.pdf on July 8, 2024.

Fink, L. (2017, December 17). *The relationship between writing and reading* [Blog post]. Accessed at https://ncte.org/blog/2017/12/relationship-writing-reading on October 5, 2023.

Fisher, D., & Frey, N. (2021). *Better learning through structured teaching: A framework for the gradual release of responsibility* (3rd ed.). Arlington, VA: ASCD.

Fleming, N. D., & Mills, C. (1992). Not another inventory, rather a catalyst for reflection. *To Improve the Academy, 11*(1), 137–155.

Fleta, T. (2017). The sounds of picturebooks for English language learning. *Children's Literature in English Language Education Journal, 5*(1), 21–43.

Foorman, B. R., Herrara, S., Petscher, Y., Mitchell, A., & Truckenmiller, A. (2015). The structure of oral language and reading and their relation to comprehension in kindergarten through grade 2. *Reading and Writing, 28*(5), 655–681.

Foorman, B. R., Koon, S., Petscher, Y., Mitchell, A., & Truckenmiller, A. (2015). Examining general and specific factors in the dimensionality of oral language and reading in 4th–10th grades. *Journal of Educational Psychology, 107*(3), 884–899.

Gajjar, B. (2023, March 8). *An ultimate guide to international business language* [Blog post]. Accessed at www.usemultiplier.com/blog/international-business-language on August 30, 2024.

Gallagher, K., & Kittle, P. (2018). *180 days: Two teachers and the quest to engage and empower adolescents.* Portsmouth, NH: Heinemann.

Galletly, S. A., & Knight, B. A. (2013). Because trucks aren't bicycles: Orthographic complexity as a disregarded variable in reading research. *Australian Educational Researcher, 40*(2), 173–194.

Gardner, H. (1983). *Frames of mind: The theory of multiple intelligences.* New York: Basic Books.

Gardner, H. (2011). *Frames of mind: The theory of multiple intelligences* (3rd ed.). New York: Basic Books.

Gay, G. (2015). The importance of multicultural education. In A. C. Ornstein, E. F. Pajak, & S. B. Ornstein (Eds.), *Contemporary issues in curriculum* (6th ed., pp. 211–217). Boston: Pearson.

Gebre, E. H., & Polman, J. L. (2020). From "context" to "active contextualization": Fostering learner agency in contextualizing learning through science news reporting. *Learning, Culture and Social Interaction, 24,* Article 100374. https://doi.org/10.1016/j.lcsi.2019.100374

Gewertz, C. (2020, January 3). How much should teachers talk in the classroom? Much less, some say. *Education Week.* Accessed at www.edweek.org/leadership/how-much-should-teachers-talk-in-the-classroom-much-less-some-say/2019/12 on October 2, 2023.

Ghazi-Saidi, L., & Ansaldo, A. I. (2017). Second language word learning through repetition and imitation: Functional networks as a function of learning phase and language distance. *Frontiers in Human Neuroscience, 11,* Article 463.

Gilbert, F. (2017, April 3). *Improving students' reading using reciprocal teaching* [Blog post]. Accessed at https://creativewritingandeducation.wordpress.com/2017/04/03/improving-students-reading-using-reciprocal-teaching on October 18, 2023.

Gilje, Ø., & Erstad, O. (2017). Authenticity, agency and enterprise education studying learning in and out of school. *International Journal of Educational Research, 84,* 58–67.

Giovanni, N. (2020). *Make me rain: Poems and prose.* New York: William Morrow.

Gonsalves, E. (2021). *Supporting reading fluency and prosody of English language learners* [Master's thesis, California State University, Stanislaus]. ScholarWorks. https://scholarworks.calstate.edu/concern/theses/qf85nh218?locale=en

González, J. M. (1974). *A developmental and sociological rationale for culture based curricula and cultural context teaching in the early instruction of Mexican American children* [Doctoral dissertation, University of Massachusetts Amherst]. ScholarWorks. https://scholarworks.umass.edu/entities/publication/52c64f25-af64-41a4-8664-112f7a9f98f8

Gonzalez, V. (2019, March 9). *Sentence stems or sentence frames* [Blog post]. Accessed at www.valentinaesl.com/blog/sentence-stems-or-sentence-frames on October 31, 2023.

Gort, M., & Sembiante, S. F. (2015). Navigating hybridized language learning spaces through translanguaging pedagogy: Dual language preschool teachers' languaging practices in support of emergent bilingual children's performance of academic discourse. *International Multilingual Research Journal, 9*(1), 7–25. https://doi.org/10.1080/19313152.2014.981775

Goswami, U., & Bryant, P. (1990). *Phonological skills and learning to read*. Hillsdale, NJ: Erlbaum.

Gottlieb, M. (2016). *Assessing English language learners: Bridges to educational equity* (2nd ed.). Thousand Oaks, CA: Corwin.

Graham, S., Kiuhara, S. A., & MacKay, M. (2020). The effects of writing on learning in science, social studies, and mathematics: A meta-analysis. *Review of Educational Research, 90*(2), 179–226.

Grande, R. (2006). *Across a hundred mountains*. New York: Atria Books.

Grant, L. T., Yoo, M. S., Fetman, L., & Garza, V. (2021). In-service teachers' perceptions of their preparation to work with learners of English. *Educational Research: Theory and Practice, 32*(1), 62–71.

Grant, M. G. (2019, October 7). *Principles of teaching writing* [Blog post]. Accessed at https://mgailgrant.com/?p=325 on January 6, 2024.

Graves, D. H. (1985). All children can write. *Learning Disabilities Focus, 1*(1), 36–43.

Grimes, N. (2022). *Words with wings*. New York: Wordsong.

Guthrie, J. T., & Humenick, N. M. (2004). Motivating students to read: Evidence for classroom practices that increase motivation and achievement. In P. McCardle & V. Chhabra (Eds.), *The voice of evidence in reading research* (pp. 329–354). Baltimore: Brookes.

Hafiz. (1999). *The gift: Poems by the great Sufi master* (D. J. Ladinsky, Trans.). New York: Arkana.

Hafiz. (2023). *The divan of Hafiz: Edition of complete poetry* (H. W. Clarke, Trans.). Dallas, TX: Persian Learning Center.

Hale, S. J. (1830). *Poems for our children*. Boston: Marsh, Capen & Lyon.

Halliwell-Phillipps, J. O. (Ed.). (1886). The three little pigs. In *The nursery rhymes of England* (pp. 37–41). New York: Warne.

Hammond, Z. (2015). *Culturally responsive teaching and the brain: Promoting authentic engagement and rigor among culturally and linguistically diverse students.* Thousand Oaks, CA: Corwin.

Hampton-Brown. (2000). *Language transfer issues: For English learners.* Carmel, CA: Author.

Hattie, J. A. C. (2012). *Visible learning for teachers: Maximizing impact on learning.* New York: Routledge.

Hattie, J. A. C. (2015). The applicability of Visible Learning to higher education. *Scholarship of Teaching and Learning in Psychology, 1*(1), 79–91. https://doi.org/10.1037/stl0000021

Hidalgo, N. M. (1993). Multicultural teacher introspection. In T. Perry & J. W. Fraser (Eds.), *Freedom's plow: Teaching in the multicultural classroom* (pp. 99–106). New York: Routledge.

Hiebert, J., & Grouws, D. A. (2007). The effects of classroom mathematics teaching on students' learning. In F. Lester (Ed.), *Second handbook of research on mathematics teaching and learning* (pp. 371–404). Charlotte, NC: Information Age.

Higgins, K. M., Harris, N. A., & Kuehn, L. L. (1994). Placing assessment into the hands of young children: A study of student-generated criteria and self-assessment. *Educational Assessment, 2*(4), 309–324.

Ho, J. (2021). *Eyes that kiss in the corners* (D. Ho, Illus.). New York: Harper.

Hopkins, E. (2004). *Crank.* New York: Simon Pulse.

Hopman, E. W. M., & MacDonald, M. C. (2018). Production practice during language learning improves comprehension. *Psychological Science, 29*(6), 961–971. https://doi.org/10.1177/0956797618754486

Huynh, T. (2022, February 9). *Incorporating students' native languages to enhance their learning.* Accessed at www.edutopia.org/article/incorporating-students-native-languages-enhance-their-learning on September 18, 2024.

Illinois State Board of Education. (n.d.). *Collaborative learning guide.* Accessed at www.isbe.net/Documents/collaboration-guide.pdf on September 16, 2024.

Intercultural Development Research Association. (n.d.). *The six levels of culture.* Accessed at www.idra.org/resource-center/the-six-levels-of-culture on August 30, 2024.

International Center for Language Studies. (2024, August 20). *Most spoken languages in the world* [Blog post]. Accessed at www.icls.edu/blog/most-spoken-languages-in-the-world on August 30, 2024.

IRIS Center. (2011a). Page 2: Second language acquisition. In *Teaching English language learners: Effective instructional practices* [Module]. Accessed at https://iris.peabody.vanderbilt.edu/module/ell/cresource/q1/p02 on September 6, 2024.

IRIS Center. (2011b). Page 9: Differentiate instruction. In *Teaching English language learners: Effective instructional practices* [Module]. Accessed at https://iris.peabody.vanderbilt.edu/module/ell/cresource/q2/p09/#content on September 6, 2024.

IRIS Center. (2015). Page 3: Importance of home language maintenance. In *Dual language learners with disabilities: Supporting young children in the classroom* [Module]. Accessed at https://iris.peabody.vanderbilt.edu/module/dll/cresource/q2/p03 on September 6, 2024.

IRIS Center. (2018). *Fundamental skill sheet: Wait-time.* Accessed at https://iris.peabody.vanderbilt.edu/wp-content/uploads/misc_media/fss/pdfs/2018/fss_wait_time.pdf on September 2, 2024.

Irujo, S. (n.d.). *What does research tell us about teaching reading to English language learners?* Accessed at www.readingrockets.org/article/what-does-research-tell-us-about-teaching-reading-english-language-learners on May 8, 2023.

Ivey, G., & Johnston, P. H. (2015). Engaged reading as a collaborative transformative practice. *Journal of Literacy Research, 47*(3), 297–327. https://doi.org/10.1177/1086296X15619731

Jaggars, S. S., Edgecombe, N., & Stacey, G. W. (2013, April). *Creating an effective online instructor presence.* Accessed at https://files.eric.ed.gov/fulltext/ED542146.pdf on October 29, 2024.

K12Reader. (n.d.). *The relationship between reading and writing.* Accessed at www.k12reader.com/the-relationship-between-reading-and-writing on September 18, 2024.

Katz, S. B. (2012). *My mama Earth* (M. Launay, Illus.). Cambridge, MA: Barefoot Books.

Katz, S. B. (2022). *Strong girls in history: 15 young achievers you should know.* Oakland, CA: Rockridge Press.

Kaur, H. (2018, June 15). *FYI: English isn't the official language of the United States.* Accessed at www.cnn.com/2018/05/20/us/english-us-official-language-trnd/index.html on September 2, 2023.

Kawasaki, J. (2020, July 8). *What is TPR for teaching English and how can I use it?* [Blog post]. Accessed at https://bridge.edu/tefl/blog/what-is-tpr-for-teaching-english-and-how-can-i-use-it on August 24, 2023.

Keene, E. O., & Zimmermann, S. (2007). *Mosaic of thought: The power of comprehension strategy instruction* (2nd ed.). Portsmouth, NH: Heinemann.

Kennedy Center. (n.d.). *Your brain on music: The sound system between your ears.* Accessed at www.kennedy-center.org/education/resources-for-educators/classroom-resources/media-and-interactives/media/music/your-brain-on-music/your-brain-on-music/your-brain-on-music-the-sound-system-between-your-ears on August 11, 2024.

King, M. L., Jr. (1963, August). *Letter from Birmingham Jail.* Accessed at www.csuchico.edu/iege/_assets/documents/susi-letter-from-birmingham-jail.pdf on January 6, 2024.

Kostadinovska-Stojchevska, B., & Popovikj, I. (2019). Teacher talking time vs. student talking time: Moving from teacher-centered classroom to learner-centered classroom. *The International Journal of Applied Language Studies and Culture, 2*(2), 25–31.

Kozloff, M. (2002, September 12). *A whole language catalogue of the grotesque* [Blog post]. Accessed at http://people.uncw.edu/kozloffm/wlquotes.html on October 3, 2024.

Krashen, S. D. (1982). *Principles and practice in second language acquisition*. Elmsford, NY: Pergamon Press.

Krashen, S. D. (1989). We acquire vocabulary and spelling by reading: Additional evidence for the input hypothesis. *Modern Language Journal, 73*(4), 440–464.

Krashen, S. D. (2017, July 17). The case for comprehensible input. *Language Magazine*. Accessed at www.languagemagazine.com/2017/07/17/case-for-comprehension on May 15, 2024.

Krashen, S. D. (2018, October 26). *The case against intensive phonics*. Accessed at www.sdkrashen.com/content/articles/the_case_against_intensive_phonics_.pdf on September 12, 2023.

Krashen, S. D. (2019, December 25). *Optimal input* [Video file]. Accessed at www.youtube.com/watch?v=S_j4JELf8DA on May 8, 2023.

Krashen, S. D. (2021, January 11). *Letter to the editor: More books, not more phonics*. Accessed at www.edweek.org/teaching-learning/opinion-more-books-not-more-phonics/2021/01 on August 11, 2023.

Krashen, S. D., Lee, S., & Lao, C. (2018). *Comprehensible and compelling: The causes and effects of free voluntary reading*. Santa Barbara, CA: Libraries Unlimited.

Krashen, S. D., & Mason, B. (2022). Foundations for story-listening: Some basics. *Language Issues, 1*(4), 1–5.

Krashen, S. D., Mason, B., & Smith, K. (2018). Some new terminology: Comprehension-aiding supplementation and form-focusing supplementation. *Language Learning and Teaching, 60*(6), 12–13.

Kucan, L. (2012). What is most important to know about vocabulary? *The Reading Teacher, 65*(6), 360–366.

Kusfitriyatna, F., Evenddy, S. S., & Utomo, D. W. (2021). The effect of using cloze passage technique toward students' reading comprehension in narrative text. *Journal of English Language Learning, 5*(1), 49–62.

Ladson-Billings, G. (1995). But that's just good teaching! The case for culturally relevant pedagogy. *Theory into Practice, 34*(3), 159–165.

Lambert, W. E. (1974). Culture and language as factors in learning and education. In F. E. Aboud & R. D. Meade (Eds.), *Cultural factors in learning and education* (pp. 91–122). Bellingham, WA: Fifth Western Washington Symposium on Learning.

Lastiri, L. (2021, December 24). *Average reading speed by age: Are you fast enough?* Accessed at https://irisreading.com/average-reading-speed-by-age-are-you-fast-enough on October 2, 2024.

Lawrence, J. F., Knoph, R., McIlraith, A., Kulesz, P. A., & Francis, D. J. (2021). Reading comprehension and academic vocabulary: Exploring relations of item features and reading proficiency. *Reading Research Quarterly, 57*(2), 669–690.

Leonard, D. (2023, September 8). *The science of belonging and connection*. Accessed at www.edutopia.org/article/the-science-of-belonging-and-connection on December 20, 2023.

Lesley University. (n.d.). *A primer on guided reading.* Accessed at https://lesley.edu/article/a-primer-on-guided-reading on January 6, 2024.

Levins, The. (n.d.). *The Levins.* Accessed at https://thelevinsmusic.com/home on December 5, 2024.

Lewis, R. (2020, November 4). *What is comprehensible input and why does it matter for language learning?* [Blog post]. Accessed at www.leonardoenglish.com/blog/comprehensible-input on December 18, 2023.

Lexia. (n.d.). *Lexia LETRS professional learning (pre-K–5).* Accessed at www.lexialearning.com/letrs?gclid=CjwKCAjwoIqhBhAGEiwArXT7K-Oxxx0F-q4sLCY3fffmds19SKYKi9YSsIf3vzMgRhoHJveZ9XBW4BoCc78QAvD_BwE on July 8, 2023.

Liberman, I. Shankweiler, D., Fischer, F. & Carter, B. (1974). Explicit syllable and phonemes segmentation in the young child. *Journal of Experimental Child Psychology, 18,* 201–212.

Lindstrom, C. (2020). *We are water protectors* (M. Goade, Illus.). New York: Roaring Brook Press.

Literacy Minnesota. (2017, July). *Lower the affective filter.* Accessed at www.literacymn.org/lower-affective-filter on July 12, 2023.

López, L. M., & Páez, M. M. (2021). *Teaching dual language learners: What early childhood educators need to know.* Baltimore: Brookes.

Lov, A. (2023). *The overidentification of ELLs as special education students* [Master's thesis capstone project, State University of New York Brockport]. SUNY Open Access Repository. Accessed at https://soar.suny.edu/handle/20.500.12648/11070https://scholarworks.calstate.edu/downloads/j9602601n on April 4, 2023.

Lubliner, S., & Hiebert, E. H. (2011). An analysis of English–Spanish cognates as a source of general academic language. *Bilingual Research Journal, 34*(1), 76–93. https://doi.org/10.1080/15235882.2011.568589

The Madera Tribune. (n.d.). *New way of thinking, learning at Madera elementary school.* Accessed at www.maderatribune.com/single-post/2017/10/04/new-way-of-thinking-learning on October 21, 2024.

Makalela, L. (2015). Moving out of linguistic boxes: The effects of translanguaging strategies for multilingual classrooms. *Language and Education, 29*(3), 200–217. https://doi.org/10.1080/09500782.2014.994524

Marshall, B., & Drummond, M. J. (2006). How teachers engage with assessment for learning: Lessons from the classroom. *Research Papers in Education, 21*(2), 133–149.

Marzano, R. J. (2009). Six steps to better vocabulary instruction. *Educational Leadership, 67*(1), 83–84.

Marzano, R. J., & Pickering, D. J. (n.d.). *Tips from Dr. Marzano.* Accessed at www.marzanoresources.com/resources/tips/hec_tips_archive on September 5, 2024.

Marzano, R. J., Pickering, D. J., & Pollock, J. E. (2001). *Classroom instruction that works: Research-based strategies for increasing student achievement.* Arlington, VA: ASCD.

Mason, B. (2020, June 4). Curbing implicit bias: What works and what doesn't. *Knowable Magazine.* Accessed at https://knowablemagazine.org/article/mind/2020/how-to-curb-implicit-bias on October 19, 2023.

Masrul, M., & Rasyidah, U. (2022). The Writers' Workshop impact to the writing of English foreign language (EFL) learner in Indonesia. *Tamaddun, 22*(2), 166–182.

MATHCOUNTS. (n.d.). *Salute.* Accessed at www.mathcounts.org/sites/default/files/Salute_1.pdf on May 15, 2023.

Mattos, M., Buffum, A., Malone, J., Cruz, L. F., Dimich, N., & Schuhl, S. (2025). *Taking action: A handbook for RTI at Work* (2nd ed.). Bloomington, IN: Solution Tree Press.

McEwan, E. K. (n.d.). *Root words, suffixes, and prefixes.* Accessed at www.readingrockets.org/topics/spelling-and-word-study/articles/root-words-suffixes-and-prefixes on September 6, 2024.

McGraw Hill. (2017, August 14). *Flags and holidays won't make your classroom multicultural.* Accessed at https://medium.com/inspired-ideas-prek-12/flags-and-holidays-wont-make-your-classroom-multicultural-cc57775c36ba on October 20, 2023.

McGraw Hill. (2021, November 10). *How to teach English learners based on the science of reading: An interview with Dr. Jana Echevarría.* Accessed at https://medium.com/inspired-ideas-prek-12/how-to-teach-teaching-english-learners-based-on-the-science-of-reading-df6be2c5b052 on December 20, 2023.

McSpadden, K. (2015, May 14). You now have a shorter attention span than a goldfish. *TIME.* Accessed at https://time.com/3858309/attention-spans-goldfish on September 2, 2024.

Merrill, S., & Gonser, S. (2021, September 16). *The importance of student choice across all grade levels.* Accessed at www.edutopia.org/article/importance-student-choice-across-all-grade-levels on September 2, 2023.

Merrimack College School of Education and Social Policy. (2019, May 8). *5 reasons reading is so important for student success.* Accessed at https://online.merrimack.edu/student-literacy-important-for-student-success on January 8, 2024.

Miles, J., & Bailey-McKenna, M.-C. (2016). Giving refugee students a strong head start: The LEAD program. *TESL Canada Journal, 33*(10), 109–128. Accessed at https://teslcanadajournal.ca/index.php/tesl/article/view/1249/1072 on December 19, 2023.

Miller, D. (2017, October 15). *On the level* [Blog post]. Accessed at https://nerdybookclub.wordpress.com/2017/10/15/on-the-level-by-donalyn-miller on September 18, 2024.

Minocha, T. (2024, February 6). *The U.S. education system fails to support non-native speakers.* Accessed at https://emorywheel.com/the-u-s-education-system-fails-to-support-non-native-speakers on February 27, 2024.

Mittal, R. (2014). Teaching English through poetry: A powerful medium for learning second language. *IOSR Journal of Humanities and Social Science, 19*(5), 21–23.

Montelongo, J. A., Hernández, A. C., & Herter, R. J. (2016). English-Spanish cognates in the Charlotte Zolotow Award picture books: Vocabulary, morphology, and orthography lessons for Latino ELLs. *Reading Horizons, 55*(1), 1–15.

Morgan, C. (n.d.). *How to write objectives for lesson plans with embedded language support* [Blog post]. Accessed at www.theallaccessclassroom.com/how-to-write-objectives-for-lesson-plans-with-embedded-language-support on October 22, 2023.

Moss, C. M., Brookhart, S. M., & Long, B. A. (2011). Knowing your learning target. *Educational Leadership, 68*(6), 66–69.

Musanti, S. I., & Rodríguez, A. D. (2017). Translanguaging in bilingual teacher preparation: Exploring pre-service bilingual teachers' academic writing. *Bilingual Research Journal, 40*(1), 38–54. https://doi.org/10.1080/15235882.2016.1276028

Najarro, I. (2023, February 21). The English learner population is growing. Is teacher training keeping pace? *Education Week.* Accessed at www.edweek.org/teaching-learning/the-english-learner-population-is-growing-is-teacher-training-keeping-pace/2023/02 on February 26, 2024.

Najarro, I. (2024, April 30). English learners' proficiency scores are still in decline, data find. *Education Week.* Accessed at www.edweek.org/teaching-learning/english-learners-proficiency-scores-are-still-in-decline-data-find/2024/04 on July 3, 2024.

National Assessment of Educational Progress. (n.d.). *National achievement-level results.* Accessed at www.nationsreportcard.gov/reading_2017?grade=4 on October 29, 2024.

National Board for Professional Teaching Standards. (n.d.). *Five core propositions.* Accessed at www.nbpts.org/certification/five-core-propositions on February 27, 2024.

National Center for Education Statistics. (2024, May). *English learners in public schools.* Accessed at https://nces.ed.gov/programs/coe/indicator/cgf on October 20, 2023.

National Center on Improving Literacy. (2022). *The science of reading: The basics* [Infographic]. Washington, DC: Author. Accessed at https://improvingliteracy.org/brief/science-reading-basics/index.html on September 5, 2024.

National Clearinghouse for Bilingual Education. (2000, January). Why is it important to maintain the native language? *IDRA Newsletter.* Accessed at www.idra.org/resource-center/why-is-it-important-to-maintain-the-native-language on October 18, 2023.

National Education Association. (2020, July). *English language learners.* Accessed at www.nea.org/resource-library/english-language-learners on January 6, 2024.

National Geographic Learning. (2020). *WIDA PRIME 2020: Publisher report.* Accessed at www.eltngl.com/assets/downloads/lift_pro0000009186/lift_wida_prime_2020.pdf on March 18, 2024.

National Governors Association Center for Best Practices & Council of Chief State School Officers. (2010). *Common Core State Standards for English language arts and literacy in history/social studies, science, and technical subjects.* Washington, DC: Authors. Accessed at https://learning.ccsso.org/wp-content/uploads/2022/11/ELA_Standards1.pdf on October 22, 2023.

National Institutes of Health. (2021, June 8). *Study shows how taking short breaks may help our brains learn new skills.* Accessed at www.nih.gov/news-events/news-releases/study-shows-how-taking-short-breaks-may-help-our-brains-learn-new-skills on January 23, 2023.

National Reading Panel. (2000). *Teaching children to read: An evidence-based assessment of the scientific research literature on reading and its implications for reading instruction.* Bethesda, MD: Author.

Newell, W. W. (1884). *Games and songs of American children, collected and compared by W. W. Newell.* New York: Harper & Brothers.

New York State Education Department. (n.d.). *Multilingual learner/English language learner (MLL/ELL) classroom observation tool.* Accessed at www.nysed.gov/sites/default/files/programs/bilingual-ed/classroom-observation-tool-appendix-b-final-a.pdf on December 22, 2023.

NGSS Lead States. (2013). *Next Generation Science Standards: For states, by states.* Washington, DC: The National Academies Press.

Nickelsen, L., & Dickson, M. (2019). *Teaching with the instructional cha-chas: Four steps to make learning stick.* Bloomington, IN: Solution Tree Press.

Nickelsen, L., & Dickson, M. (2022). *The literacy triangle: 50+ high-impact strategies to integrate reading, discussing, and writing in K–8 classrooms.* Bloomington, IN: Solution Tree Press.

Ninsuwan, P. (2015). The effectiveness of teaching English by using reading aloud technique towards EFL beginners. *Procedia: Social and Behavioral Sciences, 197,* 1835–1840.

Northwest Evaluation Association. (2023). *Building fluent readers lesson plan tool.* Portland, OR: Author. Accessed at www.nwea.org/resource-center/guide/79209/building-fluent-readers-lesson-plan-tool.pdf on September 6, 2024.

Nyong'o, L. (2019). *Sulwe* (V. Harrison, Illus.). New York: Simon & Schuster Books for Young Readers.

Octavio, C. (2018). *Hispanic children thrown into limbo: Language ideologies of Spanish heritage speakers and their English peers in a monolingual and a bilingual school in Indiana* [Doctoral dissertation, Purdue University]. Purdue e-Pubs. https://docs.lib.purdue.edu/open_access_dissertations/2038

Ogle, D. M. (1986). K-W-L: A teaching model that develops active reading of expository text. *The Reading Teacher, 39*(6), 564–570.

OnTESOL. (2021). *Five reasons why the 70/30 rule is useful in ESL conversation class.* Accessed at https://ontesol.com/blog/how-to-teach-english/teaching-english-conversation/five-reasons-why-the-70-30-rule-is-useful-in-esl-conversation-classes on October 29, 2024.

Orr, R. B., Csikari, M. M., Freeman, S., & Rodriguez, M. C. (2022). Writing and using learning objectives. *CBE—Life Sciences Education, 21*(3), Article fe3.

Oteir, I. N., & Al-Otaibi, A. N. (2019). Foreign language anxiety: A systematic review. *Arab World English Journal, 10*(3), 309–317.

Owen-Hill, A. (2024, June 11). *Why listening is important for language learners* [Blog post]. Accessed at www.fluentu.com/blog/learn/the-importance-of-listening-in-language-learning on September 6, 2024.

Oyler, D. R., & Romanelli, F. (2014). The fact of ignorance: Revisiting the Socratic method as a tool for teaching critical thinking. *American Journal of Pharmaceutical Education, 78*(7), 144.

Padeliadu, S., & Giazitzidou, S. (2018). A synthesis of research on reading fluency development: Study of eight meta-analyses. *European Journal of Special Education Research, 3*(4), 232–256.

Paris, D. (2012). Culturally sustaining pedagogy: A needed change in stance, terminology, and practice. *Educational Researcher, 41*(3), 93–97.

Pearson, D. P., Palincsar, A. S., Biancarosa, G., & Berman, A. I. (2020). *Reaping the rewards of the reading for understanding initiative.* Accessed at https://naeducation.org/wp-content/uploads/2020/07/NAEd-Reaping-the-Rewards-of-the-Reading-for-Understanding-Initiative.pdf on October 29, 2024.

Pendergast, M., Bingham, G., & Patton-Terry, N. (2015). Examining the relationship between emergent literacy skills and invented spelling in prekindergarten Spanish-speaking dual language learners. *Early Education and Development, 26*(2), 264–285.

PEN International. (2024, April 23). *PEN's global community condemns book bans around the world.* Accessed at www.pen-international.org/news/pens-global-community-condemns-book-ban-around-the-world on September 5, 2024.

Pepler, D. J., & Bierman, K. L. (2018, November). *With a little help from my friends: The importance of peer relationships for social-emotional development.* University Park, PA: Edna Bennett Pierce Prevention Research Center. Accessed at https://prevention.psu.edu/wp-content/uploads/2022/05/rwjf450248-PeerRelationships-1.pdf on September 5, 2024.

Piaget, J. (1936). *Origins of intelligence in the child.* London: Routledge & Kegan Paul.

Piaget, J. (2001). *The language and thought of the child* (3rd ed.; M. Gabain & R. Gabain, Trans.). New York: Routledge.

Pinkney, A. D. (2021). *Bright brown baby: A treasury* (B. Pinkney, Illus.). New York: Orchard Books.

Poole, G. A., & Sahakyan, N. (2024, April). *Examining English learner testing, proficiency, and growth: Continued trends since the COVID-19 pandemic* (WIDA Research Report No. RR-2024-1). Madison, WI: Wisconsin Center for Education Research. Accessed at https://wida.wisc.edu/sites/default/files/resource/Research-Report-Examining-English-Learner-Testing-Proficiency-Growth-2024.pdf on September 5, 2024.

Prutting, C. A., & Kirchner, D. M. (1987). A clinical appraisal of the pragmatic aspects of language. *Journal of Speech and Hearing Disorders, 52*(2), 105–119.

Ramirez-Espinola, M. (2023, July 11). *Teaching Tuesday: How poetry can support ELLs and diverse learners* [Blog post]. Accessed at www.gcu.edu/blog/teaching-school-administration/teaching-tuesday-how-poetry-can-support-ells-and-diverse on November 9, 2023.

Raymond, P. (1988). Cloze procedure in the teaching of reading. *TESL Canada Journal*, 6(1), 91–97. Accessed at https://files.eric.ed.gov/fulltext/EJ387352.pdf on June 19, 2023.

The Reading League. (n.d.). *What is the science of reading?* Accessed at www.thereadingleague.org/what-is-the-science-of-reading on October 21, 2024.

The Reading League. (2023). *Curriculum evaluation guidelines: Reviewer workbook.* Accessed at www.thereadingleague.org/curriculum-evaluation-guidelines on October 29, 2024.

The Reading League & National Committee for Effective Literacy. (2023). *Joint statement: Understanding the difference—The science of reading and implementation for English learners/emergent bilinguals (ELs/EBs)*. Accessed at www.thereadingleague.org/wp-content/uploads/2023/09/TRLC-ELEB-Understanding-the-Difference-The-Science-of-Reading-and-Implementation.pdf on September 5, 2024.

Regional Educational Laboratory Program. (2021, March 2). *Writing with authenticity and choice are more important than ever* [Blog post]. Accessed at https://ies.ed.gov/ncee/rel/Products/Region/midatlantic/Blog/30150 on July 18, 2024.

Reinhart, M. (2023). *Teeth, tentacles, and tail fins: A wild ocean pop-up.* San Rafael, CA: Insight Kids.

Relocate Magazine. (2022). *Comparing the US and UK education systems.* Accessed at www.relocatemagazine.com/reeditor-09-d3-2015-7523-comparing-the-us-and-uk-education-systems on October 20, 2024.

Resnick, L. B., Asterhan, C. S. C., & Clarke, S. N. (2018). *Accountable Talk: Instructional dialogue that builds the mind.* Geneva, Switzerland: UNESCO International Bureau of Education. Accessed at https://unesdoc.unesco.org/ark:/48223/pf0000262675 on January 6, 2024.

Richardson, J. (n.d.). *Resources.* Accessed at www.janrichardsonreading.com/copy-of-sample-meal-plan on January 6, 2024.

Richardson, J. (2023, November 28). *How to address text complexity and help students understand what they read* [Blog post]. Accessed at www.nwea.org/blog/2023/how-to-address-text-complexity-and-help-students-understand-what-they-read on September 6, 2024.

Riches, A. (2021, April 27). *Classroom pedagogy: Why talk is more important than ever.* Accessed at www.sec-ed.co.uk/content/best-practice/classroom-pedagogy-why-talk-is-more-important-than-ever on September 2, 2024.

Ross, J. A., Hogaboam-Gray, A., & Rolheiser, C. (2002). Student self-evaluation in grade 5–6 mathematics: Effects on problem-solving achievement. *Educational Assessment*, 8(1), 43–59.

Ross, J. A., & Starling, M. (2008). Self-assessment in a technology-supported environment: The case of grade 9 geography. *Assessment in Education, 15*(2), 183–199.

Rowe, M. B. (1972, April). *Wait-time and rewards as instructional variables, their influence in language, logic, and fate control* [Paper presentation]. National Association for Research in Science Teaching meeting, Chicago.

Rucker, N. W. (2019, December 10). *Getting started with culturally responsive teaching.* Accessed at www.edutopia.org/article/getting-started-culturally-responsive-teaching on February 25, 2024.

Rumi, J. A.-D. M. (2004). *The essential Rumi* (New expanded ed.; C. Barks, Trans.). San Francisco: HarperOne.

Sahadeo-Turner, T., & Marzano, R. J. (2015). *Processing new information: Classroom techniques to help students engage with new content.* West Palm Beach, FL: Learning Sciences.

Saleem, A., Rana, S., & Bashir, M. (2022). Role of non-verbal communication as a supplementary tool to verbal communication in ESL classrooms: A case study. *Propel Journal of Academic Research, 2*(2), 39–52.

Sanchez, C. (2017, February 23). *English language learners: How your state is doing.* Accessed at www.npr.org/sections/ed/2017/02/23/512451228/5-million-english-language-learners-a-vast-pool-of-talent-at-risk on January 6, 2024.

Scardina, K., & Johnson, J. (2024, June 20). Integrated English language development. *Language Magazine.* Accessed at www.languagemagazine.com/2024/06/20/integrated-english-language-development on September 2, 2024.

Scholastic. (n.d.). *The power of reading choice, time, and pleasure.* Accessed at http://teacher.scholastic.com/education/classroom-library/pdfs/The-Power-of-Reading-Choice.pdf?esp=TSO/ib/202104////label/card/classroom/reading on February 25, 2024.

Schütz, R. E. (2019). *Stephen Krashen's theory of second language acquisition.* Accessed at www.sk.com.br/sk-krash-english.html on December 18, 2023.

Schwartz, S. (2020, December 16). Is this the end of "three cueing"? *Education Week.* Accessed at www.edweek.org/teaching-learning/is-this-the-end-of-three-cueing/2020/12 on October 22, 2023.

Schwartz, S. (2022, April 21). The "science of reading" and English-language learners: What the research says. *Education Week.* Accessed at www.edweek.org/teaching-learning/the-science-of-reading-and-english-language-learners-what-the-research-says/2022/04 on January 8, 2024.

Schwarz, J. (2003, July 14). *Social interaction plays key role in how infants learn language, studies show.* Accessed at www.washington.edu/news/2003/07/14/social-interaction-plays-key-role-in-how-infants-learn-language-studies-show on September 16, 2024.

Sclafani, C. (2017). Strategies for educators of bilingual students: A critical review of literature. *International Journal of Education and Literacy Studies, 5*(2), 1–8.

Seidel, T., Rimmele, R., & Prenzel, M. (2005). Clarity and coherence of lesson goals as a scaffold for student learning. *Learning and Instruction, 15*(6), 539–556.

Shelley, M. W. (1818). *Frankenstein; Or, the modern Prometheus*. London: Lackington, Hughes, Harding, Mavor, & Jones.

Shute, V. J. (2008). Focus on formative feedback. *Review of Educational Research, 78*(1), 153–189.

Silverzweig, Z. (2020, October 14). *English is harder to read than other languages* [Blog post]. Accessed at https://blog.tinyivy.com/blog/why-reading-in-english-is-so-hard on September 18, 2024.

Simms, J. A., & Marzano, R. J. (2019). *The new art and science of teaching reading*. Bloomington, IN: Solution Tree Press.

Simon & Simon. (2024, January 10). *7 tips to improve your listening comprehension* [Blog post]. Accessed at www.simonandsimon.co.uk/blog/7-tips-to-improve-your-listening-comprehension on September 6, 2024.

SimpleK12 Staff. (2023, April 23). *Auditory learning style: Characteristics, benefits and strategies*. Accessed at www.simplek12.com/learning-theories-strategies/auditory-learning-style on October 4, 2024.

Singer, T. W. (2018). *EL excellence every day: The flip-to guide for differentiating academic literacy*. Thousand Oaks, CA: Corwin.

Skinner, B. F. (1953). *Science and human behavior*. New York: Macmillan.

Skinner, B. F. (1957). *Verbal behavior*. New York: Appleton-Century-Crofts.

Snow, C. E., & Hoefnagel-Höhle, M. (1978). The critical period for language acquisition: Evidence from second language learning. *Child Development, 49*(4), 1114–1128.

Sonoma County Office of Education. (2006, January). *Providing language instruction*. Santa Rosa, CA: Author. Accessed at www.scoe.org/docs/ah/AH_dutro.pdf on December 19, 2023.

Soto, G. (1993). *Too many tamales* (E. Martinez, Illus.). New York: Putnam.

Spelling City. (n.d.). *Multiple meaning words/homonyms lists*. Accessed at www.spellingcity.com/multiple-meaning-words.html on September 18, 2024.

Srinivas, R. P. (2019). The significance of writing skills in ELL environment. *ACADEMICIA, 9*(3), 5–17. https://doi.org/10.5958/2249-7137.2019.00035.1

Staake, J. (2023, September 26). *130 interesting persuasive essay topics for kids and teens*. Accessed at www.weareteachers.com/persuasive-essay-topics on January 6, 2024.

Staake, J. (2024, August 7). *120 useful English idiom examples everyone should know*. Accessed at www.weareteachers.com/idiom-of-the-day on September 16, 2024.

Stahl, R. J. (1994, May). *Using "think-time" and "wait-time" skillfully in the classroom* (ED370885). ERIC. https://files.eric.ed.gov/fulltext/ED370885.pdf

Statistics Canada. (2022, August 17). *While English and French are still the main languages spoken in Canada, the country's linguistic diversity continues to grow.* Accessed at www150.statcan.gc.ca/n1/daily-quotidien/220817/dq220817a-eng.htm on July 2, 2023.

Stavely, Z. (2024). *English learner advocates in California oppose 'science of reading' bill.* Accessed at https://edsource.org/2024/english-learner-advocates-oppose-science-of-reading-bill/707178 on October 29, 2024.

Storch, N., & Aldosari, A. (2013). Pairing learners in pair work activity. *Language Teaching Research, 17*(1), 31–48. https://doi.org/10.1177/1362168812457530

Sugarman, J. (2019, April). *The unintended consequences for English learners of using the four-year graduation rate for school accountability.* Washington, DC: Migration Policy Institute.

Swain, M. (1995). Three functions of output in second language learning. In G. Cook & B. Seidlhofer (Eds.), *Principle and practice in applied linguistics: Studies in honour of H. G. Widdowson* (pp. 125–144). Oxford, England: Oxford University Press.

Swain, M. (2000). The output hypothesis: Just speaking and writing aren't enough. *The Canadian Modern Language Review, 50*(1), 158–164.

Swain, M. (2005). The output hypothesis: Theory and research. In E. Hinkel (Ed.), *Handbook of research in second language teaching and learning* (pp. 495–508). New York: Routledge.

Tangel, D. M., & Blachman, B. A. (1992). Effect of phoneme awareness instruction on kindergarten children's invented spelling. *Journal of Reading Behavior, 24*(2), 233–261.

Tatter, G. (2018, October 19). *English learners and reading challenges.* Accessed at www.gse.harvard.edu/ideas/usable-knowledge/18/10/english-learners-and-reading-challenges on March 25, 2023.

Taylor, V. (2018, April 8). *Having conversations with your kid is the best way to develop language skills, study finds.* Accessed at www.romper.com/p/having-conversations-with-your-kid-is-the-best-way-to-develop-language-skills-study-finds-8726116 on July 10, 2024.

Teachers College Reading and Writing Project. (n.d.). *Case studies and reports.* Accessed at https://advancingliteracy.tc.columbia.edu/resources/case-studies-and-reports on June 10, 2024.

TeacherVision Staff. (2019, November 15). *Your secret weapon: Wait time.* Accessed at www.teachervision.com/teaching-strategies/your-secret-weapon-wait-time on September 2, 2024.

TeachThought Staff. (n.d.). *The definition of a Socratic seminar.* Accessed at www.teachthought.com/critical-thinking/definition-of-socratic-seminar on September 5, 2024.

TEDx Talks. (2016, March 18). *The windows and mirrors of your child's bookshelf | Grace Lin | TEDxNatick* [Video file]. Accessed at www.youtube.com/watch?v=_wQ8wiV3FVo on September 18, 2024.

TEDx Talks. (2020, January 31). *Mirrors, windows, & sliding doors | Akhand Dugar | TEDxMountainViewHighSchool* [Video file]. Accessed at www.youtube.com/watch?v=oGz2q9M86Cs on September 18, 2024.

Terada, Y. (2021, January 7). *Why students should write in all subjects.* Accessed at www.edutopia.org/article/why-students-should-write-all-subjects on November 13, 2023.

Terada, Y. (2022). *We drastically underestimate the importance of brain breaks.* Accessed at www.edutopia.org/article/we-drastically-underestimate-importance-brain-breaks on October 29, 2024.

Thomas, W. P., & Collier, V. (1997, December). *School effectiveness for language minority students.* Washington, DC: National Clearinghouse for Bilingual Education.

Thompson, S. (2021, December 10). The U.S. has the second-largest population of Spanish speakers—how to equip your brand to serve them. *Forbes.* Accessed at www.forbes.com/sites/soniathompson/2021/05/27/the-us-has-the-second-largest-population-of-spanish-speakers-how-to-equip-your-brand-to-serve-them/?sh=79e2fa3e793a on May 15, 2023.

Tolisano, S. R. (2015, June 14). *An update to the upgraded KWL for the 21st century* [Blog post]. Accessed at www.linkedin.com/pulse/update-upgraded-kwl-21st-century-silvia-rosenthal-tolisano on September 3, 2015.

Towell, R., Hawkins, R., & Bazergui, N. (1996). The development of fluency in advanced learners of French. *Applied Linguistics, 17*(1), 84–119.

Treiman, R. (1983). The structure of spoken syllables: Evidence from novel word games. *Cognition, 15,* 49–74.

Treiman, R. (1985). Onsets and rimes as units of spoken syllables: Evidence from children. *Journal of Experimental Child Psychology, 39,* 161–181.

Triebold, C. (2020, Spring). The importance of maintaining native language. *Forbes and Fifth, 16.* Accessed at www.forbes5.pitt.edu/article/importance-maintaining-native-language on October 18, 2023.

Tutt, P. (2023, September 1). *17 brain breaks tailored for high schoolers.* Accessed at www.edutopia.org/article/17-brain-breaks-tailored-for-high-schoolers on September 2, 2024.

Twinkl. (n.d.). *Discussion group role cards.* Accessed at www.twinkl.co.th/resource/us2-e-66-discussion-role-cards on January 3, 2025.

Uitti, J. (2023, June 20). The meaning behind the sad yodeling song "Oh My Darling, Clementine." *American Songwriter.* Accessed at https://americansongwriter.com/the-meaning-behind-the-cartoonish-yodeling-song-oh-my-darling-clementine on November 2, 2023.

Umejima, K., Ibaraki, T., Yamazaki, T., & Sakai, K. L. (2021). Paper notebooks vs. mobile devices: Brain activation differences during memory retrieval. *Frontiers in Behavioral Neuroscience, 15.* https://doi.org/10.3389/fnbeh.2021.634158

UNICEF. (2021, April). *Migration.* Accessed at https://data.unicef.org/topic/child-migration-and-displacement/migration on February 25, 2024.

University of Tokyo. (2021, March 19). *Study shows stronger brain activity after writing on paper than on tablet or smartphone.* Accessed at www.sciencedaily.com/releases/2021/03/210319080820.htm on July 14, 2023.

U.S. Department of Education. (2019). *Academic performance and outcomes for English learners: Performance on national assessments and on-time graduation rates.* Accessed at www2.ed.gov/datastory/el-outcomes/index.html#introText on February 26, 2024.

van der Wilt, F., Bouwer, R., & van der Veen, C. (2022). Dialogic classroom talk in early childhood education: The effect on language skills and social competence. *Learning and Instruction, 77,* Article 101522.

Vanessa Flynn Coaching. (n.d.). *Student led reading structures.* Accessed at www.vanessaflynncoaching.com/student-led-reading-structures.html on October 2, 2023.

Vasquez, V. (n.d.). *Lowering the affective filter for English language learners facilitates successful language acquisition* [Blog post]. Accessed at www.collaborativeclassroom.org/blog/lowering-affective-filter-facilitates-language-acq on September 5, 2024.

Verga, L., & Kotz, S. A. (2013). How relevant is social interaction in second language learning? *Frontiers in Human Neuroscience, 7,* Article 550. Accessed at www.frontiersin.org/journals/human-neuroscience/articles/10.3389/fnhum.2013.00550/full on December 23, 2024.

Victoria State Government Department of Education. (2020, March 18). *Accountable Talk.* Accessed at www.education.vic.gov.au/school/teachers/teachingresources/discipline/english/literacy/speakinglistening/Pages/teachingpracaccountable.aspx on September 3, 2024.

Vogel, S., & García, O. (2017). *Translanguaging* [City University of New York]. CUNY Academic Works. https://academicworks.cuny.edu/gc_pubs/402

Vygotsky, L. S. (1978). *Mind in society: The development of higher psychological processes.* Cambridge, MA: Harvard University Press.

WestEd. (2014). *Helping English learners rise to the challenge of complex texts.* Accessed at www.wested.org/wp-content/uploads/2016/11/1390502203article_HelpEnglishLearners_RD143-3.pdf on June 29, 2023.

Western Sydney University. (n.d.). *Strategy: 10-2 strategy.* Accessed at https://lf.westernsydney.edu.au/engage/strategy/10-2-strategy on December 20, 2023.

WIDA. (2020). *WIDA English language development standards framework, 2020 edition: Kindergarten–grade 12.* Madison, WI: Board of Regents of the University of Wisconsin System. Accessed at https://wida.wisc.edu/sites/default/files/resource/WIDA-ELD-Standards-Framework-2020.pdf on September 2, 2024.

Will, M., & Najarro, I. (2022, April 18). What is culturally responsive teaching? *Education Week.* Accessed at www.edweek.org/teaching-learning/culturally-responsive-teaching-culturally-responsive-pedagogy/2022/04 on September 1, 2024.

Willis, J. (2016, December 7). *Using brain breaks to restore students' focus.* Accessed at www.edutopia.org/article/brain-breaks-restore-student-focus-judy-willis on December 19, 2023.

Willmar Public Schools. [pointlake]. (2013, December 17). *I can statements as classroom objectives* [Video file]. Accessed at www.youtube.com/watch?v=Tr3uqF7YObo on December 19, 2023.

Wolf, M. K., Crosson, A. C., & Resnick, L. B. (2004, April). *Classroom talk for rigorous reading comprehension instruction* [Paper presentation]. American Educational Research Association annual meeting, San Diego, CA. Accessed at www.stat.cmu.edu/~brian/AERA04/Clasroom%20Talk_AERA04MW.pdf on September 3, 2024.

Wolf, M. K., Crosson, A. C., & Resnick, L. B. (2006, January). Accountable Talk in reading comprehension instruction (CSE Technical Report No. 670). Los Angeles: Center for the Study of Evaluation.

Woodson, J. (2018). *The day you begin* (R. López, Illus.). New York: Nancy Paulsen Books.

Woodson, J. (2016). *Brown girl dreaming*. New York: Puffin Books.

Wyman, K. (2017, February 27). *To help English learners, you need ways to reduce their affective filter*. Accessed at https://resilienteducator.com/classroom-resources/affective-filter-english-learners on July 12, 2023.

Yang, X. (2017). The use of body language in English teaching. *Theory and Practice in Language Studies, 7*(12), 1333–1336.

Ybarra, S. E., & Hollingsworth, J. R. (n.d.). *Integrated or designated ELD: 6 things to know about ELD instruction*. Accessed at https://dataworks-ed.com/research/6-things-know-integrated-designated-eld-instruction on September 2, 2024.

Yurtbaşı, M. (2015). Building English vocabulary through roots, prefixes and suffixes. *Global Journal of Foreign Language Teaching, 5*(1), 44–51.

Yusa, N., Kim, J., Koizumi, M., Sugiura, M., & Kawashima, R. (2017). Social interaction affects neural outcomes of sign language learning as a foreign language in adults. *Frontiers in Human Neuroscience, 11*. Accessed at www.frontiersin.org/articles/10.3389/fnhum.2017.00115/full on July 11, 2023.

Zaatar, M. T., Alhakim, K., Enayeh, M., & Tamer, R. (2024). The transformative power of music: Insights into neuroplasticity, health, and disease. *Brain, Behavior, and Immunity—Health, 35*, Article 100716. https://doi.org/10.1016/j.bbih.2023.100716

Zacarian, D., Alvarez-Ortiz, L., & Haynes, J. (2017). *Teaching to strengths: Supporting students living with trauma, violence, and chronic stress*. Arlington, VA: ASCD.

Zaff, J. F., Margolius, M., Varga, S. M., Lynch, A. D., Tang, C., & Donlan, A. E. (2021). English learners and high school graduation: A pattern-centered approach to understand within-group variations. *Journal of Education for Students Placed at Risk, 26*(1), 1–19.

INDEX

NUMBERS
10/2 strategy, 58, 82

A
academic vocabulary. *See also* vocabulary development
    English learners and, 165
    informational or expository writing and, 138
    partner and group conversations and, 198
    strategies and activities for reading and, 167–168
    SWIRL framework and, xiv
accountability
    Accountable Talk, 80
    interacting and, 147
    listening strategies and, 191
    writing and, 128
accuracy, 164, 179
acquisition-learning hypothesis, 35. *See also* Krashen's theory of second language acquisition, hypotheses of
acrostics, 131. *See also* poetry
active listening and body language, 191–194. *See also* strategies and activities for listening
active observations, 199
adaptations, 71–73, 74
affective filters and affective filter hypothesis, 36, 43, 83. *See also* Krashen's theory of second language acquisition, hypotheses of
along the lines, 102–103. *See also* strategies and activities for speaking

anchor charts, 58, 71, 116, 121, 168–169
assessments
    assessments to ascertain EL levels, 39–40
    example rubric to assess student work in the solar system unit, 61
asset-based education, 17, 18, 20, 43
audience, 114, 127

B
back channeling, 193
balanced literacy, 161
basic interpersonal communication skills (BICS), 79
bias, 21–22
bilingualism, xiii–xiv, 16, 17
biographies, 132–133, 141. *See also* strategies and activities for writing
Bishop, R., 170
body language, active listening and, 191–194. *See also* strategies and activities for listening
book clubs, roles for, 172–173, 174. *See also* strategies and activities for reading
books, example list of multicultural books, 170–171
brain breaks, 73
bridging, 16–17, 38

C
chants, 168, 191
checking comprehension, 180–182. *See also* strategies and activities for reading
choice. *See* student voice and choice

chunked audio and video for processing, 197. *See also* strategies and activities for listening
classroom feud, 150. *See also* strategies and activities for interacting
classrooms. *See* setting up the classroom to SWIRL
clock partners, 198–199, 202
cloze activities, 118–119, 196
cognates
    about, 25–27
    bridging and, 16
    informational or expository writing and, 138
    lesson planning and, 49, 50
    story as input and, 195
cognitive content dictionary, 92, 95–97, 98, 107. *See also* strategies and activities for speaking
Cohen, G., 87
collaborative conversations, 58
compound, root, and base words, 177–178. *See also* strategies and activities for reading
compound words, 138
comprehensible input debate, 40–43
comprehensible output theory, 42
comprehension
    checking comprehension, 180–182
    English learners and, 164, 165
    making connections, 171–172
    reading and, 164
concepts of print and language structure transfers, 28–29
conferencing, 123–127. *See also* writers' workshop
connections, making, 171–172. *See also* strategies and activities for reading
content objectives
    interacting and, 146
    language objectives and, 51–52, 52–53
    lesson planning and, 50
    verbs for, 64
cooperative strip paragraphs, 133–136. *See also* strategies and activities for writing
critical consciousness, 19
critical thinking, xiv, 152
critique groups, 128–129
cultural competence, 19

culturally responsive and sustaining teaching. *See also* setting up the classroom to SWIRL
    about, 18–19, 21
    active listening and body language and, 192
    cultural connections, 23–24
    implicit bias and, 21–22
    pedagogical and instructional practices and, 22–23
    products and traits of culturally responsive and sustaining asset-based classrooms, 20
    reading and, 165
    strategies to reinforce, 25–29
Culturally Responsive Teaching and the Brain (Hammond), 19, 21
culture and language. *See also* setting up the classroom to SWIRL
    about, 14
    culture, three levels of, 14–16
    experiences while learning a new language, 17–18
    home languages, benefits of maintaining, 16–17
current events and news, 24

D

desirable difficulty, use of term, 34
dialectic discourse, 151. *See also* Socratic seminars
dialogic classrooms, 143–144
dice discussions, 151. *See also* strategies and activities for interacting
differentiation, xviii, 13, 123–127
discourse, 81
dual immersion programs, 16, 84, 120, 126

E

Echevarría, J., 92, 164–165
elements of learning a new language, 11. *See also* language acquisition and proficiency levels; planning lessons; setting up the classroom to SWIRL
emergent multilingual students (EMSs), use of term, 7. *See also* multilingual learners (MLs)
English language
    difficulty of for writing, 114–115
    English language development (ELD) instruction, 44–47

playground English, 79
speaking, importance of in learning, 82
English learners (ELs). *See also* multilingual learners; newcomers
  assessments to ascertain EL levels, 39–40
  listening and, 189
  long-term ELs, 67
  phonemic awareness and, 163
  reading and, 164, 165
  speaking and, 82
  statistics on, 4
  SWIRL framework and, xviii, 5–6
  who multilingual/English learners are, 7–8
English Learners Success Forum, 116
Enhanced Core Reading Instruction (ECRI), 166
environmentalists, 33
experiences while learning a new language, 17–18
extending language, 44

F
feedback, 44, 127, 128–129
fishbowls, 148, 199. *See also* think-pair-share
fluency, 163, 164, 165, 180
four corners, 156–157. *See also* strategies and activities for interacting
functionalists, 33

G
García, O., 7
GLAD strategies, 95, 104, 133
gradual release of responsibility, xviii, 50, 72, 188
Greenwald, A., 21
grouping students
  home languages and heritage languages and, 146
  jigsaw activity, 87
  partner and group conversations, 197–199
  purposeful partnerships, 84–86
  scaffolds, interventions, and adaptations and, 72

H
haiku, 131. *See also* poetry
Hammond, Z., 19, 21
hand up, stand up, 86–87. *See also* strategies and activities for speaking
Harvard University, 3
Hidalgo, N., 15
hidden curriculum, 81
home languages and heritage languages
  asset-based education and, 7, 8
  benefits of maintaining, 16–17
  cognates and, 195
  culturally responsive and sustaining teaching and, 18, 20
  culture and language and, 14
  grouping students and, 146
  newcomers and, 65
  partner and group conversations and, 198
  reading and, 162, 164, 165, 204
  think-pair-share and, 82, 148–149
  turn-and-talk and, 58, 82
  writing and, 117
homonyms and homophones, 183–184. *See also* strategies and activities for reading
hot seat, 103. *See also* strategies and activities for speaking
Huynh, T., 117

I
I can statements, 50, 67–70
idioms, 182–183. *See also* strategies and activities for reading
implicit bias, 21–22
informational or expository writing, 137–138. *See also* strategies and activities for writing
input hypothesis, 34, 35–36. *See also* Krashen's theory of second language acquisition, hypotheses of
interacting. *See also* strategies and activities for interacting; SWIRL
  about, 143–144
  activities and strategies for, 146–160, 208
  components of quality interactions, 147
  conclusion, 160
  importance of, 204
  research on, 144–145
  speaking and interacting activity overlaps, 86
  in SWIRL, 5, 6
interactive journaling, 120–122. *See also* strategies and activities for writing
interventions, 71–73
introduction
  how to use this book, 8–9

who multilingual/English learners are, 7–8
why SWIRL works for multilingual/English learners, 5–6
why this book is crucial, 2–4
invented spelling, 125–126

J

jigsaw activity, 87–88, 89, 156–157. *See also* strategies and activities for speaking
journaling, interactive, 120–122. *See also* strategies and activities for writing

K

knowledge demands, 176
Krashen, S., 42, 189
Krashen's theory of second language acquisition, hypotheses of, 34–37
Kuhl, P., 145
KWHLAQ chart, 93, 94
KWL chart, 92–95, 106. *See also* strategies and activities for speaking

L

language acquisition and proficiency levels
  about, 31
  assessments to ascertain EL levels, 39–40
  comprehensible input debate, 40–43
  conclusion, 47
  instructional approaches: designated, integrated, and systematic ELD, 44–47
  Krashen's theory of second language acquisition, hypotheses of, 34–37
  language acquisition proficiency stages, 37–39
  language theory in brief, 32–34
  motivation, self-esteem, and anxiety and, 43–44
  speaking and, 79
  writing difficulties and, 115
language awareness, 72
language clarity, 176
language conventionality, 176
Language Essentials for Teachers of Reading and Spelling (LETRS), 166
language form, 61, 62
language function, 61, 62
language objectives
  content objectives and, 51–52
  example for, 53–54, 70
  function and form and, 61–63
  interacting and, 146
  lesson planning and, 50
  multilingual learners and, 70–74
  rigor and, 63–67
  student-friendly wording, 67–70
  verbs for, 63, 64
  writing, 54–57, 60
language structure transfers, 28–29
language targets. *See* language objectives
listening. *See also* strategies and activities for listening
  about, 187–188
  activities and strategies for, 190–201, 208
  conclusion, 201
  importance of, 204
  purposeful partnerships, 86
  reading and, 189
  reproducibles for, 202
  research on, 189–190
  in SWIRL, 5, 6
literature and cultural connections, 24
long-term ELs, 67. *See also* English learners (ELs)

M

Mason, B., 189
memory, xiv, 158–159. *See also* strategies and activities for interacting
Migration Policy Institute, 67
Miller, D., 34
mirrors, windows, and sliding glass doors, 169–171. *See also* strategies and activities for reading
Molina, R., 17
monitor hypothesis, 35. *See also* Krashen's theory of second language acquisition, hypotheses of
morphology, 81
motivation, self-esteem, and anxiety, 43–44
multicultural books, example list of, 170–171
multilingual learners (MLs). *See also* English learners (ELs)
  differentiation and, 13
  phonemic awareness and, 163
  science of reading and, 162
  speaking and, 82
  statistics on, 2
  strategies for, 70–74

SWIRL framework and, 5–6
who multilingual/English learners are, 7–8
why this book is crucial, 2–4
multilingualism, benefits of, xviii–xiv
music, impact of, 169, 191. *See also* songs

N

narrative input, 199–200. *See also* strategies and activities for listening
nativist, 33
natural order hypothesis, 36. *See also* Krashen's theory of second language acquisition, hypotheses of
newcomers. *See also* English learners (ELs); multilingual learners (MLs)
 experiences while learning a new language, 17, 18
 language objectives and, 53, 64–67
 speaking and, 79

O

Ogle, D., 92
one-to-one correspondence, 158, 163
oral language, 80, 165. *See also* speaking

P

pacing, 87
paint chip vocabulary strips, 97, 99–100. *See also* strategies and activities for speaking
pandemic slide, 162
parakeet partners, 84–86
parents and families
 culturally responsive and sustaining teaching and, 18
 newcomers and, 66
 who multilingual/English learners are, 7–8
partners. *See also* grouping students
 activities and strategies for interacting and, 146
 clock partners, 198–199, 202
 parakeet partners, 84–86
 partner and group conversations, 197–199
 purposeful partnerships, 84–86
pedagogical and instructional practices, 22–23
peer editing, 128–129. *See also* strategies and activities for writing
peer learning, 144. *See also* interacting
persuasive essay writing, 137. *See also* strategies and activities for writing

phonemic awareness, 80–81, 161, 162, 163, 164
phonetics, 5
phonics
 English learners and, 164
 phonics phones, 124, 125
 research on reading and, 163
 Rime Magic, 173
 science of reading and, 161–162
physical clues, 145
picture walks, 180, 194–195
Pillars, W., 83
place mat note-taking, 129–130, 140. *See also* strategies and activities for writing
planning lessons
 about, 49–50
 conclusion, 75
 turning content objectives into language objectives, 51–52
 writing language objectives, 52–74
playground English, 79
poetry
 anchor charts and, 168–169
 listening strategies and, 191
 strategies and activities for writing, 130–132
pop culture, 24
pragmatics, 81
predictions, 181
prefixes, 178
print, concepts of print and language structure transfers, 28–29
print-rich environments, 44
prior experiences, 193
process grids, 104, 111. *See also* strategies and activities for speaking
productive struggle, use of term, 34
professional development, 3
pronunciation, 178–179. *See also* strategies and activities for reading
Pruett, K., 100
purposeful partnerships, 84–86. *See also* strategies and activities for speaking

R

read-alouds, 195–197
reading. *See also* strategies and activities for reading
 about, 161–162
 activities and strategies for, 167–184, 208

conclusion, 184–185
importance of, 204
listening and, 189
research on, 163–167
science of reading, 161–162
in SWIRL, 5, 6
writing and, 113, 114, 161
reproducibles for
    clock partners, 202
    cognitive content dictionary, 107
    Four Layers of the Rain Forest song, 109
    KWL chart, 106
    note-taking place mat, 140
    Octopi Have Tentacles song, 108
    process grid, 111
    Sweet Harriet song, 110
    writers' workshop conference tool, 139
    writing a biography, 141
response to intervention (RTI), 71
rhyming families, 118. *See also* poetry
rigor, 63–67
Rime Magic, 173, 175. *See also* strategies and activities for reading
roles for book clubs, strategies and activities for reading, 172–173, 174
rubrics, example rubric to assess student work in the solar system unit, 61
Rucker, N., 18, 21

S

salute, 159. *See also* strategies and activities for interacting
scaffolding
    comprehensible output theory and, 41, 42
    extending language and, 44
    integrated ELD, 45
    interacting and, 146–147
    language objectives and, 53
    lesson planning and, 49, 50
    multilingual learners and, 71–73
    reading and, 166–167, 180, 181
    sentence frames, starters, and stems, 59, 71, 88, 90
    story as input and, 194
    technology and, 74
    use of term, 32
    writing and, 116–117, 138
scenarios, 157
schemata, 193

science of reading, 161–162. *See also* reading
second language acquisition, 34–37, 40. *See also* language acquisition and proficiency levels
semantics, 81
sentence frames, starters, and stems
    extending language and, 44
    language objectives and, 59
    lesson planning and, 50
    partner and group conversations and, 199
    scaffolding and, 71
    story as input and, 194
    strategies and activities for speaking, 88, 90–92
    think-pair-share and, 149
setting up the classroom to SWIRL
    about, 13–14
    conclusion, 29
    culturally responsive and sustaining teaching and, 18–24
    culture and language and, 14–18
    strategies to reinforce culturally responsive and sustaining teaching, 25–29
    SWIRL framework and the culturally sustaining classroom, xviii
SMART goals, 52
snowballs, 157. *See also* strategies and activities for interacting
social language, 79
Socratic seminars, 81, 151–154. *See also* strategies and activities for interacting
songs, 100–101, 169, 191. *See also* chants; music, impact of; strategies and activities for speaking
speaking. *See also* strategies and activities for speaking
    about, 79–80
    activities and strategies for, 83–104, 207
    conclusion, 105
    importance of, 203
    reproducibles for, 106–111
    research on, 80–82
    slowing down, 71
    speaking and interacting activity overlaps, 86
    in SWIRL, 5, 6
special education, 3, 67
spelling, invented spelling, 125–126
Stanford University, 176

story as input, 194–197. *See also* strategies and activities for listening
story elements, 181
strategies and activities for interacting. *See also* interacting
   about, 146–147
   classroom feud, 150
   dice discussions, 151
   four corners, 156–157
   memory, 158–159
   salute, 159
   snowball, 157
   Socratic seminars, 151–154
   swimming the spectrum, 154–156
   think-pair-share, 148–149
   who am I?, 159–160
strategies and activities for listening. *See also* listening
   about, 190–191
   active listening and body language, 191–194
   chunked audio and video for processing, 197
   narrative input, 199–200
   partner and group conversations, 197–199
   story as input, 194–197
   total physical response (TPR), 200–201
strategies and activities for reading. *See also* reading
   about, 167
   academic vocabulary, 167–168
   anchor charts, 168–169
   checking comprehension, 180–182
   compound, root, and base words, 177–178
   homonyms and homophones, 183–184
   idioms, 182–183
   including informational, nonfiction, and complex texts, 175–177
   making connections, 171–172
   mirrors, windows, and sliding glass doors, 169–171
   pronunciation, accuracy, and fluency, 178–180
   Rime Magic, 173, 175
   roles for book clubs, 172–173, 174
strategies and activities for speaking. *See also* speaking
   about, 83–84
   along the lines, 102–103
   cognitive content dictionary, 92, 95–97, 98
   hand up, stand up, 86–87
   hot seat, 103
   jigsaw activity, 87–88, 89
   KWL T-chart, 92–95
   paint chip vocabulary strips, 97, 99–100
   process grids, 104
   purposeful partnerships, 84–86
   sentence frames, starters, and stems, 88, 90–92
   songs, 100–101
   trivia, 101–102
strategies and activities for writing. *See also* writing
   about, 116–118
   biographies, 132–133
   cooperative strip paragraphs, 133–136
   informational or expository writing, 137–138
   interactive journaling, 120–122
   peer editing, 128–129
   persuasive essay writing, 137
   place mat note taking, 129–130
   poetry, 130–132
   word families, 118–120, 121
   writers' workshop, 122–128
strategies for multilingual learners, 70–74. *See also* multilingual learners
strategies to help onboard newcomers, 65–66. *See also* newcomers
strategies to reinforce culturally responsive and sustaining teaching, 25–29. *See also* culturally responsive and sustaining teaching
student learning, 19
student menu, 59
student voice and choice
   affective filters and, 43
   reading and, 162, 165, 167
   SWIRL framework and, xiv
   writing and, 114, 115, 122–123
student-friendly wording, 67–70
students with interrupted formal education (SIFE), 65
subtractive bilingualism, 17
suffixes, 178
swimming the spectrum, 154–156. *See also* strategies and activities for interacting
SWIRL. *See also* setting up the classroom to SWIRL

impact of framework, xiii, xiv
implementing, 6
lesson planning and, 50
SWIRL elements, 77–78. *See also specific SWIRL elements*
why SWIRL works for multilingual/English learners, 5–6
syntax, 81

T

tanka, 131–132. *See also* poetry
teacher talk
    comprehensible input strategies and, 41–42
    listening strategies and, 190
    ratio of, 83–84, 144–145, 204
    systematic ELD and, 46
technology, 73–74. *See also* strategies for multilingual learners
texts, including informational, nonfiction, and complex, 175–177. *See also* strategies and activities for reading
think time, 72–73
think-alouds, 172
think-pair-share
    partner and group conversations and, 198
    speaking and, 58, 82
    speaking and interacting activity overlaps, 86
    strategies and activities for interacting, 148–149
think-write-pair-share, 198
total physical response (TPR), 200–201. *See also* strategies and activities for listening
transferability of skills, xiv
translanguaging, 7
trauma, 18, 66
trivia, 101–102. *See also* strategies and activities for speaking
turn-and-talk, 58, 82

U

understanding language acquisition and proficiency levels. *See* language acquisition and proficiency levels

V

visual memory, 158. *See also* memory
visuals and gestures, 71, 145
vocabulary development. *See also* academic vocabulary
    affective filters and, 43
    checking comprehension, 181
    English learners and, 164
    Frayer model for vocabulary development, 43, 44, 92
    reading and, 164
    steps for vocabulary instruction, 96
    story as input and, 194
Vogel, S., 7

W

wait time, 72–73
who am I?, 159–160. *See also* strategies and activities for interacting
WIDA proficiency-level descriptors, 38
word banks, 116
word families, 118–120, 121. *See also* strategies and activities for writing
writers' workshop, 122–128, 139. *See also* strategies and activities for writing
writing. *See also* strategies and activities for writing
    about, 113–115
    activities and strategies for, 116–138, 207
    conclusion, 138
    importance of, 203–204
    reading and, 113, 114, 161
    reproducibles for, 139–141
    research on, 115–116
    in SWIRL, 5, 6
    writing before responding, 59
    writing process, 123
Wyman, K., 155

Z

zone of proximal development (ZPD), 34, 40

Coaching for Multilingual Student Success
Karen Johannesen Brock
Understand how to intentionally involve instructional coaches to equip teachers to successfully implement high-impact strategies that meet the unique learning needs of multilingual students. Gain tools and practices to design professional learning plans that incorporate targeted strategies with the support of an instructional coaching program.
BKG172

Cultivating Competence in English Learners
Margarita Espino Calderón and Lisa Tartaglia
This research-backed guide offers evidence-based strategies core content teachers can use immediately to improve daily practice. The authors explore the importance of SEL application to the English learning process and how to connect essential instructional elements to cultivate active, engaged learners.
BKG001

Coaching Teachers in Bilingual and Dual-Language Classrooms
Alexandra Guilamo
Gain the skills you need to coach teachers in bilingual and dual-language classrooms. In this practical guide, you will discover a proven process for creating a fair and effective observation and feedback cycle to help support teachers in this important work.
BKF918

STEM Is for Everyone
Darlyne de Haan
With culturally responsive teaching, scaffolding, and scientific approaches such as Claim, Evidence, Reasoning (CER), author Darlyne de Haan proposes general education STEM teachers can seal the leaky STEM pipeline that impacts many multilingual students, providing all students with equitable instruction and opportunity.
BKF968

Solution Tree | Press
a division of

Solution Tree

Visit SolutionTree.com or call 800.733.6786 to order.

GL⦾BAL PD

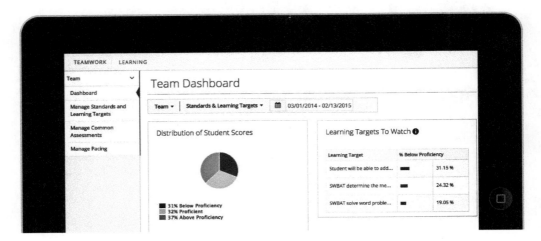

The **Power to Improve**
Is in Your Hands

Global PD gives educators focused and goals-oriented training from top experts. You can rely on this innovative online tool to improve instruction in every classroom.

- Get unlimited, on-demand access to guided video and book content from top Solution Tree authors.

- Improve practices with personalized virtual coaching from PLC-certified trainers.

- Customize learning based on skill level and time commitments.

▶ **REQUEST A FREE DEMO TODAY**
SolutionTree.com/GlobalPD